本书获得以下项目支持

◎ 2019年度教育部人文社会科学研究规划基金项目"基于定量分析的国内科技翻译教材研究（1978—2017）"（19YJA880004）

◎ 2020年度湖南省哲学社会科学基金重点项目"后疫情时代来华留学生科技汉语教材评价与研发"（20ZDB032）

◎ 中南大学教材立项项目

U0716825

通识
科技语言
探索

主　编⊙单　宇　范武邱　吴　宁
副主编⊙王　昱　李成静　王晓东

A Linguistic Approach to
General Science & Technology

中南大学出版社
www.csupress.com.cn

·长 沙·

图书在版编目（CIP）数据

通识科技语言探索／单宇，范武邱，吴宁主编.
—长沙：中南大学出版社，2023.7
ISBN 978-7-5487-5331-5

Ⅰ. ①通… Ⅱ. ①单… ②范… ③吴… Ⅲ. ①科学技术－英语－研究 Ⅳ. ①G301

中国国家版本馆 CIP 数据核字（2023）第 062297 号

通识科技语言探索
TONGSHI KEJI YUYAN TANSUO

单宇　范武邱　吴宁　主编

□出 版 人	吴湘华		
□责任编辑	谢金伶		
□责任印制	李月腾		
□出版发行	中南大学出版社		
	社址：长沙市麓山南路	邮编：410083	
	发行科电话：0731-88876770	传真：0731-88710482	
□印　　装	长沙市宏发印刷有限公司		

□开　　本	787 mm×1092 mm 1/16	□印张 12	□字数 254 千字
□版　　次	2023 年 7 月第 1 版	□印次 2023 年 7 月第 1 次印刷	
□书　　号	ISBN 978-7-5487-5331-5		
□定　　价	36.00 元		

序言

Preface

记得 6 年前，我回祖籍湖南长沙参加学术会议，并有机会应邀到中南大学参观学习，当时范武邱教授、杨文地教授特地向我介绍了单宇、仲文明等一批年轻的博士。现在单宇教授的新著就摆在我眼前，并诚邀我为之写序，真是先睹为快，令我十分感动。

党的二十大报告中强调"加快建设高质量教育体系"，指出要"扩大国际科技交流合作，加强国际化科研环境建设"，要"全面贯彻党的教育方针，落实立德树人根本任务，培养德智体美劳全面发展的社会主义建设者和接班人"，这为我们教育事业的发展指明了方向。党的二十大报告中，将教育、科技、人才集中进行专章论述，既强调了三者之间的有机联系，又强调了三者在全面建设社会主义现代化国家中的重要作用。我们都感到欢欣鼓舞，干劲十足，正团结一致，奋勇前行。

关于《通识科技语言探索》，笔者认为：这不仅仅是一本科技语言通用教材，还是一部作者紧跟时代的步伐、精心奉献的具有新颖视角的英汉科技语言对比专著。简单地说，《通识科技语言探索》分为 8 章，另有附录 6 种，总计 20 多万字。作者在每章前还写有精练的摘要，章节分明；正文之后的附录，内容丰富，清楚实用。

上周我同范武邱、单宇有过亲切交流，彼此都感到高兴。我们都深深感到，随着科技发展与全球经济一体化的逐步深入，科技语言媒介作用得以突破。由于科技语篇内容使用域和语篇功能的特殊性，形成了科技语篇典型的文体特征。科技英语作为国际科技交流的重要工具，依托英语在语言世界的广泛性与强流通性，对国际学术和技术交流产生深远影响。同样，新型科技汉语词汇概念严谨，词义严格，专业性强，语体逻辑严密，特点突出，用简单的表达承载博大精深的思想。论述以英汉科技文体具有的天然共性为出发点，探讨微观层面的显性差异，与宏观层面的科技语境、文化思维差异理据。英汉科技语篇在词法、句法、语篇、文体、修辞层面的差异，在很大程度上制约着科技工作者的理解和语言转换，因此，强化英汉科技文体的对比研究，对中国科技工作者在学习科学的过程中体会科技精髓和精神，形成系统的思维观念进而提高对科学和技术的理解具有显著价值。对于目前科学技术体系的语言以英语语言和西方文化为主导的现实，本书辩证地认知剖析，秉持为规范的科技汉语言"走出去"提供参照与动能，丰富多源载体科技内涵。

综上简述，我认为《通识科技语言探索》具有鲜明的特色，应引起我们的格外关注：

第一，教学目的凸显，工具性与人文性统一。该书兼顾英语与汉语、国内与国际、人文与理工、课内与课外，以课程标准的总体规划为依据，以讲义的整体设计为基础，以案例学习为主要载体，体现了系统连贯的教学思路。

第二，教学案例丰富，时代性与说服力共存。该书充分利用了现代信息技术理论与实践并重的特点，选材广泛，具有时代意义。通过接地气的案例，能够更好地培养学生自主学习的能力，在实践中提升科技素养。

第三，该书在研究方法上独辟蹊径，教学受众广泛，个性化与可读性协调。该书充分考虑学生的学习兴趣以及社会和时代的要求，有助于学生自觉学习、个性化学习。

第四，全书结构设计友善，循序渐进，体现了"授之以渔"的原则，能开阔师生视野，同时有利于师生互动。本书致力于培养学生科技语言素养、培育科技爱国情怀，体现"教育、科技、人才是全面建设社会主义现代化国家的基础性、战略性支撑"的深刻内涵。

第五，该书文献基础扎实，立论和剖析均植根于本土学术土壤与坚实的理论基础。该书把握时代的脉搏，贯通理论与实践，以新颖的面目展示在读者面前。因此，《通识科技语言探索》是一部全面、包容、系统的科技英语学习工具书，对中外语言文学的学科建设、科技语言的教学研究等方面均有鲜明的启迪作用。

总之，建设一流的教学科研队伍，提供战略人才支撑，正是当下共同关注和热议的话题。《通识科技语言探索》这样一部思想纯正、结构严谨、行文畅达的著作，一定会受到社会和学校广大读者的欢迎。我愿借此机会向作者和出版社编辑老师们，表示崇高的敬意和衷心的祝贺！祝愿他们多出好书！

是为序。

中国科学院科技翻译协会副会长
中国英汉语比较研究会翻译传译委员会名誉会长
2023 年 7 月 25 日

前言
Foreword

随着国际化不断深入，我国对外科技交流也日益广泛深入，科技语言作为交流的工具，愈发受到关注。对于高等院校学生而言，科技语言是为其专业服务、进行科技交流必不可少的工具。高等学校教学质量和教学改革工程理念进一步贯彻深入，为满足新时期国家和社会对应用型复合型人才的需求，高校积极推进外语教学改革和教材建设，开展科技语言素养拓展系列课程，"科技英语"在其中占有重要位置。现实问题是科技英语课程缺乏统一完整的教学大纲，教材难度参差，较多学生对科技文体概念认知模糊，并有畏难情绪。而现在市面上科技语言教材多以科技文章阅读为主，并未对科技文体做全面系统梳理，学生在使用此类教材时缺乏对科技文体的整体把握，能力提升效果并不显著。基于此背景，经过多年的教学实践和研究，我们编写了《通识科技语言探索》，其目的是引导学生了解科技文体，领会科技文体特征，熟悉科技文体架构，掌握一定的科技文体写作方法，为未来更深层次的科研学习和工作打下坚实的科技语言基础，进而培养获取科技信息、拓宽学术视野、开展科技交流的能力。

一、编写特色

1. 贴近实际，实用性强。本教材考虑学生在未来的专业学习中对科技语言的需求，以科技文体的主要特征为着眼点，强调科技语言认知，使学生在循序渐进中熟悉科技文体语言特征，并进一步掌握相关科技文体写作技巧。针对每个知识点的讲解，教材呈现一定量的表达样例，附有多个科技文体常用表达供学生参考学习。

2. 循序渐进，系统性强。本教材涵盖科技文体的词法、句法，也涉及篇章的衔接连贯；教材覆盖科技文体特征等理论梳理，也论及实践层面的科技文本写作。覆盖面宽，深入浅出，难度适中，系统性强。

3. 选材新颖，时代性强。本教材紧贴时代发展，具有与时俱进的特点，所涉及的示例均在一定程度上反映科技成果的时代性，也加强了文本的趣味性和知识性，有利于学生取得良好的学习效果。

二、结构设计

本教材共分为科技文体特征概述、科技文本写作、科技文献检索三大部分。

第一部分包含前 6 章内容，涵盖词法、句法，也论及篇章。首先总体层面介绍了科技文体的特征，其次分别讲解了科技术语、科技语句表述、科技语篇结构，重点介绍了术语的特征、构成和翻译，以及科技文体中常见的定义表达法、描述表达法、分类表达法等多种表达方法。此外还介绍了科技文体中数字与数学、图形与图表的表达。

第二部分包含第七章。聚焦关联科技活动的科技文本写作，梳理了科研简历、期刊论文摘要、研究计划、研究报告等常见实用性科技文本的写作框架与写作技巧，同时附有中英样例供学生学习参考。

第三部分为第八章。围绕科技文献检索主题介绍中英文数据库及检索方法、科技报告的检索，为科技工作者和当代大学生开展科研和学习提供有效手段。

三、使用建议

本教材涵盖内容比较广泛，教师可根据所在学校的课程设置和学生的实际情况，选择全部和部分章节内容用于教学。教材供一学期使用，每周两学时，可采取教师讲解、学生讨论、学生讲解等教学模式。

四、使用对象

本教材不仅适用于非英语专业本科生使用，还可作为英语专业科技英语类课程的教材，或研究生、科技工作者以及科技语言爱好者学习的教材。

在教材的编写过程中，我们将其中的材料编写成讲义，供中南大学外国语学院英语专业二年级学生在"科技英语概论"课堂上使用，学生对此表现出浓厚的兴趣，一致认为对科技文本整体特征有较好把握，对科技文本阅读和写作有较大提升作用。

教材得以付梓，离不开中南大学外国语学院多位领导和老师的支持，在此致以衷心的感谢。与此同时，在教材编写过程中，我们参考了国内外出版的相关书刊并引用了部分资料，在此一并向有关作者和单位表示诚挚的感谢。

教材出版凝聚了编写人员的心血，但由于编写人员水平有限，时间仓促，教材中错漏和浅薄之处仍恐难免，衷心希望同行专家和读者在使用过程中不吝斧正，以便使教材不断更新完善。

单宇

2023 年 4 月

目录
Contents

第一章　科技英语概论　　**1**

　　第一节　科技语言文体特征　／1
　　第二节　科技英语语法特征　／8
　　第三节　科技英语修辞特点　／14
　　第四节　汉英科技文体比较　／20

第二章　科技术语表达　　**23**

　　第一节　科技术语表征　／23
　　第二节　科技术语翻译　／33

第三章　数字与数学用语表达　　**49**

　　第一节　数字的表达　／49
　　第二节　数学用语的表达　／53
　　第三节　倍数表达法　／59

第四章　图形与图表表达　　**62**

　　第一节　科技可视化　／62
　　第二节　图形的表达　／63
　　第三节　图表的表达　／64

第五章　科技语句表达　　**73**

　　第一节　定义表达法　／73

　　第二节　描写表达法　／76

　　第三节　分类表达法　／82

　　第四节　主从关系表达法　／84

　　第五节　比较、对比、类比表达法　／88

　　第六节　其他科技语篇常用句型　／90

第六章　科技语篇结构　　94

　　第一节　中英文科技语篇结构差异　／95

　　第二节　科技语篇翻译中的衔接与连贯策略　／102

第七章　科技文本写作　　109

　　第一节　科研简历写作　／109

　　第二节　个人陈述　／116

　　第三节　科技交流信函　／121

　　第四节　期刊论文摘要　／136

　　第五节　研究计划写作　／144

　　第六节　研究报告写作　／152

第八章　科技文献检索　　156

　　第一节　中英文数据库及检索方法　／156

　　第二节　科技报告的检索　／158

附　录　　162

　　附录Ⅰ　公制单位的前缀和缩略词　／162

　　附录Ⅱ　常用希腊字母的科技文体应用　／163

　　附录Ⅲ　市制、公制、英制间的换算　／164

　　附录Ⅳ　科技文献常用动词　／165

　　附录Ⅴ　常用表达替换　／168

　　附录Ⅵ　常用科技英语词缀　／174

第一章　科技英语概论

英语不仅是一种形式丰富、成分复杂的语种，而且是世界上词汇量最大的语言之一。随着科学技术的不断发展，人类的生活也发生了日新月异的变化。这就必然使英语呈现更多适应这种变化的表达形式和用语，以满足人们各种活动的需要。科技英语（English for science and technology，缩写为 EST）泛指涉及科学和技术的英语书面语和口语，它是随着科学技术的发展而逐渐形成的一种文体，由普通英语演化发展而来，因而与普通英语相比较而言，既有共性，也有特性。本章将针对科技英语的专属特征，从文体、语法、修辞三个方面阐述英语科技文体的突出特点。

第一节　科技语言文体特征

文体是人们在不同的交际环境下，以特定的方式，同特定的交际对象，围绕特定的目的进行语言交际时所使用的不同语言形式。科技文体泛指一切论及或谈及科学和技术的书面语和口语，是随着科学技术的发展而逐步形成的一种特色文体。

（一）科技英语文体特征

1. 非人称化

科技文体第一个显著的特点就是非人称化。可以说，大多数科技文章（scientific articles）很少使用有人称的句子。这主要是由于科技文章所描述和讨论的是科学发现或科学事实。尽管科技活动系人类所为，但由于科技文章所报告的主要是这种科技的结果或自然规律，而不是报告这些结果或自然规律是由谁发现或完成的，因此，科技文章往往没有人称。例如：

①The general layout of the illumination system and lenses of the electron microscope correspond to the layout of the light microscope.

②The electron "gun" which produces the electrons is equivalent to the light source of the optical microscope.

③The electrons are accelerated by a high-voltage potential (usually 40,000 to 100,000 volts), and pass through a condenser lens system usually composed of two magnetic lenses.

④The system concentrates the beam onto/on the specimen, and the objective lens provides the primary magnification.

⑤The final images in the electron microscope must be projected onto/to a phosphor-coated screen so that it can be seen.

⑥For this reason, the lenses that are equivalent of the eyepiece in an optical microscope are call "projector" lenses.

(From Thornley G. C., *Further Scientific English Practice*)

显然，上面段落包含的6个句子都是非人称句。但需要说明的是，在科技文体中，无人称化并非绝对现象。有时由于行文要求，也会使用一定量的人称，比如使用"we"的情况是较为多见的。但总的来说，人称句在科技文章中出现频率较低。

2. 语气正式

由于科技活动本身是一件十分严肃的事情，不容含混、隐约其词，因而无论是普通科技文体还是专用科技文体，语气都较正式，语言表述完整。例如：

①The burning of coal is very wasteful of energy.

②This can be realized when we remember that one pound of coal burned in the furnace of a power station will raise enough steam to drive a generator that will produce enough current to light a one-bar electric fire for three hours.

③On the other hand, if all the energy in the atoms of a pound of coal could be released, there should be energy to drive all the machinery in all the factories in Britain for a month.

④In simple words, all this means that one pound of any element or compound of elements, if completely converted into energy by breaking up the atoms, would release the same amount of heat as the burning of 1,500,000 tons of coal.

⑤Scientists have calculated that if a bucket of sand from the beach could be completely converted into energy and if the energy so obtained was used to drive electric generators, enough current would be produced to supply the whole of Europe for five year.

⑥In other words, a bucket of sand contains enough energy to generate a thousand million pounds' worth of electricity.

（From Thornley G. C., *Further Scientific English Practice*）

从上述段落中的 6 个句子中，可以明显看出科技文章语气正式的特点。其句子结构完整，无任意省略，词语使用规范。尽管它为科技文体中正式化程度较低的科普文章，但对科技内容表述的语气与普通文章相比，较为正式。

3．语言规范、专业性强

科技文体语言规范，具体表现为语法的规范性。这与文学作品有很大不同。科技文体的语法之所以规范，是由其描述客观事物必须准确无误这一要求所决定的。科技语言是构成科技理论、科技工作者语言的基础，其语义具有严谨性和单一性。具体体现在以下三个层面：

1）数据呈现频繁

科技文体中，数据显现频繁，表达方式多样。中英文在数据表述规约方面的差异，如中文是个、十、百、千、万、十万、百万、千万、亿……，以"十"的倍数来表示；而英文则是在数字超过千以后，以"千"（thousand）的倍数来表达，"一万"（ten thousand），"十万"（hundred thousand），"百万"（million），"千万"（ten million），"亿"（hundred million）……此外，在表示倍数、长度、面积、体积、容量等单位上也存在较大差异。详见附录Ⅲ。

①It is generally accepted in the railway industry that curve resistance is approximately the same as a 0.04% upgrade per degree of curvature (which equals 0.8 lb/ton per degree of curvature) for standard gauge tracks.

②Costs can be reduced $\frac{1}{5}$ by this process.

③This process consumes 5% less fuel and produces 12% more power.

2）用词精准讲究

科技文体中的用词准确规范，存在着大量的专业词汇，即专用于某个学科或专业的词汇或术语。在科技文体中也存在普通词汇，但与它们在一般英语中的措辞是不同的，这主要是由于科技文献更加偏向于书面语，并且大词和长词的出现频率远高于一般英语文体，如表 1-1 所示。

表 1-1　通识科技英语常用大词

Big words	Small words	Big words	Small words	Big words	Small words
accomplish	do	commence	start, begin	prior to	before
acquire	get	concerning	about	demonstrate disclose exhibit indicate present reveal	show
additional	extra	consequently	so	provide	give
alteration	change	considerable	much	purchase	buy
assistance	help	construct	build	regarding	about
application	use	elevated	raised, high	remuneration	pay
magnitude	size, amount	encounter	meet	render	make
magnify	enlarge	equivalent	equal	sanguineous	bloody
maximum	highest, largest	identical	same	similar to	like
nocturnal	night	illuminate	light	sufficient	enough
numerous	many	indication	sign	termination	end
optimum	best	inquire	ask	transplant	graft

此外，科技文体里也常用规范且语义明确的书面语动词来代替普通英语中的多义且易生歧义的动词短语或动词词组，如表 1-2 所示。

表 1-2　通识科技英语书面语动词

EST	Common English	EST	Common English	EST	Common English
absorb	take in	escape	get away	reciprocate	move backwards and forwards in a straight line
aggregate	put together	evaporate	turn … into vapor	reflect	throw back

4

续表

EST	Common English	EST	Common English	EST	Common English
be precipitated	fall down	extract	take out	release	set free
eliminate	get rid of	lengthen	grow longer	rise	go up
combine	join together	liquify	turn … into liquid	replace	put back
decompose	break up	moisten	make wet	shorten	grow shorter
diffuse	spread out	neutralize	make neutral	solidify	become a solid
emerge	come out	observe	look at	survive	stay alive
ensure	make sure	overflow	pour out over the top	transmit	pass on

3）语法结构严密

在语法结构方面，科技文章里的句子一般都结构严密，语法规范，不会出现语义上模棱两可的情况。比如在下面的这个句子中，为了避免使用人称代词 it 带来的语义上的模糊性，选择了对相关名词进行重复。

If a splice is used in the manufacture of the **gasket** , the strength shall be such that the **gasket** shall withstand 100% elongation over the part of **gasket** that include the *splice* with no visible separation of the *splice*.

4. 陈述客观

科技文章是反映客观事物的，文章中不能掺杂作者个人的主观意识，对客观事物的陈述必须客观、准确。这既是科技文体的特征，也是对科技文章作者的基本要求。

1）使用名词和名词短语

为了实现客观性和正式性，在科技写作中，通常使用名词或名词短语来代替动词和形容词。试对比下列两个句子：

①The rate of evaporation of a liquid enormously depends on temperature.

②The dependence of the rate of evaporation of a liquid on temperature is enormous.

2）使用被动语态

在科技语言中，动作的执行者并没有动作本身那么重要，因为科学家们更关注的是事物和过程，而不是进行实验的人，所以多采用被动语态。试对比下列两个句子：

①We can improve its performance when we use super-heated steam.

②An improvement of its performance can be effected by the use of super-heated steam.

3）使用先行词 it

类似于被动语态的使用，在科技语言中，科学家们更喜欢用先行词 it 来表达科学家的客观态度。试对比下列两个句子：

①Some scientists suggested that this "active nitrogen" consisted of the gas in its atomic state.

②It was suggested by some scientists that this "active nitrogen" consisted of the gas in its atomic state.

5. 逻辑性强

虽然逻辑属于非语言因素的范畴，但与语言的关系密不可分。科技文章用语言表达科学理论、规律、概述以及事物之间错综的关系，阐述事理逻辑性强。例如：

The moon is a world that is completely and utterly dead, a sterile mountainous waste on which during the heat of the day the sun blazed down with relentless fury, but where during the long night the cold is so intense that it far surpasses anything ever experienced on the earth.

月球是一个毫无生机的世界，贫瘠多山。白昼赤日炎炎，烈日当空，灼热无情。而在漫长的夜晚，冰冷严寒，这极寒温度远远不是我们在地球上所能体验到的。

该句结构复杂，但关系清楚，逻辑性强。句子含有一个主句，另外含有四个分句：由关系词"that""which""where"引导的三个定语从句，以及一个 so...that 结构的状语从句。理顺主从句后，本句想要说明的月球的特性就一目了然了。

（二）科技文体分层

方梦之、范武邱（2008，2015）根据科技语域的语场、语旨和语式将科技文体分为两个类别、六个层次，科技变体Ⅰ～Ⅵ的语域特征如表1-3所示。

表1-3　科技语域分类与层次

文体	正式程度	语场	语旨	语式
普通科技文体	Ⅰ（低）	科普读物、中小学教材	专家与外行之间	自然语言 避免术语 多用修辞格
	Ⅱ（较低）	消费领域的产品说明书、使用手册、促销材料等	生产部门与消费者之间	自然语言 少量术语 句法灵活
	Ⅲ（中等）	生产领域的操作规程、维修手册、安全条例等	生产部门的技术人员、职工之间	自然语言 部分术语 句法刻板

续表

文体	正式程度	语场	语旨	语式
专用科技文体	Ⅳ（较高）	应用科学技术论文、报告、著作	同一领域的专家之间	自然语言为主辅以人工符号较多专业术语句法规范
	Ⅴ（很高）	科技论著、法律文本	高级管理人员之间、律师之间或专家之间	自然语言为主辅以人工符号较多专业术语句法严密
	Ⅵ（最高）	数学、力学等基础理论科学论著、报告	科学家之间	人工语言为主辅以自然语言较多专业术语句法严谨

1.普通科技文体

主要包括科普文章（popular science/science article）及技术文本（technical prose/document）。其语场是传播科技知识、描写生产过程、说明产品的使用方法等；语旨是内行对外行；语式是采用自然语言，偶用人工符号，用词生动，句法简易，文风活泼，多用修辞格。技术文本包括：①通信，包括电子邮件、备忘录、公司与客户之间的商务信件；②营销，包括经营管理文件和推销促销材料；③产品操作指南和使用说明书；④建议书，包括对实施新项目的建议、对改变生产过程的建议等；⑤报告书，包括请示报告、项目可行性研究报告书、实验报告、项目进行报告等。

普通科技文体的主要特点是用词平易、句式简单、多用修辞格，有较强的劝导性（persuasiveness），劝导读者做什么或不做什么、怎么做，劝导读者相信什么或质疑什么。

2.专用科技文体

主要包括技术性法律文本和科技著述。其语场包括基础科学理论、技术性法律条文，涉及科学试验、科学技术研究、工程项目、生产制造等领域；语旨是内行对内行；语式中，抽象程度很高的基础科学理论的论著的语式以人工语言为主，辅以自然语言，不是行家的翻译工作者难以理解。技术性法律文本具有法律效力，包括专利说明书、技术标准、技术合同和协议书，以及其他生产技术中有法律效力的条款、规程和章法；科技著述指有关专著、论文、科研报告等。

专用科技文体一般特点是表述客观、逻辑严密、行文规范、用词正式、句式严谨。

第二节　科技英语语法特征

作为英语语言的一部分，科技英语以其行文庄重、结构严谨、力求客观、感情色彩少而著称。对科技英语语言特点进行分析，我们可以看出语法结构的不同单位（词、句、语篇）均在时态、语态、情态、语气等方面显示出其显性的语法特征。

（一）时态因子

语法学中所说的"时"或"态"，主要是指行为发生或状态存在的时间与陈述时间之间的交互关系（傅勇林、唐跃勤，2012）。英语为印欧语系语言，时态与动词的屈折变化相关性较大，动词是讨论的重要范畴；而汉语属于典型的汉藏语系语言，汉语中动作的时间和状态并非通过动词词形变化来体现，主要通过词序及虚词来表达语法概念、明确时间关系，通过不同助词的添加来表明动作所处的不同阶段，或时态意义暗含在语义中，无任何显性标记。

科技英语具体通过三种方式来表达时态：一是单词法，如 now，then，first，finally 等；二是时间短语组合法，如 ten years ago，in the future，at the end of，after the confererce 等；三是屈折时态法，即通过助动词和谓语动词的屈折变化来体现时间关联。

（1）科技文体中最常见的时态是一般现在时态，用于表示行为或事物发生的时间与说话时间存在的匹配关系，将行为或事物从提供参照时间的任务中解脱出来，其价值体现在陈述命题内容的真实性上，例如：

①Nuclear transfer *involves* the use of two cells. The recipient cell *is* normally an unfertilized egg taken from an animal soon after ovulation.

核移植需要使用两个细胞。受体细胞通常取自排卵不久的动物的一个未受精卵。

②Electronically controlled support magnets located on both sides along the entire length of the vehicle *pull* the vehicle up to the ferromagnetic stator packs mounted to the underside of the guideway.

电子控制的悬浮磁铁贯穿车辆的两侧，这些磁铁使车辆吸住安装在导轨下方的磁铁电子元件。

（2）科技文体在陈述已发生的自然现象或已进行的活动时，通常使用一般过去时态，例如：

Antonio Navarra *said* the whole Mediterranean region *was* two to three degrees warmer than usual this summer and if the heat persisted, it *would* be consistent with the institute's climate simulations showing the potential effect of greenhouse gases.

Antonio Navarra 说,今年夏季整个地中海地区的气温比以往夏季气温高出 2 至 3 度,如果高温天气仍持续下去的话,这将与该学会所进行的关于温室气体潜在气候模拟试验结果一致。

(3)科技文体中多用一般完成时表述已经发生的动作或获得的研究成果。

①Extracellular vesicles（EVs）— nanometer sized messengers that travel between cells to deliver cues and cargo — ***are*** promising tools for the next generation of therapies for everything from autoimmune and neurodegenerative diseases to cancer and tissue injury. EVs derived from stem cells ***have already been shown*** to help heart cells recover after a heart attack, but exactly how they ***help*** and whether the beneficial effect ***is*** specific to EVs derived from stem cells ***has remained*** a mystery.

细胞外囊泡(EVs)是一种在细胞间穿梭传递信息和物质的信号分子,可用于自身免疫疾病、神经退化性疾病到癌症、组织损伤等所有病症的治疗,其下一代治疗方案前期预期较好。已经证实,干细胞**分泌出**的细胞外囊泡能帮助修复心脏病发作后的心脏细胞,但具体的机制,以及这种效果是否仅由干细胞分泌出的细胞外囊泡产生,**仍然不得而知**。

上文范例原文并不长,但采用了两种时态。陈述细胞外囊泡的客观属性时,是客观事实的阐述,用一般现在时;表达干细胞分泌出的细胞外囊泡的功效及研究现状时,用现在完成时态。

②String theorists ***have scored*** some striking successes in the study of black holes, in which matter ***has been compressed*** to catastrophic densities similar to the Big Bang, but they ***have made*** little progress with the Big Bang itself.

弦理论家们已在黑洞(在黑洞中,物质已被压缩成类似于大爆炸的灾难性密度体)研究中**获得**了一些显著成果,但对于大爆炸本身的研究,他们**并未取得**多大进展。

描述弦理论家们所获得的研究成果时,现在完成时广泛使用。

(二)语态因子

就语态而言,英语中的语态分为主动和被动两种。英语中的被动语态主要通过语序变换、动词形态变化等语法手段来实现。英语被动语态的使用在客观上可以满足科技文体的如下表达要求:

(1)文体客观性要求。科技文体陈述的主体往往是从事某项工作的人或装置,而客体通常为客观事物、现象或过程,被动语态强调对客观的陈述,使读者注意力集中在被陈述的事物上,而非动作的发出者身上。

(2)凸显受事者要求。被动语态的使用可以强化受事者的表达,将它置于句子的前部以突出信息重心和关注焦点。

(3)语篇连贯性要求。被动语态的表达易连接上句,形成完整的语篇逻辑。

（4）礼貌原则要求。被动语态在特定语境中，回避主观武断的表达，利于表明作者的客观态度。

①In terms of numbers, the alliance today *is outmanned*, *outgunned*, *outranked and outplaned.*

②A knowledge of statistics *is required* by every type of scientist for the analysis of data.

③Many advances in computer technology took place in the twenty years after 1950. They *are generally classified* into four stages or generations.

④This text *has* also *been* successfully *used* to teach students in other fields of engineering.

被动语态强调的是动作的对象或动作的过程，因此在科技英语里一般都把施动者或行为者略去，但在某些特定情形下，施动者得以保留，如施动者属于某种动物、植物或物质，施动者为某一组织或机构，施动者是一种自然过程，施动者为某种情况或原因，施动者为赖以进行动作的手段或方法等。

（三）情态因子

人们对世界认知的有限性和使用语言的主观性，使人们对世界的陈述具有主观色彩，因而语言输出的客观性只是一个相对概念。在科技文体中，为了强化或者强调这种相对客观性，作者会有意识地、主动地使用能愿/情态动词以凸显自己的视角、情感和个体认知体验，使读者明白其情感意愿，正视并认可其陈述的相对性。英语科技文体的不同情态意义通过不同情态动词来体现，如表1-4所示。

表1-4　英语情态动词与情态意义

英语情态动词	情态意义
be able to, could, can	能力
shall, may, will	提议、建议
have to, should, must	必须、应该
used to, would, will	习惯
could, can, might	允许
must, will, ought to	推论、肯定
would, will	意愿

表达时需特别注意情态、能愿动词在表达说话人对某种可能性感到肯定或不肯定时，不同情态动词的使用体现意愿程度上的差别，以把控不同的情态。例如：

①The bearing capacity of this axially compressed short column *is* 2 tons.

这根轴压短柱的承载力达2吨。

②The bearing capacity of this axially compressed short column *can be* 2 tons.

这根轴压短柱的承载力能达2吨。

③The bearing capacity of this axially compressed short column *could be* 2 tons.

这根轴压短柱的承载力可达2吨。

④The bearing capacity of this axially compressed short column *should be* 2 tons.

这根轴压短柱的承载力应该能达2吨。

⑤The bearing capacity of this axially compressed short column *may be* 2 tons.

这根轴压短柱的承载力可能能达2吨。

⑥The bearing capacity of this axially compressed short column *might be* 2 tons.

这根轴压短柱的承载力或许能达2吨。

（四）语气因子

语气表示说话人对某一行为或事情的看法或态度，是思想感情运动状态支配下语言的形式。英语中的语气分为陈述语气、疑问语气、祈使语气和虚拟语气四种。汉语的语气即说话的口气，表示陈述、疑问、祈使、感叹的语法范畴，通过语气词（如"吗""呢""吧""啊"）和语调来实现。科技文体语气的选择同样基于对客观命题或事实真实性的判断，目的在于陈述事实，应依据作者的主观态度，选择符合实际情况的语气。下文重点解释祈使语气与虚拟语气在科技文体中的使用。

1. 祈使语气

多用于公式图表说明、产品说明书、操作规程、作业指导、程序建议及注意事项等英语无主句表达中。文体语言精练、简短，叙述条理清晰、简洁、客观。如公式图表说明中，常用的英语动词有 find（求）、show（证明）、solve（解）、evaluate（计算）、compute（计算）、prove（证明）、determine（确定、计算）、draw（画出）、construct（做图、画出）等。例如：

① *Solve* these equations for the unknowns.

② *Observe* the resin manufacturers' recommendations about mixing and application of the resin.

2. 虚拟语气

英语中的虚拟语气可分为三种：表示与事实相反、不可能实现或难以实现的事，表示主观愿望、要求、建议等，表示语气委婉或主观推测。科技文体中，虚拟语气常用于表示与事实相反、不可能实现或实现的可能性不大的事，主要有以下五种结构。

1）if 引导的虚拟条件句（表 1-5）

表 1-5　if 引导的虚拟条件句

假设时间	条件句中的谓语形式	主句谓语形式
与现在事实相反	过去时 ①一般动词用过去式 ②be — were/was	过去将来时 should/would/could/might+v.
与过去事实相反	过去完成时 had+pp.	过去将来完成时 should/would/could/might+have+pp.
与将来事实相反 （推测与告诫）	①should+v. ②were to do	过去将来时（不易实现的事） 一般将来时/一般现在时（能够实现的事）

例如：

①What *would happen if* the boy on the bridge *had thrown* the stone at 20 m/s exactly horizontally instead of vertically?

② *Were* an error to exist, *it is amplified* and *applied* to a motor drive.

2）"that（从句引导词）+should+v.（从句谓语）"的结构（表 1-6）

表 1-6　"that（从句引导词）+should+v.（从句谓语）"的结构

形容词	necessary, essential, important, imperative, possible, impossible, natural, desirable, reasonable, better, preferable 等	It+is+*adj.*+that S+v.+it+*adj.*+that
及物动词	require, demand, suggest, desire, propose, order, recommend, request, necessitate 等	It+v.（passive）+that S+v.（active）+that
名词	requirement, suggestion, necessity, importance, desire, recommendation, request, order, condition, constraint, restriction, restraint, philosophy, time, idea, proposal, motion 等	It+is+*n.*+that *n.*+is+that+v.（passive）

例如：

①极为重要的是，每一步测量得准确。

It is of paramount importance（*extremely important*）*that* correct measurements **be carried out** at every step.

②他们认为，重要的是应注意距离、速度和加速度的代数符号。

They consider *it important that* proper attention *be paid* to the algebraic signs of distances, velocities, and accelerations.

③建议立即修改这一设计。

It is suggested that this design *should be modified* at once.

④国际电工技术委员会建议，应该放弃这一标准而采用基于载流导体之间磁力的一种标准。

The International Electrotechnical Commission has *recommended that* this standard *be abandoned* in favor of one based on the magnetic forces between current-carrying conductors.

⑤读者用袖珍计算器来做基础电子学中所要求的数学计算。

It is recommended that the reader *use* a pocket calculator to do the mathematical work required in basic electronics.

⑥$x-a$ 能够除尽分子的条件是，$x=a$ 是一个根。

The *condition* that $x-a$ divide the numerator is that $x=a$ *be* a root.

3)用于某些固定表达中（如 provided that, unless, without, under, by, but for = were it not for, in the absence of 等）

①Everything on the earth will lose its weight *provided* there be no gravity.

② Some things, like satellite communications, would be impossible *without* semiconductors.

③ *But for* the binary system, the electronic computers might have been much more complicated.

④ *In the absence of* gravity, there would be no air around the earth.

4)用于某些固定结构中(表1-7)

表1-7　虚拟语气用于某些固定结构中

英文标志词	从句中的谓语形式
as if as though	涉及现在：过去时 涉及过去：过去完成时
whether … or …(省略 whether 需倒装) no matter …	(should)+v. (should)+v.
lest, in case, for fear that	(should)+v.
in order that/so that	(should/could/would/might)+v.
if only wish would rather	涉及现在/将来：过去时 涉及过去：过去完成时

例如：

①In this case, the leaves of the electrometer will diverge just **as if** they **had been charged** from a body electrified by contact.

②After all, all living creatures live by feeding on something else, **whether** it be plant **or** animal, dead or alive.

③The electron speed must be that given by Eq. (35-2) **in order that** the electrostatic attraction of the nucleus **not pull** the electron into it.

④Batteries should be kept in dry place **lest** electricity (should) leak away.

⑤政府提议，每个餐厅老板都应装备接纳残疾人用餐的设备。

It is the government's proposal that owners of restaurants should equip them to admit disabled people.

5）虚拟式动词原形用于正式文体

动词原形作为虚拟时态一般用在正式文体中。

（1）用于条件从句中，所表的假设是可能实现的，其结果主句应用直陈语气。如：

If the heart **be** malformed, the condition may be ascertained by the x-ray examination.

（2）用于目的与让步状语从句中。

Let us act and net shrink for fear our motives **be** misunderstood.

（3）虚拟式动词原形置于主语之前，如：

All magrets behave the same, **be** they large or small.

（4）虚拟式动词原形用于主语从句和宾语从句中，如：

I would like to suggest newspaper reporters **not write** this kind of article any more.

（5）虚拟式动词原形用于独立句中，如：

Long **live** the People's Republic of China!

第三节　科技英语修辞特点

西方对语体、文体的研究已经成为现代修辞研究的基础。实际上，众多修辞格的选择并非此有彼无的问题，而是在不同文体中使用频率与使用场合的问题。科技文章用于客观阐明事理和论述问题，要求文体清晰、准确，语言精练、严密，个人风格和感情色彩渗入较少。英语科技文体中，修辞格在科学论著、技术文本和科普文章等中都有不同程度的应用。科技文体(尤其是科普文章)中常使用明喻、暗喻、提喻、拟人等修辞格，将抽象的事物具体化、形象地展现给读者，同时使文章更具有简洁性、可读性和趣味性，从而更好地反映科技英语文体严谨、表达确切而不失灵活性的特点。翻译过程中，首选对应修辞格，但由于两种语言修辞格构成以及使用场合和方法不一，有时需进行修辞格的转换。

（一）明喻

明喻可使复杂的技术词汇或者概念更加形象、具体、精练，因此在科技英语中应用广泛。

1. 词

①如 H-beam，V-belt，H-post，R-sweep，T-beam，J-scope，O-ring。
②如 U-bend，U-steel，U-shaped spring。

2. 句

科技英语中还经常使用 like，unlike，as，seem，as if/as though，similar to 等显性标志性词语构成明喻，使形象思维与逻辑思维相结合，使抽象的事物具体化、形象化，把深奥的道理说得通俗、浅显、明白，鲜明地刻画事物。

①When the propeller turns，it pushes the ship forwards ***just as*** a wood screw goes forwards into a piece of wood when it is turned.

② ***Like*** a solidly hit fast ball，the *Big Bang* is going-going-going.

（二）隐喻

科技英语中，科技概念抽象性较高，为便于科技传播与知识推广，经常使用隐喻描述读者不太熟悉的事物的性能、特点和用途，本体和喻体之间不用比喻词，只是在暗中打比方。这有助于创造一种非形象性语言所不具备的感染力。

1. 术语的隐喻

1）形态转移

如 butterfly bolt（蝶形螺栓），eagle nose pliers（鹰嘴钳），sunflower disc（葵盘），snail wheel（蜗形轮）。

2）性质转移

如 mother machine（工作母机），balance wheel（平衡轮），sister metal（同类型金属），high blood（贵族血统）。

3）动作转移

如 dog course（追踪航线），monkey driver（捶式打桩机），grass-hopper conveyor（跳跃式运输机），catfish efficacy（鲇鱼功效/效应）。

4）结构转移

如 sandwich concrete（夹层混凝土），cylinder wall（汽缸壁），party branch（党支部），axis of evil（邪恶轴心）。

5）功能转移

如 cyberholic（网迷），airbrush（喷枪），carrier rocket（运载火箭），mixing bowl（公路交叉点）。

6）领域转移

如 word processing（文字处理），digital nervous system（数字神经系统），plus or minus（增减），a catalyse for social change（促进社会变革）。

2. 明喻与隐喻喻体认知与翻译

语言是与概念结构一致的象征符号系统，概念结构也会反映在语言中。不同民族的语言使用者在认知客观世界的过程中会产生类似的概念结构。英汉两种语言所具有的相同或相似的认知方式会产生两种语言相同或相近的喻体，成为两种语言转换的前提。在实际翻译过程中，常采用直译喻体、转换喻体、直译加注、取代喻体四种处理方式。

1）直译喻体

网络空间包括飞速发展的无线通信系统：微波发射塔、通信卫星和低飞的卫星。其中，微波发射塔传送着大量的蜂窝电话信号和数据，通信卫星像串珠一样与地球在同步轨道上运行，而低飞的卫星就像忙碌的蜜蜂往返穿梭于全球，使得因相距遥远或行距不定而无法使用有线通信器材的人们取得联系。

It (Cyber space) includes the rapidly expanding wireless services: microwave towers that carry great quantities of cellular phone and data traffic; communications satellites strung *like beads* in geosynchronous orbit; low-flying satellites that will soon crisscross the globe *like busy bees*, connecting folks too far-flung or too much on the go to be tethered by wires.

译文采用直译喻体的翻译方法，保留原文中将通信卫星比作串珠（beads）、低飞的卫星比作蜜蜂的表达，串珠和蜜蜂在两种语言中认知喻体相近，直接译出，形象生动。

2）转换喻体

It was something too earth-shaking to handle with *kid gloves*, and Jaunte was anxious to make his name immortal.

这个事件是如此惊世骇俗，用小儿科的办法来研究显然不够，而且强特也急于想让自己的名字流芳百世，所以无论什么方法他都愿意配合。

原文中 kid gloves 的原意为"羊羔皮手套"，喻指娇弱之物。原文中 handle with kid gloves 字面意义为"犹如处理娇弱之物"，隐含"小心谨慎地应对"之义，结合语境，译为"用小儿科的办法（来研究）"，是进行了喻体的转换，更符合目的语读者的认知习惯。

3）直译加注

Is cloning technology becoming the sword of **Damocles** to human beings?

克隆技术是否正日益成为人类头上的一柄达摩克利斯剑，无时无刻不在威胁着人们的安全呢？

达摩克利斯剑（the sword of Damocles）喻指临头的危险。传说叙拉古（Syracuse）的暴君狄奥尼修斯（Dionysius）邀达摩克利斯饮宴时，在其头顶用线悬一出鞘之剑，以表示尽管大权在握但常朝不保夕。译文采用直译加注的方式，在直译出"达摩克利斯剑"后，加文内注"无时无刻不在威胁着"作为补充说明，使语义明确，易为读者所接受。

4）取代喻体

① The **babel** of their plan to invent a perpetual motion machine must terror to the ground.

他们想发明永动机的计划是空想，到头来必然落空。

原文中的 babel，意为"上帝之门"，直译为"巴别塔"，译文将其翻译为"空想"，源于《圣经》中 Babel 的典故：远古时人们意欲建城、修塔（"the tower of Babel"），但上帝担心世人会像神一样无所不能，于是不等他们把塔建成，就让人类使用不同的语言，使他们不能彼此交流，并将他们分散在世界各地，最终结果是城和塔都未成形。babel 现多用来喻指"混乱的情况"或"空想的计划"，这里的翻译舍弃了喻体，译为"空想"，易于被读者接受。

② The ADAM and EVA mathematical models were used in the calculation in which 18 kinds of organs or tissues for ADAM and 20 for EVA were considered respectively.

采用 ADAM 和 EVA 两种拟人模型，考虑了男性 18 种和女性 20 种器官或组织。

根据《圣经·旧约·创世纪》记载，神耶和华按照自己的形象创造了人类的祖先——男人亚当（Adam），亚当再用自己的一根肋骨创造了女人夏娃（Eva）。原文《圣经》中两个人物名称，翻译为大写的 ADAM 和 EVA，喻指拟人模型，转换原有文化符号概念，体现形式上的变化；另一处译为男性和女性，舍弃了喻体本身，符合译入语目标读者期待。

（三）提喻

提喻在科技文体中也称为替代修辞，主要指词汇的替代关系。在科技英语中，名词或名词短语的替代居多，其作用：避免形态上的简单重复；避免使用 it、they/them、one 等代词可能带来的理解上的随意性；能明确替代与被替代词语之间的所属关系。

①The exact composition of **the corrosion product** depends upon the atmosphere so that **the patina** may be protected or permit further corrosion leading to deep and penetrating attack.

在科技文献中，物质的命名一般根据其结构或者特点，主要使用学名，有时也会使用俗称。这样就有了等义词的替代方式。此句中的 corrosion product 与 patina 是等义词，the corrosion product 是学名，patina 为俗称。

②The list of **nondestructive testing methods** in Table 1 provides a range of proven tools for a variety of test conditions and materials. Yet we are aware that there are many other methods and modifications of the **methods** we've discussed.

提喻修辞结构中的"定语+中心词"或"中心词+定语"的词组常由中心词所替代。此句中定语（nondestructive testing）+中心词（methods）由中心词（methods）所替代。

（四）拟人

拟人赋予动植物和其他非生命的事物以人的特征，在科技英语翻译中，应尽量保留这种风格，与原文保持一致。例如：

①Since the early 1950s, when naval missiles **came of age**, the way in which the different navies evaluated the level of importance to be attributed to naval gun has been marked by ups and downs.

句中的 came of age 一般用来描写人，表示"成熟，到法定年龄"，但在这里用来说明舰载导弹的发展情况。

②The programme ready for computers to "**read**" is prepared in a specially designed language.

句中的 read 本应由人发出，这里使用拟人修辞手法，表达形象生动。

（五）排比

为了使结构匀称、节奏鲜明、重点突出，在严谨的科技文章中也采用排比。例如：

①物质可分为两类：单质和化合物。单质是一种不能分解为其他物质的物质。化合物是由两种或两种以上元素按一定重量比化合而成的物质。

Substances can be classified into elements and compounds. **An element is a substance** which has not been decomposed into other substances. **A compound is a substance** composed of two or more elements chemically combined in definite proportions by weight.

原文中的排比句式在译文中得以传递。

②Learning a foreign language needs **intelligence, confidence, diligence and perseverance**.

学习外语需要才智、信心、勤奋和坚持不懈。

（六）头韵

押韵包括头韵（alliteration）和尾韵（end rhyme）。头韵指相同的词首辅音在一组词、一句话或一行诗中重复出现。尾韵指相同的词尾辅音在一组词、一句话或一行诗中重复出现。英语科技文体的文章标题、引言部分常采用头韵，翻译时常作变通处理。例如：

①**Starts** with **S**, **Ends** with **Ex**.

怎一个"性"字了得

这则新闻标题采用头韵的修辞手法，又有英语单词特有的拆字法（将 sex 拆分）。

②Desperate **Need**, Desperate **Deed**.

燃眉之急，非常行动

③It is, basically, a response to propaganda, something like the **panic-producing pheromone** that slave-taking ants release to disorganize the colonies of their prey.

这大致是对信息传递的一种反应，像奴蚁释放诱致惊恐的信息素，以使其捕食的群体陷入混乱。

例③所示，汉译后，原文中的头韵辞格无法体现。尽管汉语也有 25 个辅音，但汉字主要用于表义，音义难以兼得。

（七）借代

借代是用 A 事物的名称来代替 B 事物的名称。A、B 两事物在某方面有着密切的联系，说到 A 自然会想到 B。这种修辞格在英语科技文体中较为常见。例如：

More often, the heart disease process progresses silently until symptoms occur because the **pump** is not supplying blood in sufficient quantity to other organs.

更常见的是，这种心脏病在发作过程中并无症状，后来发生症状是因为心脏不能给其他器官供应充足的血液。

原文中用 pump 代替 heart。医学上常按功能，将心脏比作泵，将肾（kidney）比作过滤器（filter）。然而汉英借代习惯有别，本句译文使用同词反复，译出实称。

（八）反复

反复就是在句中反复使用同一个词或短语，以增强语势和感染力。例如：

①**Your** own car. **Your** own phone. **Your** own place. **Your** dad's insurance.

②可采用下列运行条件：

a.装置处于规定负载和运行条件下；

b.装置处于满负载下（情况与 a 不同）；

c.装置处于无负载下；

d.……

The following operational conditions may be appropriate：

a)**device under** specified load and operating conditions；

b)**device under** full load（if different from a）；

c)**device under** no load；

d)…

（九）低调陈述

低调陈述指故意使用有节制的措辞来陈述事物。例如：

① This structure has novel features which are of **considerable** biological interest.

这种结构新颖，具有一定的生物学意义。

② **It has not escaped our notice** that the specific pairing we have postulated immediately suggests a possible coping mechanism for genetic materials.

不能不引起我们注意的是，我们所假设的特殊配对直接表明基因物质能复制的可能。

原文是詹姆斯·沃森（James Watson）和弗朗西斯·克里克（Francis Crick）在著名英国杂志《自然》上撰文宣布他们发现 DNA 双螺旋结构时所说的话，他们的声明读来只是轻描淡写，他们选择用这种低调陈述来毫不夸耀地引起读者对重要信息的注意。

第四节　汉英科技文体比较

无论是汉语还是英语，科技文体与非科技文体在语言选择上均存在差异。而汉、英语两种语言的科技文体也存在一定的差异。语言的对比研究有助于探讨语言的共性和个性，推动两种语言和文化间的交流和碰撞。科技文体译者"作为游走于两种语言之间的行者"，必须掌握两种语言的文体知识。本节以语言学为研究视角，将重点放在语言对比之上，从词汇、句法以及语篇特征三个层面立体呈现两种语言的共通点与特殊性。

（一）汉、英语科技文体共性

汉、英语两种非亲属语言可以进行转换，原因如下：其一，语言是全人类所共有的，各种发达的语言有许多相似的地方，这就是共性，是两者进行比较与转换的基础。其二，思维是人类对客观事物的认识能力，人类的思想意识和科学知识总有相通之处，因而语言的互译成为可能。

由于科技文体内容、使用域和语篇功能的特殊性，以及科技工作者长期以来的语言使用习惯，汉、英语科技文体具有一些共有的特点，可大致概括如下：一是客观性。科技类文章主要用于解释不断发展变化的客观科学事实，科技名词术语的推陈出新就是一个很好的说明。钱三强曾指出："科技名词术语是科学概念的语言符号。人类在推动科学技术向前发展的历史长河中，同时产生和发展了各种科技名词术语，作为思想和认识交流的工具，进而推动科学技术的发展。"二是精确性。科技文本表述精确，特别是专业科技文本一般不会出现含糊表达，形容词和副词类修饰词语使用有限，尽管科技文本的表达在不断变化，但精确性的原则始终如一。三是权威性。

科技文本需要权威性，术语表达要符合行业规范，语法和结构的表达也要符合语法规范。四是关联性。如科技论文所揭示的是自然界事物的规律及其本质，形成包括很多定义、定理、定律和结论的逻辑关联体。表达这样的内容，要求叙述严密、周到，句子凝练、准确。某些复杂现象间的依存关系往往要注意前后的关联，有时甚至是跨越某一篇文章的，是前期研究与后期研究的关联。也正是这样的功能目的性使得科技文本在语言学视角上形成了其独特的文体特征。

（二）汉、英语科技文体差异

汉、英语不是亲属语言，汉语属汉藏语系，英语属印欧语系。尽管汉、英语科技文体在整体趋势上有着共性，但是在具体的微观层面还是存在着许多差异，突出表现在词法、句法和语篇层面上。

1. 汉语科技文体特点

汉语科技文体是汉语在科学技术领域内使用的一种文体。它的语言材料是现代汉语。

1）词汇层面

科技文体中大量使用单义性、抽象词、文言词（尤以保留运用单音节动词的古代用法最为常见，用最少的信息载体传递最为丰富的信息，如"具、行、呈、司、被、为、饲、营"等）、外来词、反义词及虚词。

2）句法层面

第一，主语是客观现象、事物时，多用完全的主谓句；主语泛指人时，往往可以省略。

第二，主要用于叙述自然界的客观规律及其应用时，多用陈述句，语序多为正常语序。

第三，常使用固定格式和词组，如"跟……起反应""作用在……上""如图……所示""把……分解成……""设……则……""垂直于……""用……来表示""称……为……""过……作……""由……变成……""由此可见"等。

第四，单句复杂化。其一，多使用长定语和长状语。为了深刻揭示事物的特殊矛盾，区别事物之间的界限，准确地表达概念和判断，需要从数量、性状、质料、范围和所属等方面来限定名词所表示的事物，从时间、空间、范围、情态、程度、条件和方式等方面来限定动词所表示的动作变化以及限定形容词所表示的性质或状态，因此充当定语和状语的往往不是一个词，而是几个词，尤其是常常使用各种结构形式的词组。词和各种结构形式的词组在句子的附加成分内，错综编插、层次繁复，因而定语和状语等附加成分不断地增多和延长。其二，运用复合成分。汉语科技文体表达的是逻辑思维，即从大量的现象材料中，概括归纳出本质的规律来。因此科技文体中常常使用并列结构，这就是复合成分。

第五，大量应用复句。人类对自然现象及其规律的认识日益深入，用来表达思维逻辑的句法结构越来越精密化、复杂化。复句，特别是偏正复句常用来表达精密复杂的思维关系，常用的有：假设句"如果……那么……""若……则……""假设……则……"等；条件句"只要……就……""只有……才……""除非……不……"等；转折句"虽然……但是……""尽管……但是……""……而……"等；让步句"即使……也……""就是……也……"等；因果句"因为……所以……""……因此……""……之所以……是因为……""……以致……"等。这些在汉语科技文体中大量运用。

3）语篇层面

汉语科技文体是在科学技术领域内使用的一种语体。汉语科技文体叙述的对象是客观事物、现象。它的任务是论证自然规律及其应用。科技文体反映的是逻辑思维，逻辑思维是通过概念的形式，从现实中个别的具体的事物中抽象出它们本质的规律，以建立普遍性的公式、定律和定理等。因此，科技文体的语言必须做到概念准确、论证严谨、说理清楚、层次分明。汉语科技语篇注重客观性、公正性并着重陈述事实，避免主观性、随意性表述，不注重句子与句子之间逻辑关系的显性表达，强调句子与句子之间的语义连贯。

2. 英语科技文体特点

英语科技文体的主要特征：词汇含义深，用词简洁、准确，语句关联紧密，语法结构严谨，语气正式，陈述客观，逻辑性强，专业术语较多等。

1）词汇层面

科技英语文体用词规范，通常大量使用专业和半专业词汇，名词化倾向明显，较多用抽象名词来表示动作，拉丁语词源的动词和合成词用得多，常常使用缩写词、符号、公式和图表等，短语动词及表达主观行为和情感的动词使用少，很少使用夸张、拟人等修辞手法。

2）句法层面

科技英语文体常常使用固定句型、被动语态、名词化结构、名词连用（复合名词）结构、非限定性动词短语等，时态常用一般现在时、一般将来时等。

3）语篇层面

科技英语文体强调描述清晰客观、概念准确、逻辑性强、文辞简洁、条理井然、结构严谨等。

科技时代科学技术理论系统化，科学技术成为生产力第一要素，科学技术成果广泛用之于生活，科学技术研究成为重要的社会活动。人们的信息交流包含了更多的科技内容，人们的社会活动更多地体现了科学精神，人们的思维方式更加趋于科学化，科技语言也始终作为一个变量存在于广袤的多语环境中。

第二章　科技术语表达

索绪尔认为，任何语言符号都是由概念(所指，signified)和音响形象(能指，signifier)结合而成。词是最小的可以独立运用的语言单位，具有一定的表达形式，传递一定的意义，是兼具语音、意义、语法特色的整合语言体。在科技文体中，科技词汇是主要信息的载体，而科技术语是指在自然科学、社会科学和工程技术等领域使用的科技词汇，是科学技术领域中的专有词或表达方式。一般认为，科技英语文章中的术语(含科技新词和转义词)所占比率介于4%到5%，而随着新学科、新技术、新材料、新设备、新工艺的不断出现，科技新术语激增，目前使用的专业词典更新较慢，尚不能满足需求。

第一节　科技术语表征

(一)科技术语概念

任何语言符号都是由概念(所指，signified)和音响形象(能指，signifier)组合而成。词是最小的可以独立运用的语言单位，是集语音、意义和语法特点于一身的统一整体。科技术语就是科学技术领域中的专用词或表达方式，是在自然科学、社会科学和工程技术领域使用的科技词汇。与普通词汇不同的是：科技术语主要用于解释概念、定义现象、推导数据、归纳总结，其语义外延是根据所指关系而不是能指关系来确定；科技术语伴随科学技术的发展而变化，描述新现象、新事物、新成果的科技新词不断涌现，对科技术语的研究演变为突破二元对比范畴、动静皆宜的系统化研究。

术语一般具有以下特征。

（1）确切性（accuracy）：术语要确切地反映概念的本质特征，符合构词规则。

（2）单义性（monosomy）：一词一义、一专一义为普遍特征。

（3）系统性（systematization）：特定领域术语须处于明确的层次结构中，共同构成一个系统。

（4）简洁性（conciseness）：术语要简明扼要，易懂易记。

（5）延展性（extensibility）：术语要"取之有道"，"延而有势"。

（6）稳定性（stability）：术语审定发布后，不宜轻易改动。

（二）科技术语来源

参照国际标准 ISO/DIS 704，我们将英语术语的构成方式归纳为下列几种。

1. 普通词汇转化

来源于普通词汇的专业词汇，词汇形式基本不变，但语义被赋予了新的内涵。例如，power 一词作普通词汇使用时，其基本词义已相当丰富，如"能力、力量、权力、强国等"，该词被广泛运用于科技术语表达中，与不同词汇搭配、在不同的专业领域中被赋予了不同的意义，例如：

【物理】动力；电力；功率。如 horsepower（马力）；power source（电源）；power network（电力网）；rated power（额定功率）；power gain（功率增益）；power coefficient（功率系数）。

【化学】能，能力。如 chemical power（化学能）；catalytic power（催化能力）；the combining power（化合价）。

【光学】倍率，放大率；（透镜的）焦强。如 1000-power microscope（千倍显微镜）；telescope of high power（高倍望远镜）。

【机械】力，动力。如 brake power（制动力）；power shaft（动力/传动轴）；power gas（动力气体）。

【数学】乘方，幂；指数。如 the fourth power of x（x 的四次幂）

在术语翻译实践中，普通词汇语义外延而形成的科技术语，容易造成译者对某些专业术语的理解偏差，成为汉英翻译的难点和重点。因此，在翻译实践过程中，遇到术语化的普通词汇，译者应根据该词的基本语义进行专业化推测并依托专业词典进行查证，切不可随意揣测，任意而为。

2. 外来词汇移植

直接使用外来词或外来词中的某些词素或语素，通过构词法创造科技术语。科技术语中的长词、大词主要来自外来词（以拉丁语、法语和希腊语为主），在医学、化学、生物学、药物学等领域广泛使用。直接借用或移植扩容外来词是 20 世纪术语生成的主要方式之一；而 21 世纪以来，在"语言有限符号无限运用"（Von Humboldt）的认可下，不断挖潜，对外来词的吸收体现为对词素或语素的吸收。例如：

hydrogen（氢）（源自希腊语）⇒ hydrogenation（加氢，氢化作用）；hydrogen peroxide（过氧化氢）；sulfureted hydrogen（硫化氢）。

又如：

electric（电的，导电的，电动的，发电的）（源自拉丁文）⇒ electricity（电，电流）；electrics（电学）；electrician（电工，电气技师）；electrification（电气化，带电，充电）；electrify（使电气化，使充电，使触电）；good electric conductor（电的良导体）；electric arc（电弧）；electric automobile（电动汽车）；electric battery/cell（电池）；electric blanket（电热毯）；electric chair（电刑）；electric charge（电荷，电费）；electric clock（电钟）；electric bell（电铃）；electric fan（电扇）；electric heater（电暖器）。

3. 构词法生成

利用语言中固有的词素或语素，通过词缀法、缩略法、词类转换法、合成法的重新排列组合创造科技术语是现代科技术语形成和扩展的主要途径。例如：double-curved arc bridge（双曲拱桥）；bipolar code with zero extraction（零提取双极性码）。

1）词缀法：用词根（实语素）与词缀（虚语素）结合构成词语

desarmement（裁军）：des（非、不）+armement（词根）⇒名词

stability：stable（形容词）+ity（后缀）⇒名词

2）缩略法：单词或词组缩合而成

MTI：Master of Translation and Interpreting

3）词类转换法：将一种词类改变成另一种词类

output 产量（n.）⇒输出（v.）

4）合成法：由语素合成单词型术语，或由单词合成词组型术语

sound-proof construction（防声建筑）

cast-in-place（现场浇注）

anti-freeze agent（防冻剂）

（三）科技术语的分类

对于那些在相关领域中具有很少或没有特定专业知识的人来说，科技英语中术语的理解是第一道障碍。根据上述科技英语词汇的来源途径，可将科技英语词汇分为两类：一类是纯科技词汇，另一类是半科技词汇。

1. 纯科技词汇

1）意义高度专业化

科学技术的快速发展，需要新的术语来定义新现象和解释新事物，所以必须发明合适的术语。在几个世纪以来，科学家们不停地延伸各学科的词汇，这些词汇词

意大多精确、高度专业化。例如：sonoluminescence（声波发光）；tank crystallizer（槽式结晶器）；octave analyzer（倍频程分析器）；aberration（像差）；acetaldehyde（乙醛）。

2）使用词缀

很多科技专业术语来源于拉丁语或希腊语，带有前缀和后缀。例如polytetrafluoroethylene（聚四氟乙烯）这个词由五部分组成：poly-（前缀，有"多""复""聚"的意思）、tetra-（"四"）、fluoro-（"氟"）、eyhyl-（"乙基"）以及-ene（后缀，"烯属烃"）。因此，了解前缀和后缀的含义能够更好地帮助理解词意。科技英语常用的前缀和后缀，如附录Ⅵ所示。

2. 半科技词汇

1）普通名词专业化

这类名词具有两个特点：一是普通名词专业化后，实现普通含义的专业语义外延；二是同一个词汇，不同的专业领域有不同的阐释。例如，科技汉语中"反应"一词在不同场合具有不同的含义：某人在听到家人发生意外时的反应（日常生活）；氨与二氧化碳反应形成另一种物质（化学）；核链反应（核物理学）；梁对于梁上负载重量的反应（土木工程）。

科技英语中存在着大量的半科技专业术语，以下是一些常见的例子：

①probability

一般意义：可能性

【物理学】概率。如 probability current（概率流）

【数学】概率。如 prior probability（先验概率）；probability analysis（概率分析）；conditional probability（条件概率）

【计算机】概率。如 probability-based quantum finite automata（基于概率的量子有限自动机）

②carrier

一般意义：搬运工；邮递员；货车

【医学】带菌者。如 AIDS carrier（艾滋病病毒携带者）

【计算机】载波；载体。如 carrier extersion bits（载波延伸位）

【化学】载波；载体。如 heat carrier（载热体）；leadless chip carrier（无引线芯片载体）；catalyst carrier（催化剂载体）

③transmission

一般意义：传播；传送

【电气工程】输送。如 unilateral transmission（单侧传动）；transmission parameter（传输参数）

【物理学】透射。如 transmission line 传输线；diffuse transmission（漫透射）

【医学】遗传，传递。如 synaptic transmission（突触传递）

④deposit

一般意义：放下；放置；储蓄；保证金

【地质】矿床；沉积物。如 iron deposit（铁矿床）；deposit sediment（沉积物）

【化学】沉积。如 carbon deposition reaction（碳沉积反应）

【电气】附着。如 equivalent salt deposit density（等值附盐密度）

2）科技词汇的俗化

（1）保留喻体意义，舍弃喻体形象。例如：

So far as the work concerned, the **pluses** overweighed the **minuses**.

就这项工作而言，其**有利因素**更胜**不利因素**。

plus 与 minus 原本是一对数学术语，经俗化后，形成隐喻，原有科技概念成为内涵，而俗化外延后，得到新的引申义"有利因素"和"不利因素"。

（2）保留喻体意义与形态。例如：

Drawing US troops out of Europe was opposed by a House of Representative subcommittee on Thursday on the ground that they are psychological **epoxy** of Alliance.

星期四，众议院的一个下属委员会反对将美军撤出欧洲，理由是美军是盟军心理上的**黏合剂**，能将他们紧紧地聚在一起。

epoxy（环氧树脂）是一个化学术语，指一种强力黏合剂，此句用于比喻美军的凝聚力，尽管此前是化学术语，但其意义内涵与此句语境非常吻合，科技语言俗化的同时，也使语言表达更加形象化。

（3）保留喻体大意，变形喻体形态。例如：

然而，事实上，所有从事翻译这项复杂工作的人都具有或隐或显的理论，尽管这种理论尚处于**萌芽状态**，或者被轻描淡写地说成忠实于作者想要说的。

In reality, however, all persons engaged in the complex task of translating possess some type of underlying or covert theory, even though it may be still very **embryonic** and described only as just being "faithful to what the author was trying to say".

embryonic 一词来源于生物学术语 embryo（植物的萌芽期或者动物的胚胎期），译者运用 embryo 一词的其他形态变体来比喻翻译工作者具有的那种或隐或显的理论，形象而生动。

（四）英汉语科技术语构词法比较

英语科技术语构词方式丰富多样，主要包含词缀法、转化法、合成法、缩略法、拼缀法 5 种；而汉语科技术语构词方式也涉及汉语词的内部形态结构，主要是词缀法、转化法、合成法、单纯词、借用词、重叠词 6 种。了解英汉语科技术语构词法，对准确理解词义、选取适当翻译词汇非常有益。

1. 相同的构词方式

1) 词缀法

词缀法（affixation）又称派生法，指的是由词根或单词加词缀，即词首（prefixes）或词尾（suffixes）构成新词的方法，英汉语词缀均具有较强的分类功能。从词缀法构词地位来看，在英语所有构词法中，词缀法构词能力最强，是英语词汇扩充最主要的方法，因而构成的单词量最大。与英语相比，汉语属于独立词，词缀少，但词根多（英语常用词根 420 个，汉语常用词根 3，630 个，且词根多带有独立意义）。从词缀的发展规律来看，在英汉语发展的历史过程中，词缀都经历了实词虚化的过程。如英语 two 与 twi-，multiple 与 multi-；汉语中的"超"与"超-"，"化"与"-化"，"秀"与"-秀"等。掌握科技词汇构成中常用的词缀结构与意义有助于科技词汇的准确转换。常用英语科技术语构词词缀表详见附录Ⅵ。

2) 转化法

在对原有词形不进行任何改变的情况下，把一个单词由一种词类转用为另一种词类的方法，叫作转化法（conversion）。英语词类转化构词法兴于 16 世纪。莎士比亚曾利用转化法创造了不少新词。这类构词法在 18 世纪受到抑制，19 世纪重新活跃，20 世纪成为英语新词创造的重要途径之一（表 2-1）。而汉语词类标志不像英语那样严格，词类之间分工不十分明确，词类与句子成分之间不一定有一一对应的关系，因此汉语的词类转化现象更为灵活，大多数词类不仅有转化功能而且多功能转化普遍（表 2-2）。词类转化现象是语言发展的必然结果。（任学良，1995：362）

表 2-1　英语转化法

原生词类	转化词类
n.	*adj.*，*adv.*，*v.*，*prep.*，*conj.*，*int.*
adj.	*adv.*，*n.*，*v.*，*pron.*，*conj.*，*prep.*，*int.*
adv.	*prep.*，*adj.*，*n.*，*v.*，*conj.*，*pron.*，*int.*
v.	*n.*，*adj.*，*adv.*，*prep.*，*conj.*，*int.*
prep.	*adv.*，*adj.*，*n.*，*v.*，*conj.*
pron.	*n.*，*adj.*，*adv.*，*int.*
conj.	*pron.*，*prep.*，*adv.*，*v.*，*n.*
num.	*n.*，*adj.*，*adv.*，*pron.*，*v.*
art.	*adv.*
onom.	*n.*，*v.*，*adv.*

2-2　汉语转化法

原生词类	转化词类
名词	动词、形容词、代词、副词、介词、量词、连词、象声词
动词	名词、形容词、副词、介词、连词、代词、数词、量词、象声词、叹词、助词
形容词	名词、动词、副词、介词、代词、连词、数词、量词
副词	形容词、连词、介词、名词、动词、代词
介词	动词、名词、副词、连词
连词	介词、副词
代词	名词、形容词、副词、介词、连词、动词
数词	名词、副词、连词、形容词、量词、动词
量词	名词、动词、形容词、副词
象声词	动词、叹词、名词、形容词、副词
叹词	动词

3) 合成法

把两个或两个以上独立的词按照一定的次序合成一个新词，这种构词法叫作合成法（composition）。这种新词叫作合成词，又称复合词。英语合成词由基本词汇提供，借助原有词汇组合而成，合成形式灵活，不受英语句法在词序排列上的限制，主要有合成名词、合成形容词、合成动词三类。复合词形式多样，有些是单个的单词形式，如 trademark；有些中间带有连字符，如 high-profile；有些则是分开的两个词，如 black hole。合成法是现代汉语构词手段中最重要的一种，现代汉语具有独立意义的词根比英语多，其 90% 左右的是双音节或双音节以上的合成词，且涉及所有词类。

（1）英语复合词。

在科技英语中，科学家们使用复合名词是为了使句子简洁，语言精确（表 2-3）。例如，他们可能会使用"high-speed data communication"来代替"the communication of data at high speed"，"an electrically-charged emitter end"来代替"an emitter end that is charged electrically"。

表 2-3　英语复合名词合成法

结构	举例
n.+n.	diesel locomotive, force pump
adj.+n.	incandescent lamp, distant signal
ing+*n.*	loading platform, rectifying stone
*n.+*ing	side-loading, rail reconditioning
*n.+*ing+*n.*	rail reclaiming plant, rail fastening broom
*n.+*ed+*n.*	dip-forged disc wheel, dip-forged solid disc wheel

续表

结构	举例
v.+particle	flyover, turnout
particle+*v.*	uprise, input
adj.+*n.*+head	narrow-gauge railway, axial piston pump
adj.+*adj.*+*n.*+head	basic direct access method, double acting stop block
adv.+*adj.*+*n.*	locally catenative sequence, functionally distributed computer system
n.+*n.*+*n.*	gauge side control, gear change lever
capital letter+*n.*	A. 大写字母表示形状、特征、性质，如：U-steel, I-beam B. 大写字母为单词缩写，如：P-waves（P＝primary），Q-factor（Q＝quality）
greek letter+*n.*	gamma decay, gamma unit
语法合成词	double-curved arc bridge, circular one-shaft vibrator, automatic route control of trains

复合形容词的组成形式有"*adj.*+*adj.*""*n.*+*n.*""*adj.*+*n.*""*n.*+*adj.*""*adv.*+*v.*""*n.*+*v.*"等。例如：desk-top（台式的）；electrically-charged（带电荷的）；general-purpose（通用的）；long-range（远程的，长期的）；flightworthy（具备飞行条件的）；white-hot（白热的）等。

（2）汉语复合词。

汉语复合词是指由词根和词根组合而形成的词。它是汉语中最主要的构词方法，大致可分为以下几类（表2-4）。

联合式：意义相近、相关或相反的语素并列组合而成。

偏正式：前一个词根修饰限制后一个词根，整个词义以后一个词根为主。

动宾式：前后词根之间的关系是支配和被支配的关系。

主谓式：前后词根是陈述和被陈述的关系。

补充式：后一个词根作为一种结果状态并补充说明前面的词根。

表 2-4　汉语复合词合成法

类型	复合名词	复合动词	复合形容词
联合型	途径、价值	联结、凝滞	干净、恒定
偏正型	范例、功率	喷射、强加	单向、多轨
补充型	上升、下降	提高、破坏	持平、充分
动宾型	结果、原因	评介、示意	临时、冰封
主谓型	风暴、氧化	吻合、应对	气压、脉冲

2. 不同的构词方式

1）英语科技术语构词

（1）英语缩略法（shortening/reduction/abbreviation）。

在不改变意义的前提下，将词或词组的某些部分省略或简化，即使用缩略法，构成缩略词。在科技英语中使用缩略词是为了达到简洁的目的，科技英语中的缩略词可分为以下几种形式。

①首字母缩略词（initialism）。

A. 用一个词的首字母代表那个词，例如：

A＝ampere（安培）

g＝gram（克）

m＝metre（米；公尺）

B. 取一个复合词中各个词的首字母，重新组合，分别发音，例如：

AI＝artificial intelligence（人工智能）

CAM＝computer-aided manufacturing（计算机辅助制造）

IC＝instruction code（计算机：指令代码）/integrated circuit（电子：集成电路）/interior communication（通信：内部通信联络）/ionization chamber（物理：电离室）

GRE＝graduate record examination（美国研究生入学考试）/ground radar equipment（地面雷达系统）

C. 取一个多音节词中关键音节的首字母，重新组合，分别发音，例如：

ET＝extraterrestrial（外星人）

UV＝ultraviolet（紫外线）

G20＝Group of 20（G20 峰会）

②首字母拼音词（acronym）。

取一个复合词中各个词的首字母，重新组合成为新词，不再保留各个首字母自身的读音，而进行拼读。

radar＝radio detecting and ranging（雷达/无线电探测器）

sonar＝sound navigation ranging（声呐/声波导航和测距装置）

③截短词（clipped word）。

通过去掉原词的某一个或数个音节，构成新词。

A. 去尾（apocopation）。

pro＝professional（专业人员）

jet＝jet-propelled plane（喷气式飞机）

disco＝discotheque（迪厅）

co-op＝co-operative store（合作社）

memo＝memorandum（备忘录）

B. 掐头(aphaeresis)。

bus＝omnibus（公共汽车）

dozer＝bulldozer（推土机）

C. 掐头去尾(front and back clipping)。

flu＝influenza（流行性感冒；流感）

tec＝detective（侦探）

D. 保留头尾(syncopation)。

exes＝expenses（费用）

specs/specks＝spectacles（眼镜）

E. 词组截短(clipped phrases)。

because＝by the cause（因为）

fire brigade＝firefighting brigade（消防队）

（2）英语拼缀法(blending)。

拼缀词又称混合词或混成词。拼缀法指对原有的两个词进行剪裁，提取其中的首部或尾部，并将意义结合后，组成一个新词。从形态结构来看，英语拼缀法可分为4种。

①提取第一个词的首部和第二个词的尾部，将其合为一个词，例如：

botel＝boat+hotel（汽艇游客旅馆）

ecocide＝ecology+suicide（生态灭绝）

②提取第一个词原形及第二个词的尾部，将其合为一个词，例如：

workfare＝work+welfare（工作福利）

lunarnaut＝lunar+astronaut（登月宇航员）

③提取第一个词的首部及第二个词原形，将其合为一个词，例如：

psywarrior＝psychological+warrior（心理战专家）

medicaid＝medical+aid（医疗补助）

④提取第一个及第二个词的首部，将其合为一个词，例如：

modem＝modulator+demodulator（调制解调器）

aerosol＝aero+solution（浮质；气溶胶）

2）汉语科技术语构词

（1）单纯词。

单纯词指只有一个语素构成的词。它包括单音节词和双音节词。其中双音节词主要有三类：联绵词、古语词、音译词。

联绵词是指从古代汉语中流传下来的古体词，其单个音节没有意义，如参差、偿还、混沌等；汉语科技术语中，有许多动植物术语的使用均为联绵词，如苤蓝、菖蒲、砗磲、玳瑁等。

古语词又称"文言词"。它是古代汉语的书面词语，是从古代沿用至今的带有文言色彩的词语。如以、之、为、辄、乃、而、故、其、因、遂、就、盖、于、方、然、顾、固、卒、举、既等。

（2）音译词。

音译词是指直接从外来语音译过来的词。如克隆、基因等。

（3）重叠词。

重叠词是指词根重叠而成的词，这是汉语里独有的构词方法。汉语中的重叠词一般不改变词性和词义，有些词会产生新的附加意义。它主要包括三种情况。

①A/B 式：和/或。

②AA 式：丝丝、渐渐。

③AABB 式：形形色色、三三两两、断断续续。

第二节　科技术语翻译

语义的分级性和模糊性是英、汉语言的基本属性。语义的分级性涉及语义在质量、数量、程度和频度方面存在的差异。相同是相对存在的，相异是绝对存在的。语义的模糊性涉及语义在内涵和外延方面的模糊界限。精确是相对的，模糊是绝对的。因此除极少数单义词、专有名词和纯科技词之外，汉、英语中完全对等的词并不多。尽管专业技术词汇的含义相对固定且单一，但各领域通用的半技术词汇所占比重较大。翻译时只有进行适当选择，才能译出其真实含义。而对我们来说，英语非母语，我们对英语语汇的涵盖范围、搭配习惯更多限于语法框架的描写，并不一定能掌握且灵活应用。科技文章具有较强的科学性和逻辑性，文章的话语、语篇往往形成一个有机的整体，词与词、句与句、段与段、篇与篇之间都不是简单的机械堆砌。且在上下文中词汇的实际意义，在词典中是没有简单对应的，因此对于术语的理解与翻译，除应考虑科技术语的一般性特征(确切性、单义性、系统性、简洁性、延展性、稳定性)外，必须分析词语搭配关系、上下文语境、事理与逻辑关系甚至作者的思维顺序。翻译科技术语时，转换过程中还应注意以下几个方面。

（一）确定搭配关系

从英汉对比的角度分析，英语词汇的语义非常灵活，词的含义广，一词多义现象普遍，词义对上下文的依赖较大；而汉语词义严谨，词的含义窄，词义精确固定，词义对上下文依赖小。准确把握合成术语的语义，关键在于正确理解掌握术语的搭配关系。

1. 无动词基市合成词

1) $n._1$ 制造/产生 $n._2$

限定词 $n._1$ 规定核心词 $n._2$ 是用什么材料做成的，即核心词是由限定词所表示的材料做成的，从而把该核心词与用其他限定词修饰的核心词的概念意义区别开来。例如：steel band 和 rubber band 两者的概念意义不同，前者的 band 是由钢做的，后者是用橡胶做的，不同的限定词把这两个概念区分开了。这种合成词的目的在于：为了表明某种物体的材质，例如 iron bar；或者为了规定与这种材料或物质没有必然联系的核心词，例如：cane sugar（蔗糖）；coal gas（煤气）；oil film（油膜）；saw dust（锯木屑）。

2）$n._2$ 制造/生产 $n._1$

限定词 $n._1$ 可以表示与核心词 $n._2$ 有联系的产品，从而把该核心词与同其他产品有联系的核心词区别开来。例如 steel mill 是"轧钢厂"，copper mill 是"轧铜厂"，paper mill 是"造纸厂"。换句话说，核心词制造、产生限定词。再看下面的例子：computer factory（计算机厂）；oil well（油井）；rubber tree（橡胶树）；tear gas（催泪毒气）。

3）$n._1$ 驱动 $n._2$

核心词 $n._2$ 可以是限定词 $n._1$ 操作的对象，限定词是操作核心词的主语，是核心词的动力来源，即驱动核心词。限定词一般是物质名词，核心名词一般是机器、设备，即含有"工具"功能的可数名词。例如：air drill（风钻）；battery car（电池汽车）；oil control（油压控制器）；spring governor（弹簧调速器）。

4）$n._1$ 含 $n._2$

限定词 $n._1$ 可以表示整体，核心词 $n._2$ 是限定词表示的整体的一部分。两个合成成分的关系是整体与部分的关系，即限定词包含核心词。例如：bed post（床架）；motor drive（电机驱动装置）；oscillator plate（振荡片）；table leg（桌子脚）。

5）$n._1$ 是 $n._2$

限定词 $n._1$ 与核心词 $n._2$ 具有同一性。例如：tape measure（卷尺），其中的 tape（卷尺）就是 measure（量具）。限定词是核心词中的子类，前者是"种"概念，后者是"属"概念。例如：gear wheel（齿轮），gear（齿轮）是 wheel（轮）这一"属"中的一"种"。又如：blinker light（闪光灯）；pine tree（松树）；poison gas（毒气）；resistor element（电阻元件）。

这种方法可以用来合成过程术语，例如：repair work（修理工作）；chock therapy（电疗）。在以上的例子中，虽然限定词表示子类，但与核心词并未构成从属关系，而是完全平行的，如 city state，fighter bomber，merchant seaman，modulator-demodulator 等。

这种方法还可以用来合成属性术语：由限定词规定属性术语有关的概念，如方法、机器设备、测量单位等。例如：crosstalk factor（串话因数）；resonance constant（谐振常数）；speed ratio（速率）；wavelength（波长）。

6）$n._1$ 用 $n._2$

限定词 $n._1$ 规定核心词 $n._2$ 的用途，即核心词供限定词用。例如：block switch

（闭塞开关）；computer language（计算机语言）；office time（办公时间）；oil way（油路）；safty valve（安全阀）。

7）n.₁ 变成 n.₂

由限定词 n.₁ 形成核心词 n.₂，并起着限制作用。限定词一般是物质名词。例如 snowflake（雪花）的语义应该是"a flake of snow"。两者具有必然的联系，不可分割。这种方法合成的新术语，在性质上没有发生根本变化。例如：code word（电码字）；dustheap（垃圾堆）；raindrop（雨滴）；rainstorm（暴风雨）；rainwater（雨水）。

8）adj. +n. 组成新词

这种形式的限定词是形容词或过去分词，表示合成名词的固有属性，且这种属性是核心词没有的。这一合成方法也常用来给动植物命名。形容词限定词规定核心词的颜色、形状、大小、感觉或味道。限定词还可以表示对比的属性，从而产生一组反义词，也可以在过去分词前加副词，共同限定核心词，表示设备等操作方式或性能。例如：black pigment（黑颜料）；blank bill（空白票据）；dark room（暗室）；square coil（矩形线圈）；finished product（成品）；semi-finished product（半成品）；fixed point（定点）；floating point（浮点）；separately excited generator（他励发电机）；separately ventilated machine（他励通风式电机）；vertically-polarized wave（垂直极化液）；functionally distributed system（功能分布式系统）；most significant bit（最高有效位）；most favored price（最优惠价）。

9）n.₂ 像 n.₁

限定词 n.₁ 可以把核心词 n.₂ 与其他物体比拟。例如 stirrup frame 因两个物体的形状相同而命名，所以可译为"框式机架"。这种方式构成的术语十分普遍，生动而形象。如果两个合成成分的相似性并不十分明显，可以在两者中间插入"type"，例如 clawtype clamp（爪形夹钳）。这种合成方式体现了合成术语形成的过程。从发展趋势来看，起连接作用的"-type"在逐渐消失。例如：butterfly nut（蝶形螺母）；butterfly valve（蝶形阀）；catfish（猫头鱼、鲶鱼）；H-cable（H 形电缆）；U-steel（槽钢）；V-belt（三角皮带）。

2. 非名词术语

有人认为科技术语应全归类为名词，然而这种说法有失偏颇。科技文章中不单有名词术语，英语中的非谓语动词及常用于修饰术语的形容词是术语表达泛化的体现。

1）非谓语动词术语

The transrapid accomplishes the functions of support, guidance, acceleration and ***braking*** by using non-contact electromagnetic instead of mechanical force.

磁浮列车主要是依靠无接触的电磁力，而非机械力来实现支承、导向、加速和***制动***功能。

braking 在原文中以动词化名词形式出现，此词原义为"刹车"，译文将其改为"制动"后，行文更符合科技文章的特点。

2）形容词术语

With the subsequence years, hundreds of clones from half a dozen of species have been born from this remarkable ***assisted reproductive*** technique.

此后几年中，数以百计的克隆动物（源自五六个物种）都是通过该项神奇的**助育**技术繁殖出来的。

assisted reproductive 两个形容词均修饰 technique 这一名词，原义为"人工诱导"，改译为"助育"更为简练，符合术语表达特色。

3）动词术语

中医中使用大量的术语动词来表达中医治疗理念，"止"是常见动词之一，常见搭配很多，如行气止痛、宣肺止咳、凉血止血、温中止呕等（表2-5）。

表2-5　中医动词术语"止"的英译

"止"的汉语释义	"止"的英语释义	搭配词条	搭配动词术语
1.减轻、缓解 （如：止痛、止汗、止咳） 2.消除 （如：止渴） 3.拦阻、制止、使停住 （如：止痛、止呕、止血、止痒、止呃、止泻、止遗）	1. *relieve*（to mitigate or remove pain or distress） 2. *ease*（to make sth. less painful/severe etc.） 3. *alleviate*（to make pain or suffering less intense or severe） 4. *subside*（if a feeling subsides, it becomes less strong） 5. *lessen*（to make sth. become weaker） 6. *soothe*（to make a tense or painful part of your body feel more comfortable）	痛（pain）	relieve, ease, alleviate, subside
		汗（sweating）	stop
		咳（cough）	suppress, relieve
		渴（thirst）	quench, slake
		呕（vomiting）	stop
		血（bleeding）	stop, staunch
		痒（itching）	relieve
		呃（hiccup）	stop
		泻（diarrhea）	stop

（二）分析合成语义

构词法是介于语法学和词汇学之间的一门学科。汉语构词法与西方语言的构词法有各自的特点。汉语构词法主要属于句法型构词法，通过构词法创造出来的汉语术语有主谓式、动宾式或偏正式等句法特征。在拥有词形变化的西方语言中，常见的构词类型则属于形态学类型。基于这一点，在翻译合成术语时，我们应该基于汉语词法上的特点，结合传统的音译、意译、音意结合、形译、象译等翻译方法，适当地将术语译成主谓式、动宾式或偏正式等结构。例如：

pile driving → 打桩(动宾结构)

in-track grinding → 现场打磨(偏正结构)

up-and-down hump yards → 双向驼峰编组场(偏正结构)

ballast regulating & compacting plate → 道砟整形夯实板(偏正结构)

fire retardant paint → 防火漆

cut and cover → 明挖法(偏正结构)

flyover → 立体交叉(偏正结构)

U-steel → 槽钢(偏正结构)

P-waves → 地震纵波(偏正结构)

由于受科技英语中名词化倾向(nominalization)的影响,以及名词修饰语与名词之间有时存在着深层的语义关系,也有一部分从本质上属于动宾结构的术语被译为主谓结构,如我们日常生活中常说的"电力供应"(power supply)确切地说应为"供应电力",又如 rail reconditioning 按原有顺序应译为"钢轨整修"。

以上述特征为准绳,我们在翻译合成术语时还应处理好以下几方面之间的关系。

1. 单义性与简洁性

如中文里简化的术语"数据"既可指"数值控制"(numerical control),又可指"数字控制"(digital control),在此情况下,我们应该舍弃简明性而求单义性。

2. 理据性与确切性

一般来说,科技知识相对抽象,翻译合成术语时,在不损害基本概念的前提下,我们也可增加一点理据的色彩,如将"machine tool"译为"机床"就给人一种直观的感觉。

3. 稳定性与能产性

如在将"synchronous even pressure tamping system"正确定名为"同步稳压捣固系统"后,可相应地将"non-synchronous even pressure tamping system"译为"异步稳压捣固系统"。

4. 系统性与语言的正确性

翻译合成术语时,在正确把握原文的基础上,相当重要的一点是要遵循汉语本身的构词特点和构词规律。除了通过仿造法创造的汉语术语外,在创造汉语术语时,一般来说都不能生搬硬套西方语言中术语的结构语义。此外,还必须考虑汉语的构词习惯,尤其是汉语词组的构成习惯。如在英语中,无论是"铁路"还是"铁道"都可用"railway"表示,但汉语中"铁路"这个名词在某些词组中就不能使用,而要用"铁道"这个名词取而代之,如"铁道兵""铁道学院"等,同样,在有些词组中只能用"铁路"这个名称所组成的词组来表达新概念,如"铁路局""铁路医院""铁路交通"等。上述情况的出现是由汉语中的固定搭配决定的。不过,总的来说,它既没有损害系统性,也兼顾了语言的正确性。

5.结构性与语言接受性

就字数而言,在汉语中我们偏爱使用偶数(pair characters)词和词组,尤其喜欢采用四字结构。对《英汉计算机辞典》(人民邮电出版社出版)的统计表明,几乎有三分之一(32.01%)的汉译术语为四字结构。这就牵涉一个增词和减词的问题,如我们将"bistable circuit"从"双稳态电路"改译为"双稳电路";但在翻译"dog clutch"时,出于理据方面的考虑,却将其译为"爪形离合器";又如我们没有将"rubber-metal spring"简单地译为"橡胶-金属弹簧",而是形象地译为"橡胶-金属夹心弹簧"。汉语结构特性与语言接受性的结合是对合成术语翻译的一种更高层次的要求。

翻译科技术语,尤其需要广博的专业知识。我们认为,在翻译术语时应将以上几方面密切结合起来,使汉译过来的术语既有学术味又通俗易懂,既简洁又不致产生歧义,既切中原文的基本概念又遵循汉语的词法及理据色彩,以求达到科技翻译中的"信""达""雅"。

(三)置身语境考量

在实际语言应用中,词汇意义因语境的不同而变化,只有置身于具体语境中才能确定术语的确切含义。科技词汇意义的确定,应考虑联立语境与专业语境两个方面。

1. 术语联立语境

"词无定义,随文而释。"这里的"文"就是语境。因此,翻译时必须通读上下文,根据语境仔细推敲,按词汇的联立关系确定译词。

1)词语搭配关系

词与词的搭配关系就是词与词之间的横向组合关系,亦为同现关系。英汉两种语言体系不同,词汇搭配关系有异:英语一词多义现象普遍,汉语词语独立性强、搭配灵活。例如下面四个句子中均含有"facility"一词。

①Modern communication *facilities* were equipped in each fishing boat, so the fishermen could get in touch with each other at any place.

每条渔船都装有先进的通信设备,因此渔民们在任何地方都能保持联系。

②Regulations regarding the handing of hazardous wastes have become more stringent and complex. *Facilities* can no longer ignore their wastes.

有关有害废物处理的条例已更严厉、更复杂,厂家再也不能对其产生的废物置之不理了。

③All the *facilities* in this lab should not be taken out without permission.

未经允许，所有**器材**不能带出实验室。

④The site ideally should have sufficient lands to provide a buffer zone between the *facility* and the public surrounding it.

理想的处理现场在**设施**及周围公共环境之间应有足够的隔离区域。

facility 词义较多，可译为"工厂""设施""设备""器材"等。但从语义学的角度看，译为"工厂"语域最宽，内涵最广，由"工厂"到"器材"，其语域是依次递减并有相互包容的关系。①中 facilities 是安装在渔船上的，译为"设施"内涵太大，译为"器材"内涵又太小，因此译为"设备"比较合适。②中"有关有害废物处理的条例"显然不是针对"设备""设施""器材"的，况且它们也不能对"产生的废物"置之不理，译为"厂家"才合乎语境。③中从实验室拿走的往往是一些"器材"。④是有关环保的内容，把 facility 译为"工厂"内涵过大，译为"设施"较为贴切，因为"设施"的语域既可以包括设备、器材，同时也可将建筑物包含在内。

2) 词语语法功能

在处理较纯粹的科技语篇时，翻译的困难有时并不是在专业术语上，而是在普通词语的上下文和语法关系上。首先需要根据词语在句子中的词性确定词义；其次是根据句子结构确定词义。如：

①Bricks are also produced in many different colors and with various *finishes*, particularly those used for decorative purpose.

砖也可以烧制成许多不同的颜色，具有不同的**光洁度**，尤其是那些用于装饰的砖。

finish 一词常用作动词，表示完成、结束，此句中的词性发生了改变，用作名词。

②The method of propulsion is basically similar in the two systems. In both cases the train *effectively rides on* an electromagnetic wave.

两种系统的推进方式基本相同，在两种情况下，列车**实际上**都是**依靠**电磁波行进的。

effective 原义为"有效的"，原文中 effectively 为副词，在不考虑其修饰动词短语 ride on 的前提下，应译为"有效地"；ride on 本义为"乘着、驾驭"，而本句中这一动作的发出者为 the train，因此 effectively rides on 应译为"实际上依靠"。

2. 术语专业语境

1) 普通词汇专业化

普通词汇专业化是指同一词语词义的多专业化，即同一英语单词被不同的专业采用来表达各自的专业含义。科技英语词汇沿用大量日常词汇，这些词汇具有一词多义和一词多类的特征，且同一表达用于不同场合、不同学科或专业领域中，其含义有所不同。科技翻译涉及数学、物理、化学、电子、机械、计算机等诸多领域。一个词在不同领域中的运用，意思可能大相径庭。如 end 的常用义是"末端""结束"，但其在科技英语中有更多的专业意义：soluble end 溶解范围（化学）；variable short end 可变短路器（电工学）；the overseas end of Bell Telephone Corp. 美国贝尔电话公司的海外业务部（商务）；END 则可能是 endorsement 的缩略式，指商业上（支票）的"背书"（贸易）。

2）专业词汇专业化

同一术语用于不同场合、不同学科或专业领域中，其含义有所不同。

①在本论文研究中，使用了原位反应复合技术。

In this study, in-situ *reaction* technologies were used.

②新生叶较老叶反应敏感，敏感指数高，根系较叶片反应敏感。

The response of new leaves was more sensitive than old leaves; leaves *response* was more sensitive than roots response.

③无论你暴露在什么样的烟雾环境中，你的肺部细胞都知道，并且会起反应。

No matter what level of exposure you have, your lung cells know it and will *react*.

④我们对化学反应的极限有哪些了解呢？

What do we know about extremes of chemical *reactivity*?

（四）掌握翻译准则

1. 翻译原理

在一定的学科范畴体系内，一个术语原则上只表达单一概念，术语在使用时也不宜使用其他词语代替，但在翻译时，术语概念和形式的单一性原则受到挑战，这既有译者主观方面的原因，也受英汉语言的内在差异影响。其翻译原则主要受术语稳定性及术语变体影响。

1）术语稳定性

输出方术语语言的稳定性一般不易受翻译活动的影响，但输入方如果译名标准多元化，就可能影响术语的稳定性。

（1）汉语术语地位。与英语科技术语相比，现当代汉语因长期处于词汇转换过程的净输入态势，在与英语语言国家的科技交往过程中，汉语在多数情况下是术语的输入方，英语往往是术语的输出方，是被翻译的对象，汉语在输入科学知识的同时，科技术语也成为输入的主要内容，因而汉语科技术语的命名往往是译名的需要。

（2）术语政策导向。汉语在吸收英语科技术语的长期进程中，并未注重术语使用的规范性问题，译者汉语术语的稳定性相对较低。直至 1978 年 12 月，全国科学技术名词审定委员会（原称"全国自然科学名词审定委员会"）经国务院批准成立，其任务是负责制定中国科学技术名词规范化工作的方针、政策、原则和规划；负责组织科学技术各学科的名词审定、公布及协调、推广应用工作；开展海峡两岸及华语地区科学技术名词的交流、协调和统一工作；组织开展中国术语学学科建设和国内外术语学学术交流活动。

（3）英汉语言内在差异。英汉语言文化固有特征明显，且语言翻译传统有异。

（4）译者主观因素。由于译者自身政治、历史、专业领域的隔阂，术语翻译在不同历史阶段，按照不尽相同的标准，在不同的专业领域中进行。

2）术语变体

英、汉语在各自语言内部都存在不同区域变体、社会变体及语类变体，导致术语翻译变体差异。

（1）汉语方面，由于地理、政治制度以及历史和现实的差异，科技术语翻译早期所使用的翻译方法以音译+意译的文言翻译格局为主，现行白话汉语主要采用"双音节"构词法，音意兼备；我国各地区虽然都使用中文，但在表达形式上差异明显，比如台湾、香港、澳门。如：

Aluminum 铝［音译"阿吕金内姆"，太长。掐头去尾为"吕金"，缩短为"吕"，创造新形声字"铝"，读音为"吕"，部首为"金"（属于金属）］

aspirin 阿司匹林

penicillin 盘尼西林（音译）；青霉素（意译）

streptomycin 链霉素（意译）

Reagan，中国大陆译"里根"，中国台湾译"雷根"

Bush，中国大陆译"布什"，中国台湾译"布希"

（2）英语方面，也存在英式和美式两大变体，二者在科技术语的拼写、选词方面显示出一定的差异。这也给英汉科技翻译造成了困难。

变速箱：gearbox（英式），transmission（美式）

电梯：lift（英式），elevator（美式）

上述术语稳定性和语言变体影响问题成为术语翻译工作的主要障碍，若译者对这些差异缺乏认识及必要的语言规范意识，极易造成翻译过程中的疏漏，特别是对于汉译英而言：第一，译者无法正确理解原文中涉及地区差异的词语；第二，译者难以根据翻译服务对象的语言背景选用合适的译文用语。

2．翻译方法

1）音译

音译是语言间，特别是文字系统不同的语言间常见的一种词语借用方式，即用目的语文字材料模拟源语词汇的语音，实现词汇的语际借用。

hertz：赫兹

Teflon：特氟龙

radar：雷达

2）直译

直译指在保留原文内容的前提下，力求译文与原文在用词、句式结构、修辞和文体风格等方面尽可能趋于一致，使译文能够用相同的表达形式体现原文的内容，并且产生同样的效果。直译也可以理解为语义关系上的一种借译，其直接结果是目的语中出现仿造词，从而客观上丰富目的语表达。

iron：铁

clone：克隆

ferrous metal：有色金属

horsepower：马力

bluetooth：蓝牙

3）意译

意译指在不背离原文意思的前提下，对原文的词语、句子结构做适当调整，进行灵活的翻译处理。

LASER（light amplification by stimulated emission of radiation），包含光线、放大、刺激、散发、辐射五个义素。音译："莱塞"（中国大陆）、"雷射"（中国台湾，带有意译味道，而且与"雷达"类似）。意译："激光"（取原文的"光线、刺激"两个义素）。

4）直接借用

直接借用指源语词汇以其原有的文字形态被目的语直接借用。汉语书面语对字母文字具有相当的兼容性，因此在某些情况下汉语行文中可以直接借用罗马文字形式的英语词；而英语语言的发展尽管也极具包容性与开放性，但一般不会接纳汉字，其所接纳的常为罗马化的汉语拼音形式。

4C：carat-cutting-clearance-color

DNA：deoxyribonucleic acid（脱氧核糖核酸）

MTV：Music Television（音乐电视）

斤：*jin*

两：*liang*

豆腐：tofu

功夫：Kungfu

（五）使用翻译工具

译名不易，定名更难。术语翻译除非是首译，译者基本上不可能凭借纯粹的语言功底，借助名称的形态线索（语义、语音以及文字形式）把名称"翻译"出来，无论是汉-英语境，还是英-汉语境，术语和专有名词与其说是"译"出来的，不如说是通过纸质或计算机检索"查"出来的。在现实语言中，正常流通使用的译名，往往是经过长时间的讨论与验证才得以正名的，所以说，术语翻译与常规意义上的翻译能力关联度不高，译者的科技背景知识、资料检索的意识能力才是解决问题的关键所在。

1. 翻译软件

计算机辅助翻译软件(Computer Assistant Translation, 缩写为 CAT)不是机器翻译软件。它不是金山快译, 也不是译典通, 更不是网站上的自动翻译, 而是一种人机互动的充分利用计算机的计算、记忆能力强和人的创造性强的特点的辅助翻译软件。下文着重介绍"主流"CAT 工具与"小众"CAT 工具。

1) 主流 CAT 工具

通过查阅文献、搜索翻译技术网站和论坛, 我们发现在国内外的公司企业、政府部门、国际组织、译员、翻译公司中使用较为广泛的"主流"CAT 工具有以下 10 种。

(1)SDL Trados 德国公司开发(付费)。

(2)Wordfast 美国公司开发(付费)。

(3)Across 德国公司开发(付费, 自由译员免费)。

(4)Déjàvu 法国公司开发(付费, 试用版免费)。

(5)StarTransit 瑞士公司开发(付费)。

(6)Alchemy Catalyst 爱尔兰公司开发(付费)。

(7)MemoQ 匈牙利公司开发(付费, 高校师生免费)。

(8)VisualTran 韩国公司开发(付费, 高校师生免费)。

(9)雅信 CAT 中国公司开发(付费)。

(10)Transmate(桌面版) 中国公司开发(免费)。

TRADOS 是由 1984 年成立于德国的一家公司开发的, 2005 年被 SDL 公司收购后, TRADOS、SDLX、SDL Passolo 都已整合进了 SDL Trados 产品中。在所有用户群体中, SDL Trados 都是使用率最高的 CAT 工具, 这说明了它的市场主导地位。对于翻译人员, 尤其是翻译技术学习者而言, 市场的技术风向往往对于学习哪一种 CAT 软件具有重要影响。除了 SDL Trados 这种主导产品之外, Across、Déjàvu、MemoQ、VisualTran 以及 Transmate(桌面版)这样可以提供免费版本的 CAT 软件也是不错的选择。

2) 小众 CAT 工具

主流 CAT 工具数量有限, 除上述 10 种主流 CAT 软件之外, 可供企业用户、自由译者以及高校教学选择的小众化 CAT 软件也有一定数量, 之所以称其"小众", 主要是因为发布时间和地域等导致其市场占有率不高, 及其在 CAT 软件商业领域中的市场追随者角色。而事实上, 这些软件之中, 如 Omega T、Okapi、Idiom、雪人、传神等, 因其全面的功能以及实行部分免费的获取方式而在自由译者以及 CAT 技术研究人员中有着良好的口碑和巨大的潜力(周兴华, 2013: 94)。

(1)Omega T (免费, 开源)。

(2)Okapi (免费, 开源)。

(3)OpenLanguage Tools (免费, 开源)。

（4）Tansolution（免费，开源）。

（5）Lionbridge Logoport（免费）。

（6）MemSource Editor（免费）。

（7）Idiom（免费）。

（8）Babylon（免费）。

（9）Appletrans（免费）。

（10）Bitext（免费）。

（11）火云译客 iCAT（免费）。

（12）TransWhiz（免费）。

（13）Linear B Searchable Translation Memories（付费）。

（14）MetaTexis（付费）。

（15）MLTS（付费）。

（16）Globalsight（付费）。

（17）MultiCorpora MultiTrans（付费）。

（18）MultiLing Fortis（付费）。

（19）MadCap Lingo（付费）。

（20）TransAssist（付费）。

（21）Translatum（付费）。

（22）SMILIS（付费）。

（23）T-Remote Memory（付费）。

（24）Systran(桌面版)（付费）。

（25）Eurolang Optimizer（付费）。

（26）AidTrans Studio Basic（付费）。

（27）FastHelp-Windows Help（付费）。

（28）Araya Translation Editor（付费）。

（29）朗瑞（付费）。

（30）雪人 CAT（付费）。

（31）传神（付费）。

在这些小众化 CAT 工具中，除了 Appletrans、Babylon 仅适用于 Mac OSX 系统外，其他软件均适用于当前主流的 Windows 平台，而且一般都可以跨平台使用。而它们当中，有着更多的免费软件可供译员和翻译技术学习者选择。值得一提的是，这些免费软件中，Omega T、Okapi、OpenLanguage Tools、Tansolution 均为开源软件。开源软件赋予了用户极大自由，使他们能够按照自己的业务需求定制软件，有利于一些企业用户削减开支和人力成本，用户的挑错和改进反过来对开放源码软件包的完善也可以提供反哺，正可谓相得益彰。一些付费软件也同时提供丰富的免费版本，如 MetaTexis、AidTrans Studio Basic、朗瑞等均提供了免费试用版，MemSource Editor

拥有免费的个人版和学术版，雪人提供了免费的单机版和服务器版。不过，这些软件的免费版本往往在功能上都受到了一些限制。

无论是主流 CAT 工具还是小众化 CAT 工具，随着时间的推移，它们都不断地根据用户的需要进行版本的更新和优化。在软件操作方面，大多数 CAT 工具变得越来越简单便捷，例如，除 TransWhiz、Lionbridge Logoport、Omega T、MetaTexis、火云译客 iCAT 等少数几款 CAT 工具外，大多数的 CAT 工具均开始抛弃以往嵌入到文字编辑软件中的工作方式，转而采用独立的表格工作界面，原文和译文以句对形式显示在表格之中。这种工作模式具有"集成度高、稳定性好、界面整洁等优势"（徐彬、郭红梅，2012）。这些变化既降低了掌握 CAT 工具的难度，提升了 CAT 工具在译者群体和学习者之中的接受度，同时也避免了因为软件操作复杂导致翻译效率下降的问题。毫无疑问，这对于 CAT 工具的进一步推广和普及具有良好的推动效应。

2. 在线词典

1) 普通词典

（1）必应词典。必应词典是微软官方出品的英汉/汉英词典。支持本地词库及网络查询，更有快捷单词搜索、查询建议等贴心功能。本地词库包含 10 万个中英日常词汇，使用网络查询更可享用网络释义、海量例句及发音功能。输入单词可以自动匹配词条原型和变体，并提供简洁释义，方便用户快速选择要查询的词汇。

（2）欧路词典。可以下载语音库实现真人发音，独家支持 Mdict 和灵格斯词典库、生词本在线同步功能；常用英汉词条 30 万个，专业词条 40 万个，专业词库覆盖医学、经济、工程、计算机等十余个领域；具有同义词、反义词库；完整收录权威 WordNet 英英词典，包含 10 万条英英解释；50 万条常用例句库，不需联网也能搜索例句；独创 LightPeek 取词搜索功能，可以在安卓任意程序中进行取词。

（3）海词词典。海词词典，是中文在线词典网站，网易有道词典、腾讯搜搜词典、百度词典、灵格斯词霸等内容都来源于海词词典。2013 年开始，海词词典的移动客户端全面升级，配有精细讲解、优质例句、清晰发音，是涵盖初中、高中、大学、考研族、上班族等多重人群个性化的定制词典，拥有管家式每日学习提醒服务等众多功能。

（4）灵格斯（Lingoes）。灵格斯是一款简明易用的词典与文本翻译软件，支持全球超过 80 多种语言翻译，具有查询、全文翻译、屏幕取词、划词翻译、例句搜索、网络释义和真人语音朗读功能。同时还提供海量词库免费下载，专业词典、百科全书、例句搜索和网络释义一应俱全，是新一代的词典与文本翻译专家。

（5）爱词霸（iciba）。爱词霸包含词典、短句、翻译等众多在线工具，致力于英语学习交流、及时反馈英语相关问题等。它是金山著名软件产品金山词霸的互联网版本，专注于词霸网络百科全书为主的专业搜索领域。支持中、英、日、德、法五国语言查询，200 本词典，数百万词条，覆盖几十个专业领域，并且包含中文、英文真人发音和常用单词的视频讲解。

2）专业型词典

（1）化工词典（Lookchem Dictionary）。Lookchem Dictionary 是由 Lookchem 开发的在线化工词典。该软件提供海量的化学产品专业查询，可通过化学名称分子式和 cas 号快速查询产品的性质、结构式、用途、存储等专业信息。该应用数据与全球最大的化工数据库 Lookchem 同步升级，能够为化工从业者提供专业快捷的查询体验。

（2）英汉天文学名词数据库（https://nadc.china-vo.org/astrodict/）。英汉天文学名词数据库由中国天文学会天文学名词审定委员会编纂和维护。主要提供天文学名词查询功能，已收录词条 26190 条，可实现模糊检索和精确检索。

3. 搜索引擎

索引技术是搜索引擎的核心技术之一。搜索引擎要对所收集到的信息进行整理、分类、索引以产生索引库，而中文搜索引擎的核心是分词技术。分词技术是利用一定的规则和词库，切分出一个句子中的词，为自动索引做好准备。索引多采用 Non-clustered 方法，该技术和语言文字的理解有很大的关系，具体有如下几点：

（1）存储语法库，和词汇库配合分出句子中的词汇；

（2）存储词汇库，要同时存储词汇的使用频率和常见搭配方式；

（3）词汇量大，应可划分为不同的专业库，以便于处理专业文献；

（4）对无法分词的句子，把每个字当作词来处理。

索引器生成从关键词到 URL 的关系索引表。索引表一般使用某种形式的倒排表（inverted list），即由索引项查找相应的 URL。索引表也要记录索引项在文档中出现的位置，以便检索器计算索引项之间的相邻关系或接近关系，并以特定的数据结构存储在硬盘上。

不同的搜索引擎系统可能采用不尽相同的标引方法。例如 Webcrawler 利用全文检索技术，对网页中每一个单词进行索引；Lycos 只对页名、标题以及最重要的 100 个注释词等选择性词语进行索引；Infoseek 则提供概念检索和词组检索，支持 and、or、near、not 等布尔运算。检索引擎的索引方法大致可分为自动索引、手工索引和用户登录三类。

4. 行业规范指南、标准与百科知识

1）国家标准、规范

（1）标准下载网：http://www.bzxz.net/。

（2）国家标准化管理委员会网：http://www.sac.gov.cn/SACSearch/outlinetemplet/gjbzcx.jsp。

（3）强制性国家标准：http://gbread.sac.gov.cn/bzzyReadWebApp/read.action? m=frontMain。

（4）标准分享网：http://www.bzfxw.com。

2）百科知识网站

（1）百度百科是百度公司推出的一部内容开放、自由的网络百科全书，其测试版于 2006 年 4 月 20 日上线，正式版于 2008 年 4 月 21 日发布，截至 2022 年 12 月，百度百科收录词条数已近 2700 万，参与词条编辑人数高达 2.2 亿，信息几乎涵盖所有已知知识领域，创设世界最大的中文信息收集平台。百度学科强调用户参与和奉献精神，充分调动互联网交互力量，汇聚上亿用户的头脑智慧，积极交流和分享，从不同层次上满足用户对信息的需求。

（2）维基百科（www.wikipedia.org）是一项基于维基技术的全球性多语言百科全书协作计划，同时也是一部用多种语言编成的网络百科全书，其目标及宗旨是运用用户选择的语言，为全人类提供自由的百科全书。维基百科是一个动态的、可自由访问和编辑的全球知识体，并且在许多国家相当普及。截至 2021 年 4 月 18 日，英文维基百科已有 628 万个条目。全球总计 310 种语言的独立运作版本突破 5626 万条目。总登记用户超越 9552 万人，总编辑次数更是超过 29 亿次。

5. 语料库

1）HDWiki 词库—科学技术

HDWiki 词库—科学技术是科学技术名词语料库，来源于 HDWiki。

2）术语在线

术语在线（www.termonline.cn）是由全国科学技术名词审定委员会精心打造的互联网知识服务平台，提供术语检索、术语管理（纠错、征集、分享）、术语提取与标注、术语校对等服务。术语在线聚合了全国科学技术名词审定委员会发布的规范名词数据库、两岸对照名词数据库，以及权威工具书数据库等资源，累计 50 万余条规范术语，范围覆盖自然科学、工程与技术科学、医学与生命科学、人文社会科学、军事科学等学科领域。

3）其他常用语料库

（1）JDEST 上海交大科技英语语料库。

（2）国家语委现代汉语语料库：http://www.cncorpus.org/index.aspx。

（3）现代汉语语料库。

（4）北京大学中国语言学研究中心：http://ccl.pku.edu.cn:8080/ccl_corpus/。

（5）北京语言大学语言信息处理研究所 CCRL 汉语检索通：http://lib.blcu.edu.cn/qt/zy32.htm。

（6）北京语言大学的语料库：http://www.dwhyyjzx.com/cgi-bin/yuliao/。

（7）清华大学的汉语均衡语料库：TH-ACorpus：http://www.lits.tsinghua.edu.cn/ainlp/source.htm。

（8）现代汉语平衡语料库：http://www.sinica.edu.tw/SinicaCorpus/。

（9）古汉语语料库：http://www. sinica. edu. tw/ftms-bin/ftmsw。

（10）近代汉语标记语料库：http://www. sinica. edu. tw/Early_Mandarin/。

（11）树图数据库：http://treebank. sinica. edu. tw/。

（12）中英双语知识本体词网：http://bow. sinica. edu. tw/。

（13）搜文解字：http://words. sinica. edu. tw/。

（14）汉籍电子文献：http://www. sinica. edu. tw/~tdbproj/handy1/。

（15）中国传媒大学文本语料库：http://ling. cuc. edu. cn/RawPub/。

（16）哈尔滨工业大学信息检索研究室对外共享语料库：http://ir. hit. edu. cn/demo/ltp/Sharing_Plan. htm。

（17）香港教育学院语言资讯科学中心及其语料库实验室：http://www. Lvac. org/index. php?lang＝sc。

（18）中文语言资源联盟：http://www. chineseldc. org/。

（19）香港城市大学的 LIVAC 共时语料库：http://www. rcl. cityu. edu. hk/livac/。

（20）英国国家语料库：http://www. natcorp. ox. ac. uk/。

第三章　数字与数学用语表达

　　数字及数学公式是科技类文章中重要的信息载体，只有对科技类文章中出现的数字、公式、图表、图形等的表达形式有所了解，才能进行准确的语言转换。

第一节　数字的表达

　　汉语和英语都采用十进制计数法，然而在进位级数上却存在着差异。中文的计数单位依次为：个、十、百、千、万、十万、百万、千万、亿、十亿、百亿、千亿、兆、十兆、百兆、千兆、京、十京、百京、千京、垓等。中文计数是万进位的，即四位一组的进位组合，如"万（10^4）"以上的计数单位为十万、百万、千万、亿（10^8）。再往下的计数单位则有兆（10^{12}）、京（10^{16}）、垓（10^{20}）、秭（10^{24}）、穰（10^{28}）、沟（10^{32}）、涧（10^{36}）、正（10^{40}）、载（10^{44}）、极（10^{48}）等。英文中，其计数单位为三位一组的进位组合，如 thousand（10^3）、million（10^6），分别对应 10^{3n}；而再往下的计数单位如 billion、trillion 等，则根据英美计数习惯的不同，分别对应百万（10^6）的 n 次方和千（10^3）的 n 次方，但总体而言仍旧是 10^{3n}。

　　在基数的表达上，汉语中 20 以上 100 以下的基数在英语中由十位数"几十"加个位数"几"组合而成，中间加连字符。

　　在序数的表达上，汉语序数的标识词为"第"，英语序数词则依照形式化语言构词原则，在基数词词尾加 th（个别除外，如 first, second, third）。

　　小数在汉语和英语中都是以基数词加小数点表示。"．"为"点"（point），小数点左边为整数部分，右边为小数部分。

　　百分数在汉语和英语中都是以数字加百分符号表达。汉语读作"百分之几"，英语则用基数词加百分符号（％），读作 percent。

　　英语在分数的表达上，分子用基数词，分母用序数词（分子大于 1 时，分母序数词用复数）；带分数（mixed fraction），整数正常读，在整数和分数之间加上 and；当分母为十位数或更大位数，且最后一位数字是 1 或 2 时，分数线读作 over，如"9 又 21 分之 6"，英语中读作 nine and six over twenty one。汉语采用"几又几分之几"的结构。

（一）定数表达

科技英语定数表达方法见表3-1。

表 3-1　定数表达

数字类型		举例
整数 （integer）	基数词 （cardinal number）	71, 127 seventy-one thousand one hundred and twenty-seven 95, 000, 000 ninety five million 618, 000 six hundred and eighteen thousand
	序数词 （ordinal number）	12th twelfth 23rd twenty-third 856th eight hundred and fifty-sixth
小数 （decimal）		0. 5 point five 0. 01 one hundredth; point zero/nought one 0. 001 one thousandth; point zero zero one 3. 1415926 three point one four one five nine two six 4. 9 four point nine recurring 3. 0586 three point nought five eight six, eight six recurring
分数 （fraction）		2/3 two thirds 4/5 four fifths 1/4 a quarter 3/4 three quarters; three fourths $1\frac{1}{2}$ one and one over two; one and a half $125\frac{3}{4}$ a/one hundred twenty-five and three fourths/quarters
百分数 （percentage）		75% seventy-five percent 0. 72% zero point seven two percent 426% four hundred and twenty-six percent

例如：

①The range of sounds audible by man is from ***20 to 20,000*** librations per second.
人类所能听到的声音音域是 20~20, 000 赫兹。

②There may be as many as **100,000** different sorts of proteins in a man's body.
人体的不同种类的蛋白质高达**十万**种。(换算为"万")

③Halley's comet had a tail **94 million** miles long when it visited here in 1910.
当哈雷彗星 1910 年出现时，其尾部长达 9,400 万英里。

(二)不定数表达

所谓不定数是指表示若干、许多、大量、不少、成千上万等概念的词组。科技英语不定数表达方法见表 3-2。

表 3-2　不定数表达

类型	举例
大于某数的表达	more than, over/above, … or more, 基数词+odd/and odd (在整十位数后, odd 表示 0 以上的任何个位数; 在整百位数后, odd 表示 1~99 之间的任何数), up to, as … as
小于某数的表达	less than, under/below, or less
大量的表达	scores of(几十, 许多), dozens of(几十, 几打), tens/decades of(数十, 几十), numbers of(许多, 若干), lots of(许多, 大量), hundreds of(几百, 成百上千), thousands of(几千, 成千上万), hundreds of thousands of(数十万, 几十万), tens of thousands of(数万, 成千上万), millions of(千千万万, 数以百万计), a hundred and one(许多, 无数), a thousand and one(许多, 无数), millions upon millions of(数亿, 无数)
数量不确定的表达	or(or so), about, some, more or less, around, round, roundabout, somewhere round, from … to …, between … and …

例如：

①Odd days **less than** one week shall be counted as one week for calculating the liquidated.

不足一周按一周计算违约金。

②Standard punched cards can hold **up to/more than/above** eighty characters.
标准空孔卡片能够储存**多达** 80 个字符。

③The software approach can control **as many as** eight drives.
这种软件方法能控制**多达八台**驱动器。

④These measures reduced the normal death-rate to **below** 2.5 percent.
这些措施使人口的正常死亡率下降到 2.5% 以下。

⑤**Nearly** 10 percent of this load will cause a fluctuating stress.

大约10%载荷就将引起应力的波动变化。

⑥Development costs have been estimated at ***approximately*** 100 million dollars.

据估算，研制经费**大约**为一亿美元。

⑦Brazil is larger than the Continental United States by ***about*** 185,000 square miles.

巴西比美国大陆大 18.5 万平方英里**左右**。

⑧The Chinese mined and used coal ***hundreds of years*** before it was used in Europe.

中国人采煤和用煤先于欧洲**几百年**。

⑨These bones tell us that ***many thousands of years*** ago the world was inhabited by certain mammals.

这些骨头表明，**数千年**前，地球上就有过哺乳动物。

(三)用于计量的数字表达

科技英语中，用于计量的数字表达方法见表3-3。

表3-3　数字表达

类型	举例
dimensions	3678 meters above sea-level(海拔) 2 meters in length, 2 meters in width, 1.8 meters in height(长宽高) 6 feet(wide) by 4 feet (long) (长宽) 6,6000 square miles (170,939 square km) (平方英里/千米)
speed	331.7 meters per second(米/秒) 60 mph(英里/小时) 9,600 bits per second(比特/秒) 6′36″ six minutes, 36 seconds
temperature	℃=(℉-32)/1.8(摄氏度) ℉=℃×1.8+32(华氏度) 0 ℃ freezing degree 100 ℃ boiling degree 32 ℉ feezing degree 212 ℉ boiling degree
weight	3 tons(吨) 1 g(克) 2 kg(千克)

例如：

①此通道最大净空高度为3.8米，凡超过此高度的车辆一律不准通过此通道。

The maximum headroom of the passage is **3.8 m**, and the vehicles of more than this height are not allowed to use this passage.

②双发动机配置可使该船平均中等时速达45海里，顶级时速达50海里以上。

This one-two propulsion punch delivers an average cruising speed of **45 knots** with **50-plus-knot** burst of speed.

③发电机内部的燃烧室点燃空气和天然气的混合气体，把陶瓷管加温到1,400℃以上。

A burner inside the generator ignites a mixture of air and natural gas, heating a ceramic tube to more than **1,400 ℃.**

④该恐龙体重达8吨，大约比霸王龙重3吨，而且比霸王龙长约2英尺。

The **8-ton** dinosaur was estimated **3 tons** heavier and about **2 feet** longer than Tyrannosaurus rex.

第二节 数学用语的表达

在科技英语中，常用字母、数字和其他数学符号构成的等式或不等式来描述事物内部的联系，常见的运算表达如表3-4~表3-6所示。

（一）公式

表3-4 公式表达

中文	公式	英文
a 加 b 等于 c	$a+b=c$	a and/plus b is/makes/equals/is equal to c
a 减 b 等于 c	$a-b=c$	a minus b is/makes/equals/is equal to c; a from b is/leaves c
a 乘以 b 等于 c	$a×b=c$	a times/multiplied by b is/equals/is equal to c
a 除以 b 等于 c	$a÷b=c$	a divided by b makes/equals/is equal to c
a 加 b 的括号	$(a+b)$	bracket a plus b bracket closed
a 加 b 或 a 减 b	$a±b$	a plus or minus b
b 分之 a	a/b	a over b
a 与 b 平行	$a//b$	a is parallel to b
a 等于 b	$a=b$	a equals/is equal to/is b

续表3-4

中文	公式	英文
a 不等于 b	$a \neq b$	a is not equal to/is not b
a 比 b 等于 c 比 d	$a:b=c:d$	the ratio of a to b is equal to the ratio of c to d; a is to b as c is to d
a 恒等于 b	$a \equiv b$	a is identically equal to b
a 约等于 b	$a \approx b$	a is approximately equal to b
a 大于 b	$a>b$	a is greater than b
a 小于 b	$a<b$	a is less than b
a 大于等于 b	$a \geq b$	a is greater than b or equal to b
a 小于等于 b	$a \leq b$	a is less than b or equal to b
a 的平方	a^2	a square; a squared; the second power of a; a to the second power
a 的三次方	a^3	a cube; a cubed; the cube of a; the third power of a; a to the third power
a 的 n 次方	a^n	a to the nth power; the nth power of a
a 的负 10 次方	a^{-10}	a to the minus tenth (power)
a 加 b 或减 b 的平方	$(a \pm b)^2$	a plus or minus b all squared
a 的平方根	$\sqrt{a}$	square root of a
a 的立方根	$\sqrt[3]{a}$	cube root of a
a 的 n 次方根	$\sqrt[n]{a}$	nth root of a

例如：

①$[(a+b)-c \times d] \div e = f$：$a$ plus b minus c times d, all divided by e equals f

②$\sqrt{9}=3$：the square root of 9 is/equals 3

③$2a-1/ax+b$：$2a$ minus one over ax plus b

④$x^{-2/3}+\sqrt[5]{x^2}=0$：x to the minus two third plus the fifth root of x squared equals zero

⑤$a^3+b^3=(a+b)(a^2-ab+b^2)$：$a$ cubed plus b cubed equals a plus b into a squared minus ab plus b squared

⑥$(a+b-c \times d \div e) \div g$：$a$ plus b minus c multiplied by (times) d divided by e, all is divided by g

⑦$4567 \div 23 = 198$ 余 13：23 into 4567 goes 198 times, and 13 remainder

⑧$\left(8+6\dfrac{5}{8}-3.88 \times 4\right) \div 2\dfrac{1}{2}$：eight plus six and five-eighths minus three decimal /

point eight eight multiplied by four, all divided by two and a half

⑨ $a = \dfrac{V_t - V}{t}$: a equals V sub t minus V over/divided by t

(二)数字符号

符号语言是科技语言中通用的、特有的简练语言，是在人类数学思维长期发展过程中形成的一种语言表达形式。科技语言效能在很大程度上，体现为人工符号的使用。以数学符号为例，按感知规律，数学符号分为象形符号、缩写符号、约定符号。象形符号是由数学对象的空间位置结构或数量关系经抽象概括得到的各种数学图形或图式，再经缩小或改造而形成的一类数学符号。如几何学中的符号△、⊙、∥、⊥、∠等都是原形的压缩改造，属于象形符号。缩写符号是由数学概念的西文词汇缩写或加以改造而成的符号，比如函数 f（function），极限 lim（limit）、正弦 sin（sine）、最大 max（maximal）、小 min（minimal）、存在 ∃（exist）、任意 ∀（any）等符号均为此类。约定符号是数学共同体约定的，具有数学思维合理性、流畅性的数学符号，如运算符号+、×、∩、≌、⌢、>、<等均属此类。由各种符号按照数学的逻辑意义和规则而组合建立起来的各种符号串或式子则构成数学式语言或数学句子，这里的逻辑意义和规则是指数学中的一些规定或原理法则，如 a+bc 遵循的是运算次序、略写法则等。

表 3-5　数字符号表达

符号	中文	英文
∩	交集	cap
∪	并集	cup
∅	空集	emptyset
∈	包含于	is a member/is an element of/is in
⊂	子集	is a subset of
→	映射到	maps to
↔/⇔	……是……成立的充要条件	is equivalent to; if and only if
∧	和	and
∨	或者	or
¬	非	not
∵	因为	because/since
∴	所以	therefore/hence
π	圆周率	pi; ratio of the circumference of a circle to its diameter

续表3-5

符号	中文	英文
∞	无穷大	infinity
∝	成比例	varies as; is proportional to
∽	相似	is similar to
≌	全等符号	is congruent to
⊥	垂直	is perpendicular to
//	直线平行	is parallel to
∠	角	angle
( )	圆括号	round brackets; parentheses
[ ]	方括号	square brackets
< >	尖括号	angle brackets
{ }	大括号	braces; curly brackets
$\log_n x$	以 n 为底 x 的对数	log x to the base n
$\log_{10} x$	以 10 为底 x 的对数（常用对数）	log x to the base 10(common logarithm)
$\log_e x$ 或 $\ln x$	以常数 e 为底数的对数（即自然对数或讷氏对数）	log x to the base; natural logarithm; Naperian logarithm
$|x|$	x 的绝对值	the absolute value of x
$\bar{x}$	x 的平均值	the mean value of x; x bar
Σ	总和；所示项的总和；西格玛	the sum of the terms indicated; summation of; sigma
Π	所示项的乘积	the product of the terms indicated
f 或 F	函数	function
$f(x)$; $F(x)$; $\phi(x)\cdots$	x 的函数 f（或 ϕ）	function f（或 ϕ）of x
$y=f(x)$	y 是 x 的函数；y 是 x 条件下的函数	y is a function of x; y is the value of the function at x
$\vec{F}$	矢量函数	vector F
c. d. f.	累积分布函数	cumulative distribution function
p. d. f.	概率密度函数	probability density function
c. f.	特征函数	characteristic function
∫	积分	integral
$\int : X \rightarrow Y$	将 X 影射到 Y 的积分	$\int$ maps X into Y

续表3-5

符号	中文	英文
$\int_a^b$	$f(x)$ 在区间 $[a, b]$ 上的定积分	integral between limits a and b
$\overline{AB}$	线段 AB 的长度	length of line from A to B
$A \times B$	A 与 B 的向量积	vector product of A and B; magnitude of A times magnitude of B
$A \cdot B$	A 和 B 的数量积	scalar product of A and B; magnitude of A times magnitude of B times cosine of the angle from A to B

（三）标点符号

表 3-6　标点符号表达

符号	英文
P', P'', P'''	P prime, P double prime/P second, P triple prime（AmE.） P dash, P double dash, P triple dash（BrE.）
a_1, a_2, a_3	a sub one, a sub two, a sub three
P_2''	P double prime sub 2

（四）运算表达

不同的学科领域都有一些特殊的术语，它们具有科学性强、专业性强和词义精确且狭窄等特点，熟悉这些术语才能做到译文规范。常见的运算句式有：

（1）已知……：given …。

（2）求……：find/determine …。

（3）由……：be given by …。

（4）需求……：… to be obtained。

（5）求……的公式是……：the formula for … is …。

（6）解：procedure/solution of …。

（7）有……的解：have a solution for …。

（8）……是……的唯一解：… is the unique solution of …。

（9）推导出……：derive …。

（10）……忽略不计：neglect … / … be negligible。

（11）式中……：… where …。

（12）设……为……：let … be …。

（13）使……成为……：allow ... to be ...。

（14）利用……引入下列……方程式：by using ..., we introduced the following ... equations。

（15）在此引入……函数以保证：the functions ... are introduced here to guarantee ...。

（16）将……赋予……；指定……到……：assign ... to ...。

（17）将数据代入公式：plug the data into the formula。

（18）令：denote。

（19）令……为……：denote ... by ...。

（20）正：positive/plus。

（21）负：negative/minus。

（22）……约为……：an approximation for ... is ...。

（23）入、进：round up。

（24）舍：round down。

请看下列运算中的英语表达方式及其翻译：

例 1　Given that, as shown in Figure 1, D is a point line AB, $\angle A = 30°$, $\angle ADC = 120°$, $\angle ACB = 90°$.

Solution：$\angle A = 30°$, $\angle ACB = 90°$

Because the theorem of the sum of the interior angles of a triangle

Therefore，$\angle B = 180° - \angle A - \angle ACB = 60°$

$\angle CDB = 180° - \angle ADC = 60°$

Therefore，in triangle BCD, $\angle BCD = 180° - \angle CDB - \angle B = 60°$

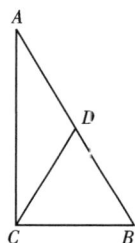

Figure 1

例 2　If $2x - 3y + 4x - 7y = 0$, then the value of y/x is?

Solution：

i：$2x - 3y + 4x - 7y$ equals to $6x - 10y$

Because $2x - 3y + 4x - 7y = 0$

Therefore $6x - 10y = 0$

ii：$6x - 10y = 0$, $6x = 10y$

Because the both side of a equation could be divided or multiplied the same number but 0

Therefore $3x = 5y$, $3/5 = y/x$

例 3　Jan is making a 3-tier（层）wedding cake for 300 guests. She will make the cake for ＄3 per serving with the following specifications（规格）：

• Each serving is 4 in.^{3}.

• Each tier must be smaller than the tier below it.

• Each square tier is 4 in. tall with a side length of 16 in., 14 in., 12 in., 10 in., 8 in. or 6 in..

What is the cost of the most economical(经济的，合算的) 3-tier cake that will serve 300 people?

Let x, y, z be the side length of the three layers of the cake where:

$\{x, y, z \mid x, y, z \in \{6, 8, 10, 12, 14, 16\}, x > y > z\}$

The volume of the cake should be at least 1200 in.^{3}(4 ∗ 300) to serve 300 people.

The volume of the cake will be ($x^2 * 4 + y^2 * 4 + z^2 * 4$)

x, y, z starts from the smallest value that satisfies the condition of the set (10, 8, 6), loop until the volume of the cake satisfies the condition (>1200):

Increase the smallest incrementable value.

Therefore, x, y, z = 12, 10, 8

Answer: 12, 10, 8,

Given that, $12 \times 12 + 10 \times 10 + 8 \times 8 = 308$, $308 \times 4 = 1232$ in.^{3}

Then, $1232 \div 4 = 308$, $308 \times 3 = 924$. ($924)

例 4　If equation(6.1) is exact, then there exists a differentiable function ϕ satisfying (6.2) in S. Since M and N are of class C^1, the function ϕ is of class C^2. Therefore,

$$\frac{\partial M}{\partial x} = \frac{\partial}{\partial x}\left(\frac{\partial \phi}{\partial t}\right) = \frac{\partial}{\partial t}\left(\frac{\partial \phi}{\partial x}\right) = \frac{\partial N}{\partial t}$$

in S, which establishes property (6.6).

Now we assume that property (6.6) holds. Integrating over t, we obtain

$$\int_{t_0}^{t} \frac{\partial M}{\partial x}(s, x)\,\mathrm{d}s = N(t, x) - N(t_0, x). \qquad (6.7)$$

Let us also consider the function

$$\phi(t, x) = \int_{x_0}^{x} N(t_0, y)\,\mathrm{d}y + \int_{t_0}^{t} M(s, x)\,\mathrm{d}s.$$

We have

$$\frac{\partial \phi}{\partial t}(t, x) = M(t, x),$$

and it follows from (6.7) that

$$\frac{\partial \phi}{\partial x}(t, x) = N(t_0, x) + \int_{t_0}^{t} \frac{\partial M}{\partial x}(s, x)\,\mathrm{d}s = N(t, x).$$

第三节　倍数表达法

　　倍数表达法通常用于物体数量、大小、体积等的比较或其增加和减少，英文表达和中文翻译之间存在差异，所以准确翻译是非常重要的。

(一)A 的大小(长度、重量……)是 B 的 N 倍,或 A 比 B 大(长、重……)N–1 倍

其表达方式主要有以下几种:

A is *N* times as large (long, heavy ...) as ***B***

A is *N* times larger (longer, heavier ...) than ***B***

A is larger (longer, heavier ...) than *B* by *N* times

例如:

①A yard *is* three ***times longer than*** a foot.

一码等于三英尺。(直译:一码的长度是一英尺的三倍。)

②The oxygen atom *is* nearly 16 ***times heavier than*** the hydrogen atom.

氧原子的重量几乎是氢原子的 16 倍。

③Mercury weighs ***more than*** water ***by*** about 14 times.

水银比水重约十三倍。

(二)倍数增加的表达法及翻译

1. 主语+double(treble,quadruple)+……

double 可译成"增加了一倍"或"翻一番",treble 可译成"增加了两倍"或"增加到三倍",quadruple 可译成"增加了三倍"或"翻两番"。

到 2010 年,中国人均国民生产总值增长率将**翻两番**。

The growth rate of GNP (gross national product) per capita for China will be ***quadrupled*** by the year 2010.

2. 增加到 N 倍=增加了 N–1 倍

其英文表达主要有以下几种:

increase *N* times

increase to *N* times

increase by *N* times

increase *N* fold

increase by a factor of *N*

温度升高100℃,半导体的导电率就**增加到五十倍**。

A temperature rise of 100℃ ***increases*** the conductivity of a semiconductor ***by*** 50 times.

(三)倍数减少的表达法及翻译

1. 减少了 N 分之 N–1=减少到 N 分之一

其英文表达主要有以下几种:

reduce by *N* times

reduce *N* times

reduce to *N* times

reduce by a factor of *N*

reduce *N* times as much（many …）as …

N fold reduction

N times less than …

注：decrease、shorten、drop、step down、cut down 等均适用上述结构。

①电压**降低了五分之四**。（或：电压为原来的五分之一。）

The voltage *has dropped five times*.

②比起老式打字机，主要的优点是重量**减轻了四分之三**。

The principal advantage over the old fashioned typewriter is *a four fold reduction* in weight.

2. 比……少一半＝比……少二分之一

其英文表达主要有以下几种：

half as much as …

twice less than …

①如果月球离地球的距离比现在**短一半**，则引力将为现在的四倍。

If the moon were only *half as* far away from the earth *as* it is, the force of attraction would be 4 times as great.

②该机器的输出功率比输入功率**小二分之一**。

The power output of the machine is *twice less than* its input.

③If you treble/triple the distance between an object and the earth, the gravitational attraction gets *nine times weaken*.

如果你把一个物体与地球的距离增加两倍，地心引力就会**减弱到** 1/9。

④When the signal has increased by 10 times, the gain may *have been reduced by* 8 *times*.

如果信号增加到 10 倍，增益就可能**降低** 7/8。

第四章　图形与图表表达

本章对科技文本中出现的可视化图形、图表的规范表达形式及其翻译进行有针对性的讲解，并列举常用句式及其翻译以供参考。

第一节　科技可视化

迄今为止，科技传播方式大致发生了三次变革：文字的出现带来了第一次变革，"历史真正成为独立的记事手段，科技发展记录方式有了一个根本性的变化，而且一直延续到现在"；摄影技术的出现引发了第二次变革，它使图像、视频成为记录科技事实的载体；虚拟现实技术的出现带动了第三次变革的萌芽，通过计算机模拟虚拟历史环境，增强科技情境沉浸感，拓展科技传播路径。

(一) 仿真可视化

虚拟现实技术 (virtual reality) 影响下的计算机动画囊括计算机、电子信息、仿真技术于一体，其基本实现方式是计算机模拟虚拟环境从而给人以环境沉浸感。教师利用仿真技术将教学内容、实验设备、学生操作与教师指导有效融合，形成一种新的操作性较强的科学实验仿真，辅助教师教学。同时，仿真技术也被应用在科技活动模拟中，对某些实验进行仿真模拟，完成了以往难以操作的一些实验，对我国的教育事业起到了很大的推动作用。计算机模拟实验主要将实验的设计思想使用仿真技术来进行现实模拟，将教学理论和实践、课内课外有效融合在一起，体现实验的主动性。学生能够在计算机模拟实验中，实现自己的设计思想，利用仿真模型来完成实验，证明自己的想法。计算机模拟实验能够激发学生的学习兴趣，让学生积极参与到模拟实验中。

（二）教育可视化

教育数据进入大数据时代。一方面，语言知识学习不再局限于文本、图片等静态资源，通过学习过程数据化、可视化可以直观、动态地加深对知识的重构。另一方面，智慧教育环境中生成了海量、异构的学习数据，多维数据可视化，便于挖掘学生学习信息，方便学生进行学习反思、教师进行教学监控，为教学管理者优化教学决策提供重要参考。

（三）知识可视化

知识可视化体现在学习过程中获得知识，并对获得知识进行加工和整理这两个阶段。调查发现，思维导图和概念图是目前支持知识可视化最具代表性的工具。思维导图是从一个核心概念开始，不断扩展和发散思维，逐步建立一个有序的知识树；而概念图则是先罗列概念，再通过连接词建立概念和概念之间的联系，从而形成一定的意义，可以有多个核心概念。

（四）信息可视化

信息可视化的研究对象是大规模非数字型信息的视觉表达（representation）问题。此类信息有软件系统之中众多的文件或者代码行、图书馆与文献书目数据库以及国际互联网上的关系网络等。

信息可视化集中关注的是以直观的方式传达抽象信息的手段和方法。可视化的表达形式与交互技术使用户能够目睹、探索以致立即理解大量的信息。

第二节　图形的表达

图形的基本要素是点、线、面，图形通过语义符号的有机组合完成意义的表达。图形中角度的表达方式有：

（1）构成一个……角：form an angle of …。

（2）一条线与另一条线成……角相交：one line cuts another at … angle。

（3）与 M 成 α 角：at an angle of α to/with M。

（4）……间的夹角：the angle included between …。

①为描述应力状态，要在接触面的中心选择参考坐标系，X 轴平行于圆柱体的轴线，Y 轴垂直于圆柱体轴线所形成的平面，Z 轴处于接触力所在的平面上。

To picture the stress state, select the original reference system at the center of the contact area with X parallel to the cylindrical axes, Y perpendicular to the plane formed by the two cylinder axes, and Z in the lane of the contact force.

②As is shown in the figure, when two lines $L1$ and $L2$ are cut by a third line $L3$, and $L1 /\!/ L2$, then the corresponding angles are equal, such as $\angle 1 = \angle 5$, $\angle 2 = \angle 6$, $\angle 3 = \angle 7$, $\angle 4 = \angle 8$; alternate interior angles are equal, such as $\angle 2 = \angle 8$, $\angle 3 = \angle 5$; the same-side interior angles are supplementary, for instance, $\angle 2 + \angle 5 = 180°$, $\angle 3 + \angle 8 = 180°$.

如图所示，两条直线 $L1$ 和 $L2$ 被第三条直线 $L3$ 所截，如果 $L1 /\!/ L2$，则同位角相等，如 $\angle 1 = \angle 5$，$\angle 2 = \angle 6$，$\angle 3 = \angle 7$，$\angle 4 = \angle 8$；内错角相等，如 $\angle 2 = \angle 8$，$\angle 3 = \angle 5$；同旁内角互补，如 $\angle 2 + \angle 5 = 180°$，$\angle 3 + \angle 8 = 180°$。

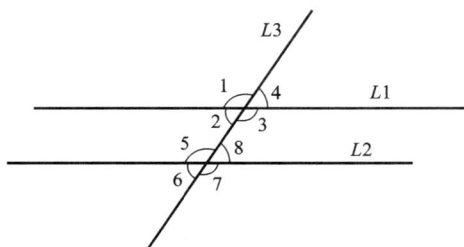

第三节　图表的表达

虽然文字是表述科技论文的主要手段，但在某些情况下，用插图或表格表述会收到文字所达不到的效果，甚至还可以简洁、准确地表达用文字无法表述的内容；插图和表格(简称图表)还具有活跃和美化版面的功能，因而在科技论文中被广泛采用。图表是科技论文的重要表述手段。

(一)图表的作用

科技论文的目的是记叙和表达实验(试验)、研究的技术方法、论证过程、分析结果和所得结论，往往涉及观测和实验数据、定量化信息的计算分析和比较等。表格能够准确地记录和提供关键的数据、定量化论据和结果，而且能够准确地表达内容的比对和逻辑关系。图形和图像则可以形象、直观地表达文字难以描述的科学思想和技术知识。另外，规范和正确地使用图表不仅可以大量省略文字，紧缩篇幅，节约版面，而且可以活跃和美化版面，使读者赏心悦目，提高阅读兴趣和效率。对于定量化论据，如果采取数据表格的形式插入科技论文中，则会非常准确、明了地呈现给读者，而且数据间排列紧凑，便于比较其大小、分布和相互关系；对于地图、大气环流形势、气象要素分布、机械构造、电路、生物形态和结构、工作或信息流程等，即使采用大篇幅的文字描述，恐怕读者也难以准确、清晰地了解，而采用图形或图片(照片)则非常简洁而直观。因此，插图和表格是文字的两个翅膀，是现代科技论文和科技书刊不可缺少的表述手段。

(二)图表的分类

科技论文中插图包括曲线图、记录图、结构图、流程图、框图、照片、布置图、地图、图版等。其中，常见的曲线图有函数关系曲线图、等值线分布图，例如，大气科学相关领域研究中常使用的气象要素时间变化曲线、空间分布曲线，以及地面气压场、位势高度场、气象要素或物理量场时间或空间剖面图等；结构图多用于呈现某一物体、机械部件的全部或部分详细构成，这一点与示意图恰好相反，示意图则不详细刻画物体细节或数量的微小变化，而只需呈现它们的总体形势和变化分布形态；流程图和框图形式相似，它们多半都由多个文字框、符号框或数据框组合构成，不同的是流程图侧重于表达事物演变和变化过程、工作或工程的步骤和顺序、信息传递方向等，而框图侧重于表达事物的构成、布局；照片则主要用于反映物体，特别是生物的外貌形态和特征。

表格按照其内容和编排形式，主要分为数据表和系统表。其中，数据表是科技论文和科技书刊中最常用的，它是以卡线表形式列出有关数据或数量，有些非数据型的符号、公式、表达式或论文中需要说明的事项也可以采用卡线表形式列出；系统表一般用于表示多个事项之间的隶属关系和层次，有时也采用类似汉语主题词表的编排格式把事项的层次关系、属性等列出。

表格(table/chart)示例如图 4-1 所示：

Table 1：The Number of Online Databases and Their Percentage

Types of websites	Number of online databases	Percentage/%
Total	169, 867	100
Government site	9, 099	5.4
Company site	92, 302	54.3
Business site	23, 951	14.1
Individual site	11, 541	6.8
Non-profit organization	15, 846	9.3
Education, science and study institutes site	11, 241	6.6
Other site	5, 887	3.5

图 4-1 表格示例

曲线图(line graph)示例如图 4-2 所示:

Total Unique Visitors（000）

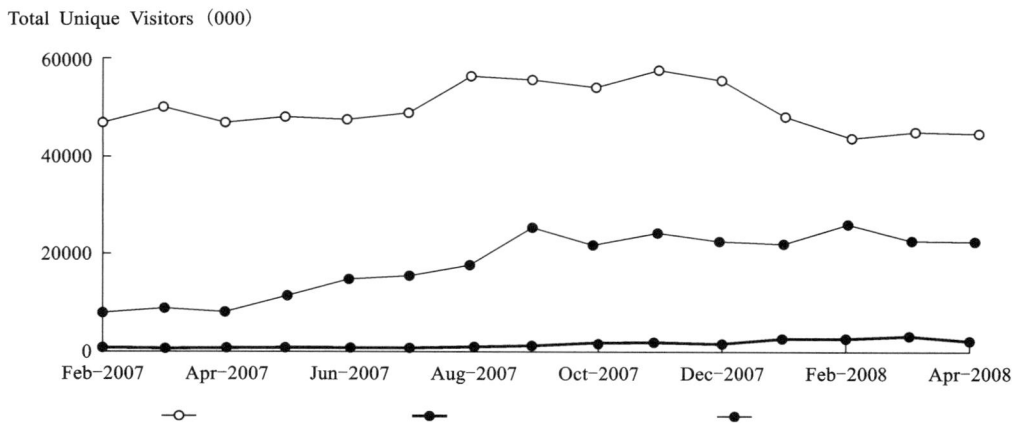

图 4-2　曲线图示例

饼图(pie chart)示例如图 4-3 所示:

Project Cost Breakdown

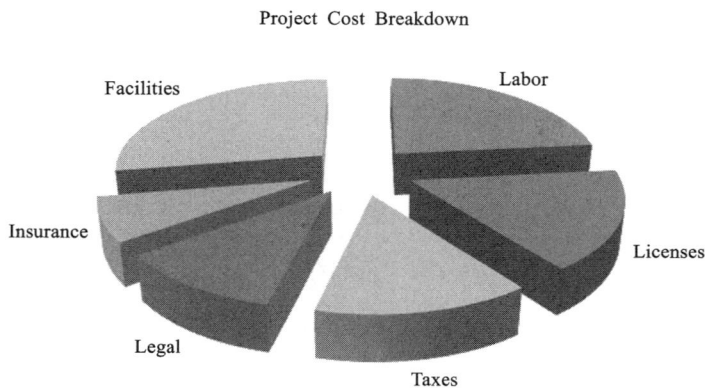

图 4-3　饼图示例

柱形图(bars)示例如图 4-4 所示:

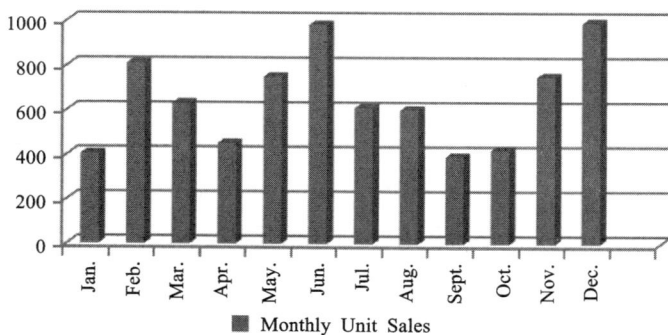

图 4-4　柱形图示例

流程图(flowcharts)示例如图 4-5 所示:

A Basic Flowchart

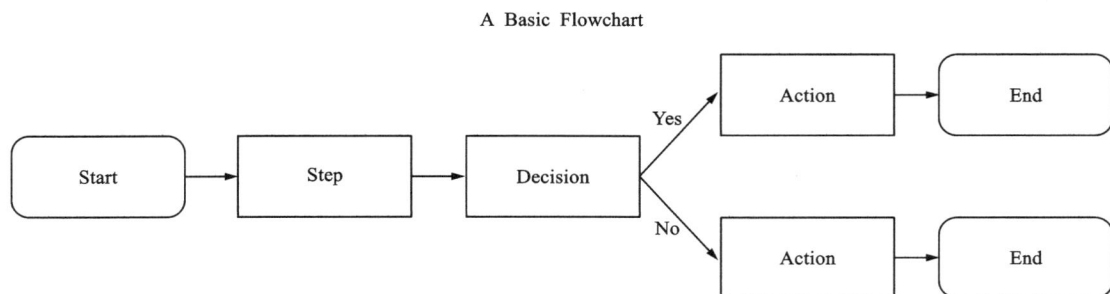

图 4-5 流程图示例

(三)图表的描述

1.常用句式

1)图表描述

(1)The graph/chart/diagram/table shows (that) …

这个图/表展现了……

(2)The table shows the changes in the number of … over the period from … to …

这个表展现了在……至……期间……的变化量。

(3)The bar chart illustrates …

这个条形图说明了……

(4)The graph features …

这个图的特点是……

(5)The graph provides some interesting data regarding …

这个图提供了一些关于……的有趣数据。

(6)This is a line graph, which describes the trend of … according to the graph.

这是个线形图,从图可看出……的趋势。

(7)As (is) shown in the graph/chart/diagram/table …

正如图/表所示 ……

(8)As can be seen from the graph/chart/diagram/table …

从图/表可看出……

(9)According to the table/chart/graph, … increased/decreased by … percent.

根据表/图,……增加/减少了……(increase/decrease to … percent … 增加到/减少到百分之……; from … to … 从……增加/减少到……)

(10)An investigation conducted by … indicates that … has reached/approached … in the past … years compared with …

通过……调查表明,……在过去的……年里与……相比达到了……

2)图表结论

(1)We can see from the figures/statistics that …

我们可以从数据中看出……

(2)It is clear from the figures/statistics that …

从这些数据很明显可以看出……

(3)It is apparent from the figures/statistics that …

从这些数据很明显可以看出……

(4)From this graph, it can be generalized that …

从这个表格,我们可以总结出……

(5)Therefore, it can be concluded that …

因此,我们可以得出……(结论)

2. 常用词汇(表 4-1)

表 4-1　图表常用词汇

中文	英文
描述上升的词	increase/raise/rise/go up/climb/boom/reach a peak/pick up
描述下降的词	decrease/go down/drop/fall/decline/slump/dip
描述变化的词	fluctuate/rebound/undulate/wave
描述不变的词	remain/stable/flat/constant/steady
描述变化速度的形容词	slow/gradual/steady/sudden/swift/quick/rapid
描述变化大的程度形容词	substantial/steep/enormous/huge/sharp/dramatic/marked/significant/considerable
描述变化小的程度形容词	minimal/small/slight/moderate

3. 案例

1)表格描述示例

Learning	Women	Men
High school diploma	$ 18,648	$ 26,766
Associate degree	$ 24,849	$ 32,349
Bachelor's degree	$ 29,284	$ 40,381
Master's degree	$ 35,018	$ 47,260

This table below shows the relationship between learning and earning and between the salaries of women and men. Write a report describing the information shown below.

Model answer

This table features the relationship between learning and earning as well as salary differences between men and women belonging to the four categories listed in the table. ***First***, for women who have a high school diploma, their average income is $ 18, 648 a year while men with the same learning earn $ 26, 766 a year. ***Next***, women who graduate with an associate degree earn $ 24, 849 a year on average while men with the same degree earn $ 32, 349 a year. ***Then***, women with a bachelor's degree earn $ 29, 284 a year and men with a bachelor's degree earn $ 40, 381 a year. ***Last***, women with a master's degree earn $ 35, 018 a year while men with the same degree earn more: $ 47, 260 a year on average. ***As we can see here***, the more one learns, the more one earns. And this accounts for the fact that students all over the world are working hard for higher degrees. ***Another fact that*** cannot be ignored is sex discrimination in pay. With the same educational background, women are earning 30% less than men on average, which is a discouraging statistic.

2）柱状图描述示例

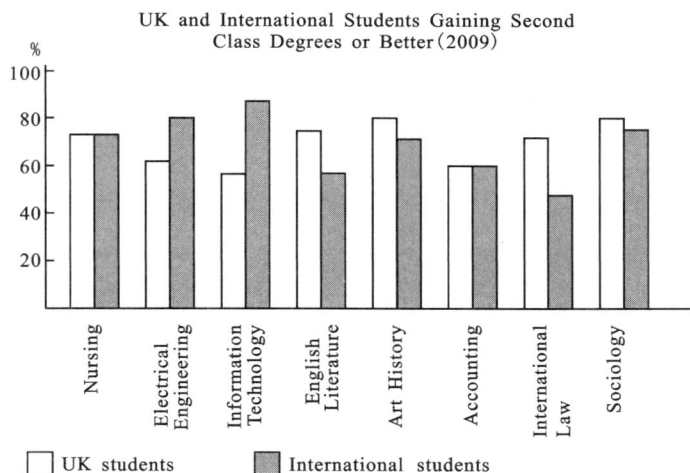

UK and International Students Gaining Second Class Degrees or Better (2009)

The bar chart shows the proportion of UK students and international students achieving second class degrees or higher in eight different subjects at a university in the UK.

Degree results were generally good for both home and international students, with well over 50 percent gaining a second class degree or better in all eight subjects except international law.

According to the chart, international students tended to do better than UK students in technology-related subjects like information technology. Over 80 percent of international students gained a good degree in IT, whereas only about half of the UK students did so.

Degree results were similar for the two groups in nursing and accounting. While in arts and social science related subjects, UK students tended to do better. The biggest gap in performance was in international law, where three-quarters of UK students gained a second class degree or better. In contrast, fewer than half of the international students attained this level.

Overall, *the chart suggests that* international and UK students had different strengths when studying for degrees in this UK university.

3) 流程图描述示例

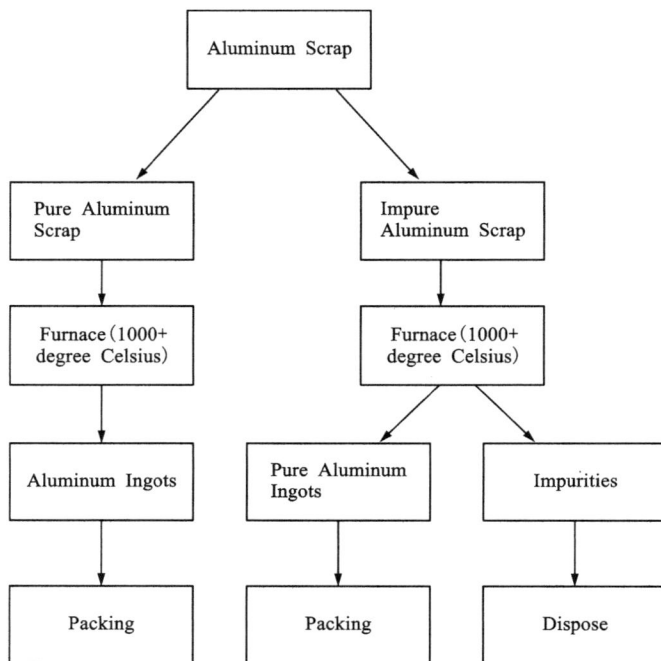

```
                    ┌─────────────────┐
                    │ Aluminum Scrap  │
                    └─────────────────┘
                      ↙            ↘
        ┌──────────────────┐   ┌──────────────────┐
        │ Pure Aluminum    │   │ Impure           │
        │ Scrap            │   │ Aluminum Scrap   │
        └──────────────────┘   └──────────────────┘
                 ↓                      ↓
        ┌──────────────────┐   ┌──────────────────┐
        │ Furnace (1000+   │   │ Furnace (1000+   │
        │ degree Celsius)  │   │ degree Celsius)  │
        └──────────────────┘   └──────────────────┘
                 ↓                  ↙        ↘
        ┌──────────────────┐ ┌──────────────┐ ┌──────────────┐
        │ Aluminum Ingots  │ │ Pure Aluminum│ │ Impurities   │
        │                  │ │ Ingots       │ │              │
        └──────────────────┘ └──────────────┘ └──────────────┘
                 ↓                  ↓               ↓
        ┌──────────────────┐ ┌──────────────┐ ┌──────────────┐
        │ Packing          │ │ Packing      │ │ Dispose      │
        └──────────────────┘ └──────────────┘ └──────────────┘
```

The flow chart describes the complete aluminum recycling process to obtain pure aluminum from the scrap. It explains all the stages that waste and alloy form of aluminum go through produce aluminum from segregation to packing stage.

To begin with, the primary process of collecting used scrap aluminum and aluminum with impurities; they are segregated into pure aluminum scrap and aluminum with impurities separately.

Both quantities of aluminum are put into two different containers. After that, there containers are introduced to different coal furnaces burning at a temperature above 1000 degree Celsius. Once the metal melts to molten state, metal contained in the pure aluminum container is condensed into the form of ingots and finally packed.

The second container is constantly observed to separate the impurities. Once the impurities are separated from the metal, the molten metal is poured in the impressions to form ingots which are delivered to the pack.

4) 线形图描述示例

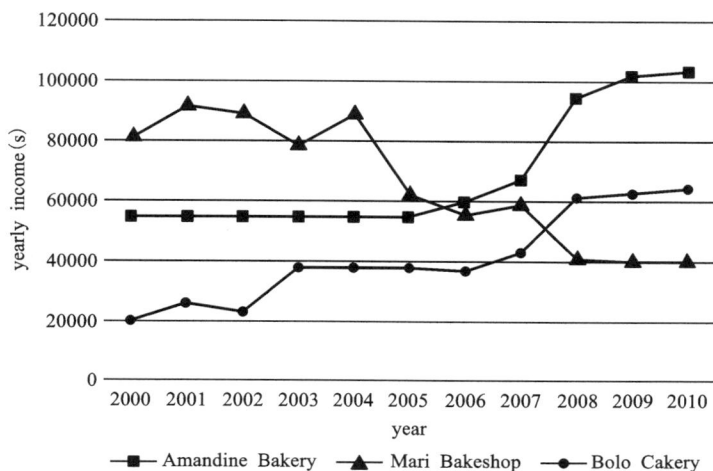

You should spend about 20 minutes on this task.

The graph shows data about the annual earnings of three bakeries in Calgary, 2000 – 2010.

Summarize the information by selecting and reporting the main features, and make comparisons where relevant.

Write at least 150 words.

Model answer

The graph shows information about the amount of money which was earned by three bakeries in Calgary, over a ten-year period between 2000 and 2010.

Overall, what stands out from the graph is that there were considerable upward trends in the income of both Bolo Cakery and Amandine Bakery, while the earnings of Mari Bakeshop saw a considerable fall over the period in question. ***Another interesting point is that*** Mari Bakeshop was the most popular bakery in 2000, but in 2010, Amandine Bakery earned more money than the others.

Looking at the details, as regards Bolo Cakery, income started at \$20,000 in 2000, then there was a fluctuation over the next three years, at which point it leveled off at just under \$40,000 until 2006. Then the figure went up significantly, finishing at around

$65, 000 in 2010. If we look at Amandine Bakery, the trend was similar. Having remained stable at approximately $55, 000 in the first half of the decade, income then rose sharply, reaching nearly $100, 000 in 2008. There was then a gradual rise to around $105, 000 in 2010.

By contrast, the income of Mari Bakeshop went in the opposite direction. Takings fluctuated around $90, 000 until 2004. After that despite falling sharply to just over $40, 000 in 2008, the figure then leveled off in the last two years.

第五章　科技语句表达

科技语言在句法方面的特点是句子结构固定，常用句型有限，表达趋于合理化、逻辑化。本章依次对科技语句中常用的定义、描写、分类、主从关系、比较、对比、类比表达法等进行说明。

第一节　定义表达法

(一)定义的概念与内涵

定义就是告诉人们"是什么"，在科技英语中被广泛应用。当科学家需要在其研究领域中解释一种新材料的本质时，就会使用定义表达法。总的来说，定义就是：陈述一个单词、短语、想法或概念的基本含义；解释某物的性质或本质特征；确定某物的界限。

一个定义通常包含三个基本要素：需要被定义的术语；该术语所属群体或类别；该术语的区别特征。

例如：

①A microscope is a scientific instrument which makes very small objects look bigger so that more details can be seen.

②Virus is a very small organism, smaller than a bacterium, which causes disease in humans, animals and plants.

③A compass is a device for finding direction which has a freely moving needle which always points to magnetic north.

④A COVID-19 vaccine is a vaccine intended to provide acquired immunity against COVID-19.

73

（二）定义的分类

定义是对一个事物或概念区别于其他所有事物或概念的解释，是揭示概念内涵的逻辑方法，即指出概念所反映的对象的本质属性。根据所提供的属概念的范围大小以及在属概念下揭示的种概念之间的差别的确切程度，定义可分为：正式定义（formal definition）；半正式定义（semi-formal definition）；非正式定义（non-formal definition）。

在科技论文中，当必须对概念做精确解释时，要用正式定义；当对概念做初步或笼统的解释时，可用半正式定义或非正式定义。根据不同的需要，对同一事物或概念可以给出严谨程度不同的定义。例如 gage 的定义：

①正式定义：A gage is a mechanical instrument which uses a scale or dial for indicating quantity. 量规是一种利用刻度或刻度盘来表示尺寸大小的机械器具。

②半正式定义：By definition, a gage has a scale or dial to indicate quantity. 量规可解释为：它用刻度或刻度盘来表示尺寸大小。

③非正式定义：A gage is an instrument or a means for measuring or testing something. 量规是一种测试器具。

（三）定义的句型

1. 英语正式定义的句型

S（主语）+be（系动词）+P（表语）+M（定语）。其中，S 是被定义的概念，用单数；P 表示属概念，是个类别词；M 修饰 P，可以是从句、分词短语或介词短语。例如：

①A knife is an instrument used for cutting things.

②Brass is an alloy containing a large proportion of copper.

2. 英语非正式定义的常见句型

（1）We can define …

（2）Sth. may be defined as …

（3）Sth. means …

（4）By … meant …

（5）By … we mean …

（6）Sth. is known as …

（7）Sth. is called/termed …

①We can define a crane as a machine which lifts heavy loads and displaces them horizontally.

②Pressure is defined as force per unit area.

③By electrolysis, we mean the process of decomposing a substance by an electric current.

3. 英语定义语篇

虽然用一个完整的句子可对一个概念从逻辑上给出定义，但对一个复杂的概念，往往不能一言以概之，而要在正式定义之后再予以补充，比如举例说明、提出主要用途、列述组成部分、或详或略地进行分析，乃至对相关概念进行对比或比较。这样，少则二三句，多则一二段，甚至整篇文章须从一个原始的、简单的定义出发，予以扩展。例如：

①A translator is a software system that transforms the statements of one computer language into statements in some other computer language. The first language is usually called the source language; the second language may be called the object language, target language, machine language, or some other descriptive name.

②A machine is a combination of rigid bodies having definite motions and capable of performing useful work. Machines vary widely in appearance, functions, and complexity from the simple hand-operated paper punch to the ship, which is itself composed of many simple and complex machines. No matter how complicated in appearance, every machine may be broken down into smaller and smaller assemblies, analysis of the operation depends upon an understanding of a few basic concepts, most of which come from basic physics.

4. 常用表达 (表 5-1)

表 5-1 定义的常用表达

中文	英文
……是一门……的科学	… is one of the … sciences which …
……是……的属性……	… is the/that property of … which/that …
……的定义是……	… is established at …
……(可)定义为……	…(may/can) be defined as …
……把……定义为……	… describe/define … as …
……被叫作(称为)……	… is/are called …; … is/are known as …
……的意思是……	… means …
所谓……指的是……	By … is here meant …
……讨论……	… treat of …
……是研究……的	… deals with …
……是用来指……	… is used to denote …

续表

中文	英文
……理解为/看成是……	… is to be understood as …
……描述为……	… is described as …
……叫作……	… is said to be …
……指的是……	… refers to …
这就是常用的……	This is … which is in common use.
另一种常用的……叫作……	Another type of … in common use is known as …
其他类型的……通常叫作……	In other types of … which are known as …
……的含义就是对……的了解	… was defined as knowledge of …

第二节　描写表达法

(一)描写的概念与内涵

描写是科技论文的主要修辞方式。与其他文体的描写不同，科技文体的描写主要分为物理描写、功能描写和过程描写。

(1)物理描写：包括对事物及其组成部分的大小、尺寸、形状、重量、容积、颜色、材料、结构等的描写。例如对铜矿石、青铜和黄铜的成分的描写：

Some ores of copper are oxides and carbonates and they have only to be reduced. Bronze, an alloy of copper and tin, was probably first discovered in some part of the world where copper and tin ores were found together, and brass, an alloy of copper and zinc, might have been similarly discovered by smelting copper and zinc ores together …

(2)功能描写：说明事物的功能、用途、特性，以及各组成部分的相互关系等。如下例描写气候对心脏病人的影响：

Climate has other implications, particularly for people who already have heart diseases. Hot, humid weather is not good for people with defective hearts and a tendency to heart failure, because it can aggravate the condition by increasing the workload on the cardiovascular system.

功能描写常把原因和结果作为描写相关事物及其信息组成部分之间的逻辑关系，把表示因果的过渡性词语，例如because、since、consequently、as a result、so that等，作为连接句子的纽带。

(3)过程描写：按行为的时间顺序，逐一说明事物在时间序列中所处的地位、状态、进程等。这特别适用于对加工工艺、实验以及事物发展的描写。现以对一组老鼠的实验描写为例：

One group of rats were taught to run through a maze. Five minutes after learning the task, they were cooled to 5 ℃, the temperature at which all electrical activity in the brain ceases. They were then kept at this temperature for 15 minutes before being allowed to return to their normal temperature. They were then run through the maze again.

在过程描写中，常伴有表示时间的连接词语，如 after、before、then、later、at this point、at that time 等。

物理描写、功能描写和过程描写三者并不互相排斥，有时其中两者(甚至三者)会出现在同一概念段落之中。

(二)分类特征描述

1.形状描述

1)平面形状
(1)圆形—round　　　　　　　　圆环—circle
　正方形—square　　　　　　　三角形—triangle
　长方形—rectangular/oblong　椭圆形—oval/ellipse
　半圆形—semicircle　　　　　 平行四边形—parallelogram
　菱形—diamond　　　　　　　 心形—heart
　月牙形—moon　　　　　　　　星形—star
　曲线形—zigzag　　　　　　　梯形—trapezoid(美); trapezium(英)
(2)四边形—quadrilateral　　　五边形—pentagon
　六边形—hexagon　　　　　　　七边形—heptagon
　多边形—polygon
2)立体形状
　立方体—cube　　　　　　　　长方体—cuboid
　球体—spheroid/sphere globe　圆锥体—cone/taper
　圆柱体—cylinder　　　　　　 半球—hemisphere

2.材质描述

1)固体
(1)固体形态：
　粉末—powder　　　　　　　　晶体，结晶体—crystal
　颗粒—granule　　　　　　　　锉屑—filing
　屑片—chip　　　　　　　　　 小(松软)薄片—flake
　刨花—shaving

（2）固体质地：

硬的，坚固的—hard　　　　　　　坚硬的—rigid

硬的，挺的—stiff　　　　　　　　结实的，牢固的—strong

坚韧的，牢固的—tough　　　　　　有弹力的—elastic

柔韧的—flexible　　　　　　　　　易弯的，柔韧的—pliable

柔软的—soft　　　　　　　　　　　（金属等）易拉长的，可延展的—ductile

有弹性的—resilient　　　　　　　易碎的，易损坏的—brittle

脆的，易碎的—fragile　　　　　　易破的，不耐用的—weak

重的—heavy　　　　　　　　　　　薄片状的—flaky

轻而薄的—flimsy　　　　　　　　　轻的—light

粉状的—powdery　　　　　　　　　晶状的，晶质的—crystalline

颗粒状的—granular　　　　　　　　透明的—transparent

半透明的—semitransparent/translucent

不透光的，不透明的—opaque

（金、银等）纯净的，（刀刃等）锋利的—fine

2）液体

（1）液体形态：

凝胶（体），胶滞体—jelly/gel　　　奶油状物，乳状悬浮液—cream

糊状物—paste

（2）液体质地：

奶油状的—creamy　　　　　　　　自由流动的—free-flowing

凝胶状的—gelatinous　　　　　　　油状的—oily

软而黏的—runny　　　　　　　　　黏性的，胶黏的—sticky

稠的—thick　　　　　　　　　　　稀薄的—thin

黏滞的，黏性的—viscous

3）气体

（1）气体形态：

层流—laminar flow　　　　　　　　过渡流—transition flow

湍流—turbulent flow

（2）常用气体：

空气—air　　　　　　　　　　　　氧气—oxygen（O_2）

氮气—nitrogen（N_2）　　　　　　氩气—argon（Ar_2）

氢气—hydrogen（H_2）　　　　　　二氧化碳—carbon dioxide（CO_2）

丙烷—dimethyl methane（C_3H_8）　　氨—hydrogen nitride（NH_3）

乙炔—acetylene（C_2H_2）　　　　液化石油气—liquefaction petroleum

3.色泽描述

（1）纯色的—pure　　　　　　　　浅色的—light

深色的—dark　　　　　　　　苍白的，暗淡的—pale

深的—deep　　　　　　　　　明亮的—bright

暗的—dull　　　　　　　　　稍黑的—blackish

略，微—faint　　　　　　　　淡薄的—diluted

不发光的—unpolished　　　　变黑的—darkened

浓的—intense　　　　　　　　有光泽的—glossy

不透明的—opaque　　　　　　略为淡色的—somewhat pale

满的—full　　　　　　　　　污的—dirty

着色的—tinged　　　　　　　鲜明的—vivid

暗色的—mat／matt／matte

有光泽的—shiny+颜色词（描述不同颜色）

（2）颜色词+-ish：

微红的，略带红色的—reddish　　　呈绿色的—greenish

微黄色的，淡黄色的—yellowish

（3）混色：颜色一-ish-颜色二。例如：

①Copper is a reddish-brown color.

②The sea is a bluish-green／greenish-blue color.

4.表面描述

（1）触觉表面：

粗糙的—coarse

粗糙的，有研磨作用的—abrasive

波纹的，缩成皱纹的，有瓦楞的—corrugated

粒状的，木纹状的，多粒的，有纹理的—grainy

有麻点的，去核的，有凹痕的—pitted

高低不平的，未经加工的，粗糙的—rough

不均匀的，不平坦的—uneven

（2）视觉表面：

杂色—variegated　　　　　　斑块状的—blocked

斑点状的—spotted　　　　　　色点的—dotted

云彩状的—clouded　　　　　　大理石花纹状的—marbled

镶嵌状的—tessellated　　　　镶边状的—bordered

有边的—edged　　　　　　　圆饼状的—discoidal

方格状的—banded

条纹状的—striped

豹纹状的—ocellated

花纹状的—painted

带纹状的—zoned

模糊状的—blurred

字母形的—lettered

5. 举例

①这种材料为蓝白色或乳白色，半透明，常用于制作首饰。

The material is ***bluish-white*** or ***milky-white***, ***translucent***, and is often used in jewellery.

②锡是一种易弯曲的白色金属，用于合金当中，并可附着于铁和钢的表面，防止腐蚀。

Tin is a soft ***white*** metal used in alloys and for coating iron and steel to prevent corrosion.

③在医药和工业中经常用到硫。它是一种浅黄色、非金属性质的固体，燃烧时产生明亮的火焰并伴有浓烈的气味。

Sulfur is often used in medicine and industry. It is a ***light-yellow*** non-metallic solid that burns with a bright flame and a strong smell.

④氮是一种无色无味的气体，该气体约占大气的4/5。

Nitrogen is a gas ***without color***, taste or smell that forms about four-fifth of the atmosphere.

⑤这种坚硬呈灰色的石头就是花岗岩，常用于建筑业。

This kind of hard ***grey-colored*** stone is granite which is often used for building.

(三) 修饰词语描写规则

1. 修饰词语的使用

科技文章的目的是分析事物，提示其发展变化的规律，所以需要用各种各样的修饰词语来描述、修饰或限制所述事物的性质(表5-2)。

表5-2　修饰词语示例

例词	语域	词语搭配
change	叙述事物性质变化	physical(物理的)、chemical(化学的)、positional(位置的)+change
	叙述事物数量变化	obvious(明显的)、negligible(可忽略不计的)、appreciable(可觉察到的)、fundamental(根本性的)、substantial(实质上的)+change
	用各种介词短语表示其变化的过程、范围和程度	change of state(物态变化)；change in weather(气候变化)

此外，如 ground station radio direction finder(地面无线电定向台)、measuring set of noise figure of TWT(行波管噪声指数测量装置)这种多重修饰现象给初学者带来诸多理解障碍，需加以注意。

2.修饰词语的顺序

英语科技文本中，修饰词语通常出现在它们修饰的名词之前，但如果用逗号分隔，它们也可能出现在名词之后，或者出现在系动词之后(表5-3)。

表5-3　修饰词语的位置

位置	英文	中文
名词前的形容词	The fluffy white clouds floated across the sky.	蓬松的白云飘过天空。
名词后的形容词	The clouds, white and fluffy, floated across the sky.	白云蓬松地飘过天空。
动词后的形容词	The clouds were fluffy and white.	云蓬松而洁白。

在英语句法中，形容词有一定的顺序(表5-4)。

表5-4　形容词顺序

限定词			数量词			评价词	实情									名词
							物理性状						其他			
冠词	所有格	指示词	数字	数量	序列	评估意见	大小	长度	状态	年龄	颜色	形状	起源	材质	种类	定语性名称	
1	2	3	4	5	6	7	8	9	10	11	12	13	14	15	16	17
The				two		comfortable			old blue						recliner	chairs
My				many		faithful, friendly			big black spotted						Labrador	retrievers

①In 1969, Ford came out with *a new*, *electronic intermittent windshield* wiper, the first in the industry.

1969 年，福特公司开始使用**一种全新的电子的间歇性挡风玻璃**雨刷。

②After several bent wings, I built *my own ultralight* with *steerable tricycle landing* gear.

经过几次弄弯了机翼之后，我终于制造了**一个超轻型飞行器**，上面有**可操纵的三轮着陆**装置。

3. 注意事项

（1）各修饰词（即形容词）可有缺项，但顺序不变。如：a small Swiss watch。

（2）当表大小（或长短）的词与表形状的词同时出现时，大小（或长短）在前，形状在后。如：a large square table。

（3）定冠词、不定冠词、指示代词、形容词性所有格、数词等位于句首。

（4）数词位于定冠词、指示代词后。数词不与不定冠词或形容词性所有格连用。

（5）分词离所修饰的名词最近。如：his new Japanese timing device；three Scottish handmade skirts。

第三节　分类表达法

（一）分类定义

分类是人们在科技论文中组织信息的一种重要修辞方式。通过分类，也就是对相关事物关系的排列组合，可以了解事物的异同与归属。分类要提供三方面的信息：类别或主体（entity）、分类项目（groups）、分类标准（criteria）。例如：

Bridges can be divided into three basic designs according to the way they bear the weight of the bridge and its load. Beam bridges are supported at their ends by the ground, with the weight thrusting downwards. Arch bridges thrust outwards as well as downwards at their ends. Suspension bridges use cables under tension to pull inwards against anchorages in the ground.

（二）分类要素与原则

在多数情况下，概念分类自成段落。段落的第一句即为分类提示句，即主题句（topic sentence），其他各句则分别为分类项目下的定义，说明其用途、功能等，以突出其有区别性的特征。

分类不限于一句或一段的表达，有时可扩大至几段，甚至统领整篇文章。例如有一篇题为"Logic Circuits"的文章即是由分类描述成文的：

To make logic decision, three basic logic circuits（called gates）are used：the OR Circuit, the AND Circuit, and the NOT Circuit.

The OR Circuit. This basic circuit has two or more inputs and a single output …

…

The AND Circuit. This circuit also has several inputs and only one output, but in this case the circuit output is at a logical state only if inputs are in the logical state simultaneously …

…

The NOT Circuit. This circuit has a single input and a single output and is arranged so that the output state is always opposite to the input state …

分类是按照种类、等级或性质对事物进行归类。检验分类有效性的基本规则是：

(1)适应性：应该符合讨论的目的；

(2)一致性：应该是一致的，因此所得到的子组是基于相同的原则；

(3)延展性：应该是排他的，使得产生的子组不重叠；

(4)完整性：应该是完整的，所以没有省略重要的子组。

我们可以使用不同的原则来对事物进行分类。例如，我们可以根据不同的原则将垃圾分类为可回收和不可回收垃圾，可燃和不可燃垃圾，纸、塑料和金属等。

分类包含三个要素：

(1)被分类的物体；

(2)划分的数目；

(3)进行分类的依据。

例如：

①Tranquilizers are divided into two categories according to the seriousness of the
　　(1)　　　　　　　　　(2)　　　　　　　(3)
mental problems they tackle — major tranquilizers and minor tranquilizers.

②Liquid pumps are divided into two main types according to the ways in which they
　　(1)　　　　　　　　　(2)　　　　　　　(3)
work— reciprocating pumps and rotary-type pumps.

有时这三个要素的位置也可以根据需要进行调换，例如：

①According to their ability to conduct electric current, all materials may be classified
　　　　　　(3)　　　　　　　　　　　(1)
into three major categories: conductors, semiconductors and insulators.
　　(2)

②Organisms may be classified on the basis of the number of cells they posses into
　　(1)　　　　　　　　(3)
single-cellular organisms and multi-cellular organisms.
　　　　(2)

偶尔第三个要素如果对要讨论的主题不是特别重要也可以省略，例如：

All matter can be divided into three classes: compounds, mixtures and elements.
　(1)　　　　　　　　(2)

（三）常用表达（表5-5）

表5-5 常用分类表达

中文	英文
……可归入几种类型	… fall into several groups …
将……分成……种	separate … into … groups
一种……；另一种……	one group … another group …
……有……种形式	… is available in … forms
大类中的主要分支是……	The major divisions within the general category were …
提出的问题中有……个需要专门评述。	Several questions were raised, … of which deserve special comment.
以……的形式	in forms of …
……给出……和……	… provides … and …
……由……组成；包括……	… consist of/include …
……可以进一步分解为……	… can be further divided into …
……由……组成	… is made up of …
……已被分成……	… has been divided into …
……的范围从……到……	… range from … to …
用……对……进行分类	… was classified by …
对……而言	for …

第四节　主从关系表达法

（一）因果关系

1.因果关系的显性连接与隐性衔接

显性连接：常见的表达因果关系的从属连词有 because、since、as、so that 等；并列连词有 for、and 等；复合连词有 now that、in as much as、in that、seeing（that）等；普通介词有 from、of、by、for、through、with 等；短语介词有 because of、due to、out of、thanks to、in view of、in consideration of、by virtue of、as a result of、by reason of、owing to、in consequence of 等；连接副词有 so、therefore、hence、thus、consequently 等。

隐性连接：很多情况下，因果关系的表达不用具体的词或结构形式，而是寓于意义、逻辑上的内在联系之中。

2.常用因果表述结构(表5-6)

表5-6 常用因果表达

中文	英文
……的原因在于……	The cause of … lies in …
将确定/准确指出/探讨/讨论……的原因。	The cause of … will be determined/pinned down/explored/discussed.
一个结果是……	One result is that …
使用……,就不难看出……	Using …, it is easy to show that …
还有其他理由促使人们期望……	There are other reasons to expect …
导致……	cause/generate/yield/bring about/give rise to/result in …
确定……以便保证……	determine/decide … to ensure that …
为了……,研究了……	To achieve …, … are examined.
为了……,……提出了……	To explain …, … proposed …
为了……的目的	for sake of …
结果是……	The consequence is …
……可归因于……	… is attributable to/determined by/decided by/caused by …
……受到……的影响	… is effected by …
试图通过……解决……	attempt to solve … by …
……由……所导致	… result from …
由于下述原因,……被认为是……	… is found to be … because of the following reasons.
可以归因于……,……,或……	… could be attributed to …, to …, or to …
除了要考虑……之外,还要考虑……	In addition to considering …, … are included.
……并不能很好地解释……	… does not provide a satisfactory explanation for …
从这些研究结果中得出的结论是,尽管……,……还是不能够……	The conclusion emerging from these studies is that… although …
不能解释……	… do not account for …

人体主要是由脂肪和水组成的。脂肪和水中含有很多氢原子,总数约占人体的63%,而氢原子核会发出核磁共振信号。**因此磁共振成像主要就是对氢原子核发出的核磁共振信号进行成像。**

The human body is primarily fat and water. Fat and water have many hydrogen atoms which make the human body approximately 63% hydrogen atoms. Hydrogen nuclei have an NMR signal. ***For these reasons*** magnetic resonance imaging primarily images the NMR signal from the hydrogen nuclei.

上述译例中文原文"因此"与英文译文"for these reasons"均采用显性词汇实现因果关系连接。

（二）主次关系

翻译过程中，正确理解是准确翻译的前提。要想透彻地理解原句，就必须明白语法结构及分句间的逻辑关系，理解句子间的主从关系，提炼句子主干。将定语、状语、补语和插入语等修饰性成分去除后，留下的主谓宾结构就是整个句子的主干。科技文章英译时，应认真分析汉语中所隐含的内在逻辑关系，依此组织译文结构，使译文形成一个各部分相互联系的整体，重点突出，主次分明。

①本文介绍了 CAPP 系统中自动生成和输出工序图的基本方法，并重点论述了比例设置，剖面线的绘制，尺寸、公差、粗糙度的标注等基本问题，其中剖面线的绘制方法是比较独特、新颖和通用的方法。

In this paper, a basic method of automatic creation and output operation figure in CAPP is introduced. ***The emphasis is laid on*** setting proportion, drawing section line, indication of size, tolerance and roughness and other basic problems, ***among which*** the method of drawing section line is not only distinctive and novel but also of universal use.

这段文字涉及如何在一系列事物中突出重点。上面的译文采用了两种方法：一种是明确用文字表示（The emphasis is laid on …）；二是使用定语从句，在其中突出主要点。

②***The fact*** that present-day cancer rates do not exhibit any generalized increase (apart from the effects of smoking) ***does not***, of course, ***guarantee*** that all, or nearly all, of the recently introduced new chemicals, pesticides, pollutants, and habits are harmless for, it may be decades before any cancer-causing effects may have become clearly evident.

虽然当前癌症发病率并未呈现普遍上升趋势（吸烟致癌除外），但这不足以说明所有或几乎所有新出现的化学物质、杀虫剂、污染物和不良嗜好都不致癌，因为致癌效应可能要过几十年才会显现。

这是一个结构颇为复杂的句子，句子主干是 The fact does not guarantee …，穿插 4 个从句。译文将原句拆成三个部分，即 does not 之前的主语部分、does not 之后的谓语动词 guarantee 加宾语从句部分以及最后的原因状语从句部分。先陈述："当前癌症发病率并未呈现普遍上升趋势"，然后再进一步进行补充说明——"这不足以说明所有或几乎所有新出现的化学物质、杀虫剂、污染物和不良嗜好都不致癌"，最后对前面这一观点进行解释和说明——"因为致癌效应可能要过几十年才会显现"。

（三）方法结果关系

方法结果关系即使用了某种方法，得出了某一结论。

本文试图从理论上说明，我国广泛采用的 XYD-I 型小液压捣固机的减振问题，并根据具体结构作减振验算，从而得出"这种减振是可行的"结论。

原译：The purpose of this paper is to explain theoretically the problem of vibration damping of Model XYD-I, a small-sized hydraulic tamping tool widely used in our country. Moreover, checks on the vibration damping are made according to certain concrete mechanism. Finally, we come to the conclusion that this mechanism of vibration damping is feasible.

改译：The purpose of this paper is to explain theoretically the problem of vibration damping of Model XYD-I, a small-sized hydraulic tamping tool widely used in our country. Moreover, checks on the vibration damping are made according to certain concrete mechanism, ***which lead to the conclusion that*** this mechanism of vibration damping is feasible.

原译中的同位语 a small-sized hydraulic tamping tool 很好地解决了它与 Model-I 型的关系问题，但原文中第二与第三部分所形成的验算方法与结果结论的表述关系，译文中分别用两个句子表达，结构略显松散，为弥补这一缺损，可将第二、三部分合并，从而实现方法与结论的紧密关联。

（四）并列承接关系

在并列承接关系中，呈现先后仅表示次序，不涉及重要性的体现。

本文将 Q 过程重新分类，得到每类 Q 过程存在、唯一性准则以及一般表达式。我们的结果在 Q 过程构造及定性理论，特别在含瞬时效的 Q 过程的构造及定性理论中，有重要应用。

原译：In this paper, Q-processes are classified in a new method. We obtain the existence and uniqueness as well as the forms of each class of Q-processes. Our result has important application in the construction and qualitative theory of Q-processes, especially, in that of instantaneous state Q-processes.

改译：In this paper, Q-processes are classified in a new method and ***the*** existence and uniqueness as well as the forms each class of Q-processes ***are obtained***. ***The result obtained*** thereby has important application in the construction and qualitative theory of Q-processes, especially, in that of instantaneous state Q-processes.

第五节　比较、对比、类比表达法

（一）基本概念

在《现代汉语大词典》中，"对比"的定义是"把两种不同的事物或情况互相比较"；"比较"的定义是"根据一定的标准，在两种或两种以上有某种联系的事物间，辨别高下、异同"。比较的对象相对比较多，而对比往往把比较锁定在两个对象之间。"类比"则重于对事物间共性的展示。类比法是将性质、特点在某些方面相同或相近的不同事物加以比较，从而引出结论的方法。

在科技文体中，**比较**是将两种类别相同或不同的事物、现象等加以比较来说明事物特征的说明方法，作用是突出强调事物的某种特征。在说明某些抽象的或者是读者比较陌生的事物时，用读者熟悉的事物与不熟悉的事物相比较来说明问题，可以将事物的特征在比较中显现出来。**对比**是把具有明显差异、矛盾和对立的双方安排在一起，进行对照比较的表现手法。对比把对立的意思或事物、或把事物的两个方面放在一起做比较，让读者在比较中分清好坏、辨别是非。对比重在对事物间的差异性的揭示，而**类比**则重在对事物间共性的展示。类比是根据一种事物的某些特征来证明另一种事物也有类似特征，或者找出类比事物和所要证明道理之间的共性的论证方法。类比将性质、特点在某些方面相同或相近的不同事物加以比较，从而引出结论的方法。

（二）常用标志词

1.比较表达

常用的比较标志词有：similarly, similar（to）, likewise, like, in the same way, both, compared with, in comparison with, one similarity … another similarity, in a similar fashion.

① ***Through the compare with*** legislation abroad, we conclude the successful experience that we can learn.

通过与国外立法**的比较**，得出我国立法需要借鉴的经验。

②Scans of his chest, abdomen, and pelvis ***likewise*** showed nothing.

扫描他的胸部、腹部和骨盆**也**没有什么发现。

③This ***similarity*** in density has long prompted speculation that the Moon split away from a rapidly rotating Earth, but this idea founders on two observations.

长期以来，这种密度上的**相似性**促使人们猜测月球是从快速旋转的地球上分裂出来的，但这种想法创始于两次观测。

2. 对比表达

常用的对比标志词有：but，however，by contrast，in contrast with，although（though），even though，while（whilst），despite，in spite of，nevertheless，whereas，on the contrary，on the one hand … on the other hand，unlike，conversely，one difference … another difference.

①Larger ones rise quickly to the surface and disappear, *whilst* smaller ones called micro-bubbles can last for days.

较大的气泡迅速上升到水面并消失，而被称为微气泡的较小的气泡可以持续数天。

②*Although* the market has been flat, residential property costs remain high. *Nevertheless*, the fall-off in demand has had an impact on resale values.

尽管市场一直疲软，房价持续偏高。然而需求的减少还是对二手房价格产生了影响。

3. 类比表达

常用的类比标志词有：as … as，than，so，either.

①Diplomacy is better *than* war.

采取外交手段胜于诉诸战争。

②Clock goes well, if second by second, and you and I are going well, if step by step.

时钟顺利，如果一秒一秒，你和我都很顺利，如果一步一步。

③The more you learn, the more you have. The more you have, the more you forget. The more you forget, the more you need to learn again.

你学的越多，你拥有的就越多。拥有的越多，忘记的就越多。你忘记的越多，你就越需要重新学习。

（三）常用表达（表5-7）

表5-7　常用比较、对比、类比表达

中文	英文
我们可以通过……进行比较。	We can structure/make/begin comparison by …
从……方面进行比较。	The comparison proceeds in … aspects.
下面的……被用来做比较。	The following … are employed for comparison.
按照……标题进行比较。	The comparison is done under … headings.

续表

中文	英文
……被用作比较……的基础。	… is used as the basis for comparing …
比较是建立在……的基础上的。	Comparisons were based on …
比较的基本标准是……	The basic criterion for comparison is …
在……之间有很大的相似之处。	Among … there is a good deal of similarity.
……与……一致	… is consistent with …
……与……吻合	… agrees/coincides with …
与……对比；对比之下	In contrast (to) …
与……相反	… is (in) opposite to …
在……和……之间存在着相似的关系。	A similar relationship exists between … and …
将……与……比较的目的在于……	… is compared with … for the purpose of (to/in order to/so that) …
然而,……在……方面表现出相当鲜明的对照特点。	However, … presents quite contrasting features with regard to …
……和……之间的差别主要是由于……(造成的)	The differences between … and … are mainly due to …
如果与……相比较,在……两侧的……就更加相似了。	The … on both sides of … are more similar when compared to …
将……与……比较,以便找出它们的共同点与不同点。	… is compared with … for similarities and differences.

第六节　其他科技语篇常用句型

　　科技语言以文字语言为主,以数字语言和工程学语言为辅,以承载科技思想为职能。在科技类文章的行文表述中,文字的表述应清晰、准确、精炼、严密,常采用某种特有的方式认证某一命题或进行计算。现将科技英语在表述数字、图形、表格、公式等时使用的语言结构、句法结构归纳如下。

（一）比例、范围的表达（表5-8）

表5-8 常用比例、范围表达

中文	英文
……的比例	the proportion of …
与……成比例	be proportional to …
与……成反比	be inversely proportional to …
从……到……不等	range/vary/differ from … to …
……的范围是……	range over …
除……之外	beyond
占……比例	account for
……覆盖（占据、跨越、包含）……	… cover/take/span/entail

（二）假设、前提（表5-9）

表5-9 常用假设、前提表达

中文	英文
设（假设）……	let/suppose/assume/imagine …
在……的条件下；倘若……	provided/providing that …
考虑……	consider that …
使……成为……	allow … to be …
假设	… is assumed that …; assuming that …
由于很难假设……	since it is difficult to assume that …
没有根据假设……	there is no basis for assuming that …
就像……所设想的那样	as is suggested by …
所假设的……是……	hypothesized … was …
……证实……的假设	… confirm the hypothesis that …
……的假设被证实了。	The assumption/hypothesis that … was confirmed.
……证明……的假设	… support/provide support for the hypothesis that …
本研究测试了……假设。	Hypotheses that … are tested in this study.
……用作反驳、修正和/或者接受假设的依据以支持这一假设。	… was used as a basis for refuting, revising, and/or accepting hypotheses, … favoring the hypothesis.

(三)程度、角度(表5-10)

表5-10 常用程度、角度表达

中文	英文
达到……	reach/attain/arrive at …
……高达……	… rise as high as …
保持……的速度/温度	keep/remain a speed of/the temperature of …
构成一个……角	form an angle of …
一条线与另一条线成……角相交。	One line cuts another at … angle.
与……成……	at an angle of … to/with …
……间的夹角	the angle included between …

(四)推导、推理(表5-11)

表5-11 常用推导、推理表达

中文	英文
假定……可推导……	assume that … we will deduce …
从……推导出……	be derived from …
将……代入……	substitute/plug … into …
求出……	… be determined
运算成……	be manipulated into …
因此……同样……	As a consequence …, similarly …
因此……	accordingly …
因此	thus/therefore/consequently/in consequence/as a result
显然;明显	obviously/apparently
……可能导致……	… might result in …
本研究/结果表明……	This study/result indicates …
这也许暗示……	This may imply that …
……的启示是……	The implications for … are …
如果……,那么……	If …, then … /If …, consequently …
如果……,……就更可能……	If …, … is more likely to …

（五）列举、举例（表5-12）

表5-12 常用列举、举例表达

中文	英文
……包括……，如……和……	… include …, such as …
下面是一个有关……的例子。	The following is an example of …
用一个例子说明……	Present … by an example.
越来越多的证据表明……	There is growing evidence of …
……是一个普遍现象。	It is common to find …
正如人们经常看到的那样，……	As is so often the case, …
……可以证明这一点。	… make the point.
然而，却没有证据表明……	There is no evidence, however, for …
作为……的一个例子是……	An example of … is …
诸如……	such … as/such as …

第六章　科技语篇结构

　　"语篇"一词在语言学中指一个任何长度的、语义完整的口语或书面语的段落。语篇是一组使用中的语言，既非小句或句子之类的语法单位，也不受长短的限制。就语法单位而言，它比句子大，但它与句子之间的关系和句子与小句、小句与词组等之间的关系是一样的，即通过成分由小单位组成大单位。语篇表达的是意义而非形式。它和小句或者句子之间不是包含与被包含关系，而是体现关系，即一种语言符号系统在另一种语言符号系统中的体现。

　　当代语言学理论的兴起和发展成为翻译研究新的巨大推动力，使之摆脱了句子结构的桎梏，推动翻译向广度和深度扩展。向广度扩展意味着从大于单句的语篇、语段来考虑翻译问题；而向深度扩展意味着从句子的内在联系和逻辑关系来研究翻译。

　　语篇与句子或小句的关系不体现在篇幅的长短上，而体现在衔接上，无论衔接以何种形式出现，这些连续的话语或句子不但必须合乎语法，而且必须意义连贯，既包含语篇内部在语言上的连贯，也包括与外界在语义上和语用上的连贯。语篇的架构，即语篇总体的宏观组织结构，包含语篇的总体安排、层次、组织，具体包括整个篇章的目的、结论，对各个要点的陈述、拓展、例证和分析，并编排各个要点的框架和次序，重构各部分之间的关系，构建全篇的框架。科技翻译研究同样应以语段或语篇为依托，其对于词义的选取、行文的组织、格调的把握均有相当的现实意义。也就是说，并非译好了每个单词就意味着译好了每个句子，就等同于译好了一篇文章。文章并非单词与句子的简单堆砌，科技语篇有其鲜明的结构、特点和风格。

第一节　中英文科技语篇结构差异

(一)中英文逻辑表述差异

科技文体具有极强的逻辑性,强调运用概念、判断、推理等方法说明需要解决的问题,要求篇章组织严密、层次清晰、前后照应、连贯一致。无论是中文表达还是英文表达均应遵循读者的期待规范。科技文体行文按时间或空间顺序为其所包含的信息提供框架,或以逻辑形式展开。语篇在提供行文信息框架的同时,也反映各项信息间的逻辑关系。

1. 自然顺序

1) 时间顺序

时间顺序指按时间先后编排信息,通常有年代时间顺序和过程时间顺序两种。

(1)年代时间顺序:将年代、日期、时间作为信息铺陈的框架。例如:

分别在1977年8月和9月发射的两个"旅行者号"探测器,原定只探测木星和土星及其卫星系,结果却大大超过了原定计划。土卫六(土星的第六颗卫星)阻碍了"旅行者1号"访问其他天体的轨道。"旅行者2号"则在得到木星和土星的引力支援后,于1986年1月成为第一个飞向天王星的人造物体。1989年8月,海王星成为"旅行者号"在太阳系内巡回大旅行访问的最后一个天体。

Launched separately *in August and September 1977*, the two Voyager spacecraft were programmed only to explore the Jupiter and Saturn systems, but they had far exceeded that original mission specification. Voyager 1's trajectory to Titan precluded its visit to any other worlds. But Voyager 2, after getting gravity assists provided by Jupiter and Saturn, became *in January 1986* the first artifact of the human species to reach the Uranus system. *In August 1989*, Neptune was the final port of call on Voyager's Grand Tour.

(2)过程时间顺序:以过程或步骤的时间顺序为基础构建信息框架,可细分为描写型和指令型两种。描写型(如例句①所示)注重连接词的使用;指令型(如例句②所示)一般不使用连接词,而将各信息按各个步骤的时间顺序分段排列。例如:

①"发育"一词包含三个过程。**首先**,通过分裂产生新细胞,这在高等植物中尽管不只是但通常是发生在称为分生组织的区域内。**其次**,是细胞生长或增大阶段。**最后**,细胞分化进入成熟和特化状态。这三个发育阶段无论是从空间上还是从时间上不一定是分开的,从一开始就了解这一点是非常重要的。

The term "development" encompasses three types of process. *First*, new cells are produced by division. In the high plant, this occurs most commonly, although not exclusively, in regions called meristems. ***Next***, there is a phase of growth or cell enlargement. ***Finally***, the cells differentiate into their mature and specialized states. It is important to grasp from the outset that these three phases of development are not necessarily separated either in space or in time.

原文采用"首先""其次""最后"（分别对应译文中的 first、next、finally），跟语篇中的其他部分衔接，按过程发生的时间顺序依次描写。

②

Conventional Restart on Windows 7 Computers

Click on the "Start" button.

On later versions of Windows, the "Start" button appears as the Windows logo.

An alternative restart method is to press the Alt+F4 on your keyboard and then scroll to "Restart" on the menu box that opens.

Navigate to the "Shut Down" option in the lower-right corner of the "Start" menu.

Click on the arrow to the right of the "Shut Down" option. A floating menu will display that contains additional options.

Select "Restart" from the options provided. Your computer will then reboot. This may take a few minutes. When it is done, it will prompt you for your Windows password just as when you turn it on.

【分析】上文 Windows 7 系统重启说明语篇中，使用了多个连续的祈使句。动词（Click、Navigate、Select 等）都是语境独立成分，其后语境独立的地点状语或宾语成分包含负载实际动态程度更高的焦点信息。

2）空间顺序

空间顺序是指按地理空间或几何空间编排信息。具体可分为明晰空间顺序和概括空间顺序两种。在概括空间顺序中，空间描述词的含义是概括性的，英语中通常使用 above、below、left、right、inside、outside 等表示空间方位的词。在明晰空间顺序中，空间描述词的含义明晰精确，例如：5 cm above、10 meters high、at 75° angle 等。两种描述顺序均可采用直译的方式。

2. 逻辑顺序

1）因果排序

中文原文多用隐含逻辑形式来表达因果关系，翻译为英文时需按因果逻辑排列信息，如常用显性逻辑形式关联词（because、as、since、due to、in the consequence of、as for）或显性词组来表达。例如：

没有（盐）这种必不可少的矿物质，人体器官就无法正常工作。**因此**在医院的特别护理部，医生会给病人静脉注射盐水；手术中，这种生命攸关的盐水还可防止病人**发生**休克。食盐过少会**导致**肌肉痉挛、恶心、抵抗力减弱。事实上，1812 年拿破仑的兵马从俄国溃退时所出现的可怕情形，**部分原因就是**他们缺少盐。士兵体内因为缺少盐分而无法抵御疾病和传染病的侵袭，导致他们当中的许多人丧命。

Without this essential mineral, our bodies could not function. *Thus*, saline solution is given intravenously in hospital intensive-care units; during surgery, this vital salt solution also prevents patients from going into shock. *With too little salt* cause muscle cramps, nausea and lowered resistance. In fact, *a lack of salt* for his men and horses *contributed to* the nightmarish conditions of Napoleon's 1812 retreat from Russia; thousands of his soldiers died when their salt-starved bodies could no longer resist disease or infection.

2）主次排序

中文原文多用隐含逻辑形式或显性逻辑次序词语来表达主次关系，如最初、起初、首先、接着、再者、然后、其次、最终、最后、总而言之等，英文则多采用主次关联词 first、second、then、next、most、in the end、second most、less、least、in short 等。

本文介绍了 CAPP 系统中自动生成和输出工序图的基本方法，并重点论述了比例设置、剖面线的绘制、尺寸、公差、粗糙度的标注等基本问题，其中剖面线的绘制方法是比较独特、新颖和通用的方法。

In this paper, a basic method of automatic creation and output operation figure in CAPP is introduced. *The emphasis is laid on* setting proportion, drawing section line, indication of size, tolerance and toughness and other basic problems, *among which* the method of drawing section line is not only distinctive and novel bust also of universal use.

上文系列事物表述中，译文采用两种方法以突出重点：一是明确文字表述（the emphasis is laid on …）；二是使用定语从句。

3）比较与对比

中文表达中孤立使用的"比"无法确定是比较还是对比关系的，需全文统筹确定后，方可进行翻译。英文中的比较表达是为了突显事物间的共性，常用比较级或固定表达 in comparison、similarly、like、likewise、in the same way、resemble、as does X、so does Y 等；而对比表达则是为了强调事物间的差异，常用 in contrast、on the other hand、however、nevertheless、although、differ 等。

（1）整体比较：作者先展现一个或一类人或事物的所有特点，然后再展现与之相比的另一个或另一类人或事物的全部特点。例如：

My hometown and my college town have several things in common. First, my hometown, Gridlock, is a small town. It has a population of only about 10,000 people. Located in a rural area, Gridlock is surrounded by many acres of farmland which are devoted mainly to growing corn and soybeans. Gridlock also contains a college campus, Neutron College, which is famous for its Agricultural Economics program as well as for its annual Corn-Watching Festival. As for my college town, Subnormal, it too is small, having a population of about 1,000 local residents, which swells to 15,000 people when students from the nearby college are attending classes. Like Gridlock, Subnormal lies in the center of farmland which is used to raise hogs and cattle. Finally, Subnormal is simmilar to Gridlock in that it also boasts a beautiful college campus, called Quark College. This college is well known for its Agricultural Engineering Department and also for its yearly Hog Calling Contest.

（2）交替进行：作者逐条比较或对照两个人或事物相同和不同的特点。例如：

I've lived in Vancouver for more than 20 years and, although I still have fond memories of Quebec City, I prefer it here. One reason is climate. Quebec City hosts a "Carnival" every winter featuring ice carving and citizens drinking Caribou (liquor) to keep warm. In Vancouver, on the other hand, winter includes blossoming cherry and plum trees in January. Another reason to prefer Vancouver is its size. Quebec City is a small capital city, much like Victoria. In contrast, Vancouver is a busting metropolis that has one of the most multi-cultural populations in the world. My last reason for preferring Vancouver over Quebec City is language. Quebecois speak French, a language I speak poorly. In Vancouver, however, people speak English, so I feel more comfortable here. Although I remember my time in Quebec City fondly, I much prefer to live in the gentle climate of Vancouver.

4）推导

推导将两类不同的事物进行排列对比，表达不同事物之间的共性。例如：

这就是我们现在面临的处境。正如毕业生人数的减少使我们更容易被自己喜欢的大学录取，犯罪人数的逐渐上升使犯罪分子送进监狱变得更难。

This is the situation we find ourselves in today. Just as the decline in the number of high-school graduates has made it *easier* to gain admission to the college of one's choice, the gradual increase in the criminal population has made it *more difficult* to get into prison.

5）例证

例证涉及相关事实、统计数据、个人经历、事件或故事，主要包括以下三类：

（1）真实示例。摆事实讲道理，在思维方式上属于归纳推理。例如我们想支撑"女性可以成为并有能力成为国家元首"的观点，就可以举例英国前首相撒切尔（Margaret Hilda Thatcher）、德国前总理安格拉·默克尔（Angela Merkel）、新西兰前总理海伦·克拉克（Helen Elizabeth Clar）、冰岛首位女总理约翰娜·西于尔扎多蒂（Jóhanna Sigurzardóttir）、印度独立 60 年首位女总统普拉蒂巴·帕蒂尔（Pratibha Devisingh Patil）。使用真实示例的优点在于示例的真实存在，益于增强说服力。

（2）假设说明。尽管不真实，但虚构或假设的实例便于清晰呈现问题的多个方面。通过某一具有典型性、代表性的假设说明，推衍诸种事物、现象的共同点和规律，由个别到一般，达到举一反三、触类旁通的效果。例如，弗吉尼亚·伍尔夫在她著名的女权主义文章《一个属于自己的房间》（A Room of One's Own）中断言，很少有

"伟大"的女性作家,这不是因为男性比女性优越,而是因为他们拥有许多特权,包括安静的阅读和写作空间。文中朱迪斯·莎士比亚是伍尔夫虚构的隐喻。她展示了女性在文学和艺术以及公共生活和文化的变迁,以此突显父权社会中的女性缺少作为知识分子思考、阅读和成长的空间,因而教育成为女性解放的关键。

(3)类比阐释。类比是将同一类事物的某些相同方面进行比较,以另一事物是否正确来证明这一事物是否正确。例如,我们可以断言语言教育改革势在必行。我们可以把目前的制度比作一座需要革新的破旧建筑。鉴于类比是两种事物之间的延伸比较,它可能是有用的,因为它通过熟悉的方式来解释不熟悉的事物。然而,教育系统几乎不像一座建筑。尽管一栋破旧的建筑的一些真实情况可能与当前的语言教育体系大致相同,但它们之间存在本质的差异。因此,我们不应将类比与证据混淆。

试比较以下两例:

①句一:The mayor is corrupt and should not be reelected.

句二:The mayor should not be reelected because he has fired two city workers who refused to contribute to his campaign fund, has put his family and friends on the city payroll and has used public employees to make improvements to his home.

②句一:Some people treat animals like humans.

句二:Give human names to their pets.

Dress pets in clothing.

Refer to themselves as "Mommy" or "Daddy".

6)图解

无论是中文还是英文,在科技文体中,都倾向使用图表或公式来解读论点。例如以下例子。

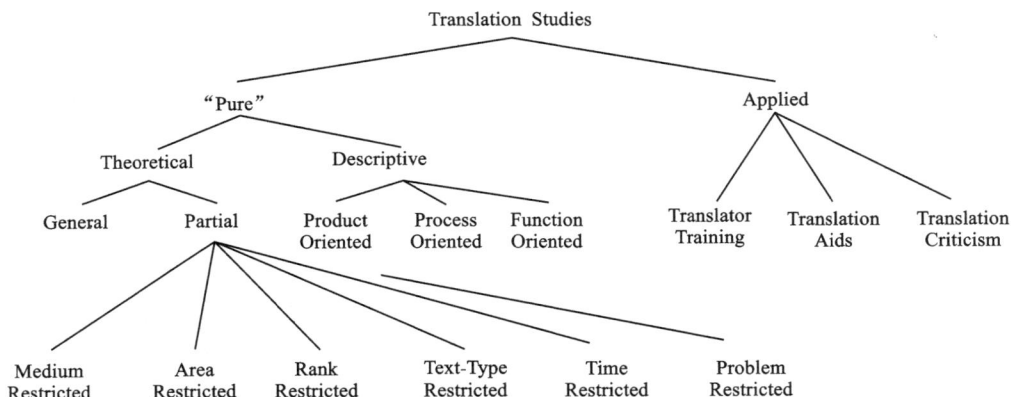

Holmes' Conception of Translation Studies (*from Toury, 1991:181*)

a. Positive

In 1972 James Holmes designed a structure of translation studies and provided the theoretical basis for the discipline to move towards independency. Later in 1995 Gideon Toury made out of it "Holmes' 'map' of translation studies", which has played a positive role in visualizing Holmes' design and propelling the development of the discipline. However, Toury's "map" has some deficiencies with several lower-order classifications omitted, the relationship between some branches misconnected, the ultimate goals of some branches excluded, and even such important branch as "study of translation studies" neglected. Such a misshaped map has hindered a full understanding of Holmes' design. The paper makes a more complete and accurate "map" of Holmes' translation studies with a closer reference to his 1972 paper. The new map, by correcting the deficiencies of Toury's map through readjusting the relationships between branches and adding the lower-order classifications, the goals of the three branches of DTS, and especially the "study of translation studies" branch, gives a thorough representation of Holmes' thought on the disciplinary structure and should help judge more objectively the historical contribution and academic value that Holmes' design deserves.

b. Neutral

James S. Holmes' seminal lecture "The Name and Nature of Translation Studies" (1972) set out to orient the scholarly study of translation. It put forward a conceptual scheme that identified and interrelated many of the things that can be done in translation studies, envisaging an entire future discipline and effectively stimulating work aimed at establishing that discipline. Historically, this was a major step forward, none the least because it involved a frontal attack on the hazy but self-assured categories that had long been used to judge translations. Holmes' categories were simple, scientifically framed, and hierarchically arranged: "applied" was opposed to "pure", the latter was broken down into "theoretical" and "descriptive", then "descriptive" divided in turn into "product oriented", "process oriented" and "function oriented", and so on. This figure shows the apocryphal graphic form these categories received later from scholars who saw it as a legitimate point of departure.

c. Negative

Maps are peculiar instruments of power. They tend to make you look in certain directions; they make you overlook other directions.

Many wonderful things found a place in this map; a few more have benefited from the modifications and variants proposed since (notably Lamber 1991, Snell-Hornby 1991, Toury 1991). Of course, translation studies cannot be reduced to this one map, and the map itself has been evolving dynamically, along with the lands it purports to represent. Yet the curious fact remains that neither Holmes nor his commentators—at least those subscribing to the map and its variants—explicitly named a unified area for the historical study of translation.

(二)语篇差异体现

无论是英文还是中文科技语篇，其架构都受其特有的思维定式和规范的影响。中文篇章架构常表现为：先设定时空和逻辑框架，再提示主题或主旨；先铺陈数据和事实，再得出结论；先分析原因，再给出结论或结果。英文篇章架构则是先表述段落的中心思想，然后分层逐点扩展说明，最后推导结论。中英文语篇架构差异基于以下两点原因：

（1）结构差异：曾有语言学家形象地将英语句子称为"葡萄形"结构，葡萄枝干很短，但果实丰硕，大小不一的果实间的逻辑关系或是通过关联词语进行显性连接，或是以形显义，句子结构严谨，缺少弹性；而中文被描绘为"竹竿形"结构，句子短小精悍，论述逐步展开，信息内容"节节"累积，以意役形，竹节间逻辑关系靠隐性连贯和叙述的整理顺序来间接显示，不用或基本不用关联词，句子结构松散，富有弹性。例如：

Perhaps the fact that many of these first studies considered only algae of a size that could be collected in a net（net phytoplankton），a practice that over-looked the smaller phytoplankton that we now know grazers are most likely to feed on，led to a deemphasis of the role of grazers in subsequent research.

也许是早期的许多研究只考虑了一种大小足以被浮游植物采集的小藻，而这种做法忽略了更小的浮游植物——现在我们知道食草动物很可能以它为生。这些事实和做法导致了在后面的研究中对食草动物的忽视。

英文表达去除"the fact"与"a practice"中的同位语从句及定语从句的修饰成分后，句子还原为一个极简的 SVO 结构，其句式中主语的复杂性主要体现在"the fact"由 that 所引导的同位语从句修饰，而同位语从句中的宾语"algae of a size"又由另一个 that 所引导的定语从句所修饰。另一并列主语"a practice"同样由 that 所引导的同位语从句修饰，而同位语从句中的宾语"the smaller phytoplankton"由 that 所引导的定语从句所修饰，形成典型的葡萄形结构。中文译文并未呈现显性关联标志词，主要通过语义连贯，实现"节节"推进，形式特征不明显，体现以意统形。

（2）形式差异：中文语篇通常没有明确的段落中心思想句，其阐述是顺着思维而自然发展的，呈流水或螺旋状向前推进。中文段落的语义具有自然流动性，首先表述现象，提出各种应该考虑的因素，然后得出结论，说明最后采取的方式和方法。而英文篇章布局通常采用总说分呈的形式，即首先表述段落中心思想，而后逐步扩展说明，最后得出结论。例如：

With the advent of space shuttle, it will be possible to put an orbiting solar power plant in stationary orbit 24, 000 miles from the earth that would collect solar energy almost continuously and convert this energy either directly to electricity via photovoltaic cells indirectly with flat plate or focused collectors that would boil a carrying medium to produce steam that would drive a turbine that then in turn would generate electricity.

　　随着航天飞机的出现,有可能把一个沿轨道运行的太阳能发电站送到距地球 24, 000 英里的一条同步轨道上去。这个太阳能发电站可以几乎不间断地收集太阳能,不仅能用光伏电池将太阳能直接转换成电能,也可用平板集热器或聚焦集热器将太阳能间接转换成电能。集热器可以使热传导体气化,从而驱动涡轮机发电。

　　英文表达仅为一句,重在解释太阳能发电站的各种能量转换,而中文处理为三个短句,分别论述太阳能发电站"建设背景""光伏电池"及"集热器"转换原理,再具体至集热器工作效能,强调语篇主旨集热器。

第二节　科技语篇翻译中的衔接与连贯策略

　　英国语言学会在翻译证书考试中提出的翻译标准是:①精确;②词语、成语、术语及语域的选择恰当;③连贯一致,组织合理;④标点使用正确。(Jeremy Munday, 2007)这一标准充分体现了基于语篇翻译层面进行翻译研究的重要性,而连贯和衔接是语篇的两大特征,因此在语篇转换过程中衔接(cohesion)和连贯(coherence)的处理变得极为重要,是两种语言在语篇的逻辑转换过程中重点考虑的因素。黄国文 (1988:7)认为:"语篇无论以何种形式出现,都必须合乎语法,并且语义连贯,包括与外界在语义上和语用上的连贯,也包括语篇内部在语言上的连贯。"语篇应该有一个论题结构或逻辑结构,句子之间有一定的逻辑联系。语篇中的话段或句子都是在这一结构基础上组合起来的。在翻译过程中处理句间逻辑关联与篇章整体架构关联的方法不尽相同。本节论述的译例选取科技论文摘要这一小型语篇翻译,从句子间逻辑关联的实现与篇章整体结构关联的确立两方面来探讨。

　　语篇(text)是指任何不受完全句子语法约束的,在一个特定的语境中具有交际功能、表示完整语义的自然语言单位。语篇涉及语言多层编码系统[语义层次(意义)──→词汇语法层次(形式)──→语音书写层次(词句)],从语义层次(意义)到词汇语法层次(形式),且词汇与语法间并无严格的区分,概括意义由语法统筹,具体意义由词汇表述。衔接是语篇的重要特征,它主要体现在语篇的表层结构上,词汇手段和语法手段均可体现结构上的黏着性,即结构上衔接。可以说,衔接是语篇的有形网络。连贯是语篇的主要特征,它指的是语篇中语义的关联,连贯存在于语篇的底层,通过逻辑推理来达到语义连接。因此可以说,连贯是语篇的无形网络。翻译的对等单位应该建立在语篇上,即翻译应寻求两种语言的语篇在同一整体情景语境中具有相同的意义和相同的功能(胡壮麟,1988)。科技语篇属于一种非常正式的语言，这是由其表意功能、篇章功能、人际功能决定的。科技语篇的显著特征就是注重行文的连贯性、清晰性和流畅性，通过严密的逻辑和客观描述来表达科学事实。科技语篇的篇章结构方面亦有着十分清楚的模式，语言程式和体例大致不变。因此，科技语篇翻译首先要注重的是两种语言间的信息转换，翻译的重要原则应是忠实，即保留原文与译文文体特点，注意其一致性，这体现在衔接与连贯两个层面。

（一）衔接

衔接是语篇的不同成分和部分之间比较具体的结构联系，属形式概念，指形成语篇的逻辑关系。当在语篇中对某个成分的意义解释需要依赖于对另一个成分的解释时，便出现了衔接。衔接关系的建立有赖于两个成分，即预设者和被预设者，其中"预设者"预设了"被预设者"，"被预设者"要到"预设者"处去寻找意义，从而获得满足，产生有效的说明，构成语篇的衔接。语篇有**组篇机制**，而其他互不相关的一组句子则没有。语篇在周围环境中体现出的整体性反映了它的组篇机制。在科技文体的汉译英过程中，需先提出预设，既而使预设得以满足，在语篇中设置某些词汇或结构，使译文语篇具有统一性，赋予它组篇机制的语言特征。

衔接项目成对出现即形成"纽带"。英语衔接中的"纽带"通常分为两种：语法衔接和词汇衔接。具体分为五种：指称、替代、省略、连接和词汇衔接（表6-1）。但英、汉语的衔接表现形式存在明显差异：英语注重句法的准确、结构的合理和完整，各种衔接手段必不可少；汉语多为隐性衔接，注重通过逻辑和事理发展的顺序来体现其中的隐性衔接。

表6-1　科技语篇衔接方法

衔接关系类型		具体表达
指称	人称指称	I、me、mine、my、one、one's
	指示指称	this、that、these、those、here、there、now、then、the
	比较指称	same、identical、equal、similar、additional、other、different、else、better、more、identically、similarly、likewise、so、such、differently、otherwise、so、more、less、equally
替代	名词性替代	one、ones、same
	动词替代	do
	小句	so、not

续表

衔接关系类型		具体表达
省略	名词性省略	特指指示语：指示词、the、所有格
		非特指指示语：each、every、any、either、no（none）、neither、a（one）、some、all、both
		后指示语：other、same、different、identical、usual、regular、certain、old、famous、well-known、typical、obvious+数量成分
		数量成分：first、next、last、second、third、fourth（省略the）
	动词性省略	动词词组可为右省略或左省略
	小句省略与复句	多见于以肯定词或否定词回答的句式中
连接	按连接语义区分	增补关系 语言补充说明
		转折关系 通过连接词连接预期相反的语义
		因果关系 因先于果、由果及因
		时空关系 事物发展的时空程序
	按抽象逻辑语义区分	详述 进一步的说明、评论或举例
		延伸 正、反面增加新的陈述及例外
		增强 时空、因果、理由、方式信息的补充
词汇衔接	重复	单词或词组的重复
	泛指词	英语：person、thing、place、fact 汉语：人、东西、物、事、地方等
	相似性	同义性（synonymity）、近义性（near-synonymity）、反义性（antonymity）
	可分类性	下义关系（hyponymy）、局部整体关系（part-whole relation）、集合关系（collectivity）、一致关系（consistency）
	搭配	倾向出现在同一语境的词项，具有语篇衔接力

在科技翻译中，要注意两种语言间意合（parataxis）与形合（hypotaxis）的转换。意合与形合是英汉语篇中的基本构成策略。所谓**意合**，指的是词语或分句之间不用语言形式手段连接，句中的语法意义和逻辑关系通过词语或分句的含义表达。所谓**形合**，指的是句中的词语或分句之间用语言形式手段（如关联词）连接起来，并表达语法意义和逻辑关系。形合与意合两种手段通常并存于一种语言中，是相辅相成的，只是汉语以意合为主，而英语以形合为主。汉语重意合是因为它是一种以分析型为主的语言。其语法关系无须通过词汇自身的形态变化来表达，而是通过虚词、词序等手段来体现，汉语篇章巧于意义支点的提取，依赖语义的配搭、语用的因素来反映

词语的组合关系，了解句子的意思；英语注重形合，是一种综合型语言，主要通过词汇本身的形态变化来表达语法意义——性、数、格、时、语态等。英语中常常通过显性连接意义的词语和结构来表示语言中结构与结构之间的逻辑语义关系。因此汉语语篇衔接多用"人称"主语，多用主动语态句、无主语句、主语省略句以及话题主语，较少注重形式规范，语篇衔接总体呈隐性；而英语语篇衔接则多用非人称主语句，被动句与主动句并重，主语一般不能省略，重形式规范，功能与形式结构规范一般可以达到契合，语篇衔接总体呈显性。例如：

①将六个山楂洗净并除去果核。把它们放在糖浆里。

译文 1：Wash and core *six cooking haws*. Put *them* into syrup. (代词回指)

译文 2：Wash and core *six cooking haws*. Put *the haws* into syrup. (定冠词回指)

②只有勇者才应得到公正。

None but *the brave* deserve *the fair*.

③头上的痛压不掉我心中的痛。

The pain in my head cannot stifle *the pain in my heart*.

④*Some* books are to be tasted, *others* to be swallowed and *some few* to be chewed and digested; that is, *some* books are to be read only in parts; others to be read, but not curiously; and *some few* to be read wholly, and with diligence and attention. (*Of Studies* by Francis Bacon)

书有可以浅尝者，有可以吞食者，少数则须咀嚼消化。换言之，有只须大体涉猎者，少数则须全读，读时须全神贯注，孜孜不倦。(王佐良译)

⑤清明时节雨纷纷，路上行人欲断魂。借问酒家何处有？牧童遥指杏花村。(杜牧：《清明》)

A drizzling rain falls like tears on the Mourning Day; The mourner's heart is going to break on *his* way. Where can a wineshop be found to drown *his* sad hours? A cowherd points to a cot' mid apricot flowers. (许渊冲译)

⑥我们现在拥有而达尔文在当时尚缺乏的资料绝不仅仅是化石。那时他还不知道猿和人会患有一样的疾病，不知道猿和人有着同样的血型；更不知道辐射的现代用法。

Fossil remains were not the only information which we now possess but which Darwin lacked. He did not know that apes have the same diseases as men, *or* have the same kind of blood. *Nor* did he know about the modern uses of radiation.

⑦世界上第一代博物馆属于自然博物馆，它通过化石、标本等向人们介绍地球和各种生物的演化历史。第二代属于工业技术博物馆，它所展示的是工业文明带来的各种成就。这两代博物馆虽然在某种程度上起到了传播科学知识的重要作用，但是，它们把参观者当成了被动的旁观者。

The first generation of museums in the world are museums of nature, *in which* all kinds of fossils and models are provided in order to introduce the history of the earth and the evolution process on it. ***The second*** are those of industrial technologies, where achievements brought by the industrial civilization are displayed. Although these two sorts of museums play a somewhat important role in spreading knowledge, they treat visitors in a passive viewer's way.

（二）连贯

连贯是词语、小句、句群在概念上、逻辑上合理恰当地连为一体的语篇特征。连贯的语篇有一个内在的逻辑结构从头到尾贯通全篇，将所有概念有机地串接在一起，达到时空顺序的明晰、逻辑推进层次分明的效果。语义连贯是构成语篇的重要标志，译者只有看清相互独立，实为相互照应的句内、句间或段间关系并加以充分表达，才能传达原作的题旨和功能。科技语篇连贯问题主要表现为：主述转换、次序调整、叙述逻辑转换。

1. 主述转换

语篇分析研究成果表明，主位推进是语篇连贯的重要体现。英汉语篇中常见的主位推进模式基本上是一致的，科技语篇自然也不例外。但是，英汉科技语篇也有着明显的差异，英语科技语篇通常采用主位同一推进模式来发展语篇，而汉语科技语篇则倾向以述位同一模式来推进语篇。因此，在翻译时，不可盲目追求与原文形式上的对等，而是要弄清原语篇的信息结构，理清作者的思路，根据译文的需要，进行必要的调整，从而实现最大程度的功能对等。

①The smaller particulates are called aerosols. The largest aerosols are just visible with a good microscope. Examples are the finer components of tobacco smoke, insect dusts, and larger viruses.

较小的颗粒物叫气溶胶。香烟烟雾的微粒、杀虫剂的粉末和大的病毒是最大的气溶胶，可用高分辨率的显微镜进行观察。

译文并没有按照原语篇的顺序进行翻译，而是将二、三句融合为一句，并将第三句的内容提到了第二句之前，使译文显得更为紧凑，逻辑更为清楚，收到了非常好的效果。

②从长远的观点来看，资助开发气体等燃料，即使价格高于自然氮氢化合液的市场价格，但为了加快减少对进口石油的依赖，这在经济上可能还是合算的。

It may be economically sound, in the long run, to subsidize their initial production, even at prices above the projected market for natural hydrocarbon fluids, in order to accelerate the deduction of dependence on oil imports.

原文是为了强调一个国家自主开发天然气的合理性，说明在这方面的投资从长远利益来看是合算的，先因后果的表述次序符合汉语思维习惯，而译文则根据英语的表达习惯，将结果提前，理由、原因后置，并使用形式主语，从而有效地避免头重脚轻。

2. 次序调整

科技英语语篇中，重要的信息往往被放在句首加以突出，以显示其重要性，而汉语则与之相反，通常是把最重要的信息放在句末，千呼万唤始出来。在翻译这类语篇时，译者要根据汉语的特点，对目的语信息结构予以相应的调整。

① Aluminum remained unknown until the nineteenth century, because nowhere in nature is it found free, owing to its always being combined with other elements, most commonly with oxygen, for which it has a strong affinity.

铝总是跟其他元素结合在一起，最普通的是跟氧结合，因为铝跟氧有很强的亲和力。由于这个原因，在自然界找不到游离状态的铝，所以，铝直到 19 世纪才被人发现。

译文通过词序调整，使之符合汉语先原因后结果的表达顺序，注重语义逻辑的行文习惯。

② 当汽缸内外的压力差达到期望值时，阀门开始驱动，被压缩气体才通过阀门进出汽缸。

Gas being compressed enters and leaves the cylinder through valves which a reset to be actuated when the pressure difference between cylinder contents and outside conditions is that desired.

译文将原语中的时间状语从句位置进行了调整，就是逆着原文的顺序进行翻译。这样的译文既符合英语的表达习惯，又显得结构清晰、语义连贯、通顺。

3. 叙述逻辑转换

在翻译实践中，通常会有这样的感觉，有的译文，若孤立地看单个句子，好像没有问题，但如果从整个语篇的角度来看，会觉得不够连贯，缺乏逻辑性，读起来费解、别扭。在这种情况下，就要求译者通篇考虑，根据目的语表达习惯，对某些部分进行调整或重构。

CO is a colorless, odorless, tasteless gas that fortunately is not known to have adverse effects on vegetation, visibility, or material objects. Its dominant environmental impact appears to be toxicity to man and animals, which arises from its well-known competition with hemoglobin in red blood cells, as in equation 3.1.

译文1：一氧化碳是一种无色、无臭、无味的气体，幸好尚未发现它对植物、对能见度或者对物质材料有什么坏的影响。它最突出的环境问题是对人体和动物体有毒，其毒性在于它与红细胞里的血红蛋白争夺氧，见反应式3.1。

译文2：一氧化碳是一种无色、无臭、无味的气体，对植物、能见度和各种物品都没有害处，可是，由于它跟红细胞里的血红蛋白争夺氧(见反应式3.1)，对人体和动物体有毒，就会造成严重的环境问题。

通过对比，可以看出，虽然译文1也将原文的意思译出来了，译文也还算通顺，但其前后逻辑关系不清，表达不够明确。译文2则不然，通过调整部分内容，使译文逻辑性非常强，因果关系明确，准确无误地传达了原语篇的信息。

第七章　科技文本写作

本章内容由科研简历写作、个人陈述、科技交流信函、期刊论文摘要、研究计划写作、研究报告写作五部分组成。涉及多学科科技活动普遍关心的科技文体写作目的、写作框架、写作内容与写作范例。本章内容旨在帮助读者了解和掌握通用科技文本的概念、作用、内容和写作要求，使读者在学习科技文体写作理论知识的同时，熟悉科技文本基本框架，通过研读写作范例，理解格式化文本写作规范，以深化对六种科技语类的认知，提升写作能力。

第一节　科研简历写作

科研简历通常是以学术会议或学术交流为目的的简历写作。个人参加国际会议时，会议组织方往往要求参会者向会议组织委员会提供科研简历，以便设置会议安排。申请国际学校、国外工作或国际学术交流项目时，如从事博士/博士后水平的研究，在外国机构担任研究员、访问学者或访问教授，均需附上科研简历以供专家参考。科研简历的作用在于建构学术身份，反映科研人员专业发展能力。科研简历是个人科研情况说明书，主要包括教育背景、研究领域、工作经验、教学内容、课题项目、发表论文、荣誉奖励、专著译著、教材编纂及资质证明等。

（一）科研简历结构

1.身份信息

身份信息一般以个人信息数据为主要内容，具体包括姓名（Name）、性别（Sex）、出生日期（Date of Birth）、籍贯（Place of Birth）、民族（Nationality）、婚姻状况（Marital

Status）、政治面貌（Party Affiliation）、健康状况（Health）、邮箱（E-mail）、地址（Address）及电话（Telephone）等。根据情况，可按实际需求进行增减。

2. 意向职位（选写）

首先说明意向职位目标，并明确表达意向志愿。

3. 教育背景

教育背景用于记录教育经历，通常包括学历、学位信息。科研简历的教育背景描述往往以最近获取的学历为表述开端。

4. 教学/研究

教学或研究经历包括从事教学或研究的职责与责任、具体研究属性、教学内容、所属工作机构、工作时长等信息。

5. 出版物/会议论文

优先呈现最新科研成果，逐项说明期刊论文、专著译著、会议论文发表的名称、出版时间、出版单位、类别等信息。

6. 专业会员资格

依次列出专业协会的会员资格及专业委员会职位。

7. 参考文献

准备详尽的参考资料清单，必要时可提供推荐人信息。

（二）科研简历技巧

英文科研简历的表述应注重：
平行结构。保持整个文档中标题或副标题结构一致，句子平衡。
易于阅读。用大写、粗体或加下划线的方式凸显标题或副标题，斜体强调主要成就，缩进副标题以创建空白。
避免错误。确保拼写、语法、格式和标点符号无误。

1. 姓名

（1）名从主人：确定名称持有者国籍或民族身份，尽量遵从其所属民族语言的发音规律，原则上按照音译表进行音译。

（2）相沿成俗：确定译名是否已在汉语中相沿成俗，有则宜沿用，不宜轻易改动。

（3）各依各规：国际汉语拼音、威妥玛式拼音（中国香港、澳门地区采用），注意符号、读音共用。（中文国际汉语拼音与威妥玛式拼音转换工具：ttps://www.chineseconverter.com/zh-cn/convert/wade-giles-to-chinese）

①李杨：Yang LI、YANG LI、Yang Li、Li, Yang、Li Yang、LI Yang.

②林郑月娥：Carrie Lam Cheng Yuet-ngor.

③杨振宁：Chen Ning Yang、Chen-Ning Franklin Yang.

④高锟：Charles K. Kao.

⑤利玛窦（意大利）：Matteo Ricci.

⑥大山（加拿大）：Mark Henry Rowswell.

⑦傅兰雅（英国）：John Fryer.

⑧白晋/白进/明远（法国）：Joachim Bouvet.

2. 地址

中文地址排列顺序由大到小：××国××省××市××区××路××号；英文地址排列顺序由小到大：××号××路（Road），××区（District），××市（City），××省（Province），××国。

（1）**地名专名**部分应使用汉语拼音，且需连写，如 Changsha 不宜写成 Chang Sha，各地址单元间要加逗号隔开，完整的地址由：行政区划+街区名+楼房号三部分组成。

（2）**行政区划**较为复杂，总体上可分为三级（表7-1）。

表7-1　行政区划

国家（State）	省级（Provincial Level）	地级（Prefectural Level）
The People's Republic of China P. R. China P. R. C China	省 Province 自治区 Autonomous Region 直辖市 Municipality directly under the Central Government，Municipality 特别行政区 Special Administration Region，SAR	地区 Prefecture 自治州 Autonomous Prefecture 市 City 盟 Prefecture 旗 Qi

3. 成就表述中动词的使用

使用动作动词来描述你的成就。以下是可能使用的动词：

Accomplish：build、create、diagnose、expand、initiate、maintain、organize、program、supervise.

Achieve：complete、customize、direct、gain、install、manage、plan、resolve、train.

Analyze：conduct、design、earn、implement、lead、manufacture、prepare、review.

Award：coordinate、develop、establish、improve、make、negotiate、present、sell.

4. 性格描述词汇表（表7-2）

表 7-2　性格描述词汇表

中文	英文
能干、活跃、适应性强、雄心勃勃、友好、善分析、有抱负、有能力、细心、有能力、自信、一丝不苟、建设性、深思熟虑、合作、创造性、敬业、灵活变通、遵守纪律、尽职、负责、充满活力的、有效、高效、精力充沛、热情、外向、内向、忠诚、诚实、坦率、友好、慷慨、温和、勤勉、勤奋、诚实、公正、幽默、独立、勤劳、主动、聪明、博学、忠诚、客观、成熟、积极、开放、原创、实际、准时、合格、合理、可靠、自觉、真诚、聪明、严格、意志坚强	able、active、adaptable、ambitious、amicable、analytical、aspiring、capable、careful、competent、confident、conscientious、constructive、contemplative、cooperative、creative、dedicated、diplomatic、disciplined、dutiful、responsible、dynamic、effective、efficient、energetic、enthusiastic、extrovert、introvert、faithful、frank、friendly、generous、gentle、diligent、hard-working、honest、impartial、humorous、independent、industrious、initiative、intelligent、knowledgeable、loyal、objective、mature、motivated、open-minded、original、practical、punctual、qualified、reasonable、reliable、self-conscious、sincere、smart、strict、strong-willed

(三) 中英科研简历常见表达 (表 7-3)

表 7-3　中英科研简历常见表达

中文	英文
①目标	① Objective
应用语言学博士后研究员	Researcher on Applied Linguistics at the postdoctoral level
天津大学法学讲师	A lecturer of law at Tianjin University
②教育	② Education
1999 年, 北京大学外语学院英语语言文学专业, 文学学士学位	B. A. in English Language and Literature, College of Foreign Languages, Peking University, 1999
2001 年, 浙江大学数学系应用数学专业, 理学学士学位	B. S. in Applied Mathematics in the Department of Mathematics, Zhejiang University, 2001
2003 年, 南开大学计算机科技专业候选人, 理学硕士	M. S. candidate in Computer Science and Technology, Nankai University, 2003
2004 年, 山东大学管理学院的工商管理硕士	M. B. A. in Management School of Shandong University, 2004
2005 年, 利兹大学生物学院博士	Ph. D. candidate in Biology, School of Biology, University of Leeds, 2005
2006 年, 墨尔本大学物理学博士学位	Ph. D. in Physics, University of Melbourne, Australia, 2006
③学术工作历史	③ Academic Work History
1992—1994 年, 利兹大学遗传学系讲师	1992-1994 Lecturer, Department of Genetics, University of Leeds

续表

中文	英文
1994—1999 年,利兹大学生物学院进化生物学准教授	1994–1999 Reader in Evolutionary Biology, School of Biology University of Leeds
1999—2006 年,利兹大学生物学院生物学教授	1999–2006 Professor of Biology, School of Biology, University of Leeds
自 2007 年起,新加坡国立大学物理系助理教授	Since 2007 Assistant Professor, Department of Physics, National University of Singapore
2006 年,新加坡国立大学物理系高级研究员	In 2006 Senior Research Fellow, Department of Physics, National University of Singapore
2001 年 12 月—2006 年 8 月,新加坡国立大学物理系研究员	December 2001–August 2006 Research Fellow, Department of Physics, National University of Singapore
2004 年山东大学经济研究讲师中心	2004 Lecturer, Center for Economics Research, Shandong University
④研究兴趣/领域	④ Research interests/areas
写作与修辞理论、文化批评、计算机中介传播、教育理论与实践、美国文学、为商务英语准备的实用写作、劳动力市场、工作组织、社会就业经济政策、妇女研究、组织社会学(性别视角)、妇女和工作、妇女和职业	Composition and Rhetorical Theory, Cultural Criticism, Computer Mediated Communication, Pedagogical Theory and Practices, American Literature, Practical Writing for Business English, Labor Markets, the Organization of Work, Social and Economic Policy on Employment and Unemployment, Women's Studies, Sociology of Organizations (a gendered perspective), Women and Work, Women and the Professions
⑤教学经历	⑤ Teaching experience
教授课程:中国现代文学、英语写作、中英翻译	Three course delivery: Modern Chinese Literature, English Writing, and Chinese-English Translation
学术写作、现代世界、环境研究	Academic Writing, The Modern World, Environmental Studies
当代诗歌、歌剧,美学	Contemporary Poetry, Opera, Aesthetics
社会研究统计	Statistics in Social Research
定量数据分析	Quantitative Data Analysis
⑥出版物	⑥ Publications
《发现:写作学习》(第二版)。亨德尔-亨特,1998 年	*Discovery: Writing to Learn*. Second Edition. Hendall–Hunt, 1998
《联系:阅读和写作》。肯达克-亨特,2002 年	*Connections: Reading and Writing*. Kendakk–Hunt, 2002
《诗歌与浪漫主义的音乐美学》。剑桥大学出版社,2007 年	*Poetry and the Romantic Musical Aesthetic*. Cambridge University Press, 2007

续表

中文	英文
《伊利诺伊州学校的文学教学》(与泰特莎·福克纳的合著。)《伊利诺伊州英语公报》,1999年冬季	*The Teaching of Literature in Illinois Schools.* (Co-author with Tetesa Faulkner) *Illinois English Bulletin*, winter 1999
《教学方案的团队》。CEA 论坛,1998年8月	*The Team Teaching Alternative.* CEA Forum, August 1998
《论社会主义市场经济中的宏观调控》。经济学研究第六期,2000年	*On Macro-modulation in the Socialist Market Economics. The 6th issue of Economics Studies*, 2000
⑦论文宣读	⑦ Conference presentations
《教学技术写作的承诺与危险》,计算机与写作会议,佛罗里达州盖恩斯维尔,2004年3月	*The Promise and Peril of Teaching Technical Writing*, Computers and Writing Conference, Gainesville FL, March 2004
《谁在接受服务?:使用网络网》,计算机和写作会议,檀香山,夏威夷,2000年5月	*Who's Being Served?*: *Using Syllawebs*, Computers and Writing Conference, Honolulu, Hawaii, May 2000
《我们在大学作文中做什么》(小组),伊利诺伊州英语教师协会,伊塔斯卡,伊L,1995年10月	*What We're Doing in College Composition* (panel), Illinois Association of Teachers of English, Itasca, IL, October 1995
《对音乐的渴望:莫扎特的唐·乔瓦尼作品中的启蒙思想》,国际比较文学协会,意大利威尼斯,2005年9月25日	*The Desire for Music*: *Enlightenment Ideals in Mozart's Don Giovanni*, International Comparative Literature Association, Venice, Italy, September 25, 2005
⑧当前工作	⑧ Work in progress
科学教育中理论评价的一个案例与方法	A case and method of theory evaluation in science education
"在态度、非认知主义和以代理人为中心的价值上的分歧"(草稿)	"Disagreement in Attitude, Non-Cognitivism, and Agent-Centered Value" in draft
《人人的正义:从大卫·休谟到亚当·史密的正义环境》正在进行中	"Justice for All: The Circumstances of Justice from David Hume to Adam Smith" in progress
⑨项目资助	⑨ Major grants
289,440美元。约翰坦普尔顿基金会的新资助,2007年8月1日至2007年12月31日	($289,440) grant PI to develop and launch a new academic minor at UNC Chapel Hill on Christianity and Culture, from the John Templeton Foundation, August 1, 2007 – December 31, 2007
396万美元。资助PI用于"美国青年的宗教实践",来自礼来捐赠公司,2001年8月1日至2005年7月31日	($3,960,000) grant PI on "The Religious Practices of American Youth", from Lilly Endowment Inc., August 1, 2001 – July 31, 2005

续表

中文	英文
25000 美元。皮尤慈善信托计划发展和评估赠款，用于对"美国公共生活的宗教和社会建设：历史和当代视角下的文化精英和制度进程"，1997 年 12 月—1998 年 4 月 1 日提出的拟议研究项目	（ $ 25, 000 ）PI on Pew Charitable Trusts Program Development and Evaluation Grant for a proposed research project on "Religion and the Social Construction of American Public Life: Cultural Elites and Institutional Processes in Historical and Contemporary Perspective", December 1997-April 1, 1998
将教学技术与基础科学方法相结合（EDDV341）。由特拉华大学 1996-1997 学年教学效率中心技术、改进教学基金资助。	Integrating Instructional Technology into Elementary Science Methods （ EDDV 341 ）. Funded by Grants for the Improvement of Instruction: Technology, Center for Teaching Effectiveness, University of Delaware, academic year 1996-1997
修订地质学内容与教学地球科学，以支持职前教师教学内容知识的发展。由布里克豪斯、希普曼、马德森承担。特拉华州公共教育部艾森豪威尔高等教育部分数学和科学教育项目资助	Revising the Content and Pedagogy of Geology and Earth Science to Support the Development of Preservice Teacher's Pedagogical Content Knowledge with N. Brickhouse, H. Shipman, & J. Madsen. Funded by Higher Education Component, Eisenhower Mathematics and Science Education Program, State of Delaware Department of Public Instruction
⑩荣誉和奖项	⑩ Honors and awards
2006 年第三次计算机程序设计大赛一等奖得主	First prize winner of the 3rd Computer Program Designer Contest, 2006
2003 年河北师范大学高级英语学生奖学金	Scholarship of Advanced English Learner, Hebei Normal University, 2003
2003 年郑州大学光华基金优秀学生	Excellent Student from Guanghua Fund, Zhengzhou University in 2003
1999 年获文化基金会奖学金	Scholarship from the Cultural Foundation, 1999
1996 年宾夕法尼亚州全国地质学教师协会的杰出地球科学教师	Outstanding Earth Science Teacher for Pennsylvania National Association of Geology Teachers, 1996
1996 年澳大利亚研究生研究奖（APRA）	Australian Postgraduate Research Award（APRA）, 1996
1994 年夏季康涅狄格大学研究生院论文奖学金	Dissertation Fellowship, University of Connecticut Graduate School, summer 1994
1993 年康涅狄格大学英语系夏季研究奖学金	Summer Research Fellowship, English Department, University of Connecticut, 1993
1995 年全国科学教学研究协会杰出论文奖	Outstanding Dissertation Award, National Association for Research in Science Teaching, 1995

续表

中文	英文
1988 年伍斯特学院威利亚姆·加尔平整体大学卓越奖	Wiliam Galpin Prize for Overall College Excellence, College of Wooster, 1988
1982—1985 年澳大利亚研究生研究奖	Australian Postgraduate Research Award, 1982–1985
⑪专业会员	⑪Professional membership
自 2000 年起担任材料研究学会副会长	Vice-President, Materials Research Society MRS since 2000
技术交流学会的会员	Member of the Society for Technical Communication
瑞士口笔译员协会和欧洲翻译协会的成员	Member of the Swiss Association of Translators and Interpreters, and of the European Society for Translation
自 2001 年以来一直担任南京计算机学会主席	President, Nanjing Computer Society since 2001
国际生物物理学会会员	Member of International Biophysics Society

第二节 个人陈述

个人陈述(personal statement)作为申请文书的必要组成部分，是用 500~1000 字的短文向委员会/机构介绍自身对特定项目或职位的兴趣、个人研究背景、研究设想、科研经验等内容。与科研简历框架式表述不同，个人陈述需用具体的范例和事实来补充说明详细信息。一份成功的个人陈述，不仅总结个人经历，还需有重点叙述，主要述清以下三点：

自身个性：自身的兴趣、价值观和动机是什么？

个人才能：我能为这个项目带来什么？

未来目标：这个项目能为我带来什么？

(一)个人陈述结构

就结构而言，个人陈述主要包括引言、正文、结语三大部分，每部分的功能及主要内容如表 7-4 所示。

表 7-4 个人陈述各部分功能及主要内容

部分	功能	主要内容
引言	引人入胜	作为个人陈述的开始，为整个陈述定下基调，并顺利进入陈述内容
正文	自我叙述	作为个人陈述的主体，需描述更多与申请动力、科研经历等内容相关的细节以此证明个人能力
结语	面向未来	需表达希望从中获得什么，是培养实践能力？还是探索理论问题？或者两者兼而有之

（二）写作技巧

1. 引言部分

1) 以具体场景开场

引言部分要做到引人入胜，需设置一个具体场景来说明自身性格或者兴趣。如可以尝试思考：改变自身观点的独特经历、难忘的老师或学习经历、不寻常或意想不到的相遇。尽量避免简单直率的描述，并提供具体细节以营造令人信服的氛围。如：

Every day on the bus home from work, we pass by a row of abandoned houses. Their windows are boarded up, the paintwork on the front doors is faded and peeling, and the front yards are overgrown with weeds. It always seems faintly tragic to me: a lonely, desolate scene of wasted potential. I think of the people who must have lived in those houses once, and the people who still could if the right approach were taken.

每天下班回家的公交车上，我们都会路过一排废弃的房子。窗户被木板封死，前门的油漆褪色剥落，前院杂草丛生。在我看来，它似乎预示着悲剧：孤独，荒凉，毫无生机。我突然想到那些住过这些房子的人，以及如果采取正确方法仍然可以住在这儿的人。

2) 以动机开场

为了强调自身的热情和承诺，可以先解释对想学习的科目或想遵循的职业道路的兴趣。仅仅说感兴趣显然是不够的，还需要弄清楚感兴趣的原因及作用。兴趣是长久以来的热情还是最近的发现？兴趣是自然而然产生的还是曾经努力实践过的？这一兴趣如何融入你的余生？它对社会有什么贡献？如：

The mind fascinates me: The way it develops, how it shapes reality, how the interactions of tiny cells in the brain shape the course of our whole lives. I have always taken an interest in what was going on inside other people's heads, but as I've come to understand more about psychology, what fascinates me the most is how blind we can be to the dynamics playing out in our minds every day.

心智让我着迷：它如何发展，它如何塑造现实，大脑中微小细胞的相互作用如何塑造我们整个生命长河。我一直对别人脑子里发生的事情很感兴趣，但是随着我对心理学的了解越来越多，最让我痴迷的是：每天在脑海中发生如此多动力，但我们却知之甚少。

总之，引言部分避免使用陈词滥调，避免使用诸如"从我还是个孩子开始……"或"只要我记得……"之类的表述。建议最后写引言部分，以此想出一个强有力的开场白，因而在撰写其余部分时，可以记下任何想到的有关引言部分有趣的想法。

2. 正文部分

1）以时间为序

最简单的策略是按时间顺序陈述申请该院校或者职位的关键经历。是什么首先激发了自身对该领域的兴趣？哪些课程、作业、同学、实习或其他活动帮助获得知识和技能？我接下来想去哪儿？这个项目如何融入我未来的计划？

需注意：不要试图把你所做的一切都陈述在内——挑选出与申请相关的亮点。正文部分旨在作一个引人入胜的陈述，展示你如何改变和积极发展自己。

My interest in psychology was first sparked early in my high school career. Though somewhat scientifically inclined, I found that what interested me most was not the equations we learned about in physics and chemistry, but the motivations and perceptions of my fellow students, and the subtle social dynamics that I observed inside and outside the classroom. I wanted to learn how our identities, beliefs, and behaviours are shaped through our interactions with others, so I decided to major in social psychology. My undergraduate studies deepened my understanding of, and fascination with, the interplay between an individual mind and its social context. During my studies, I acquired a solid foundation of knowledge about concepts like social influence and group dynamics, but I also took classes on various topics not strictly related to my major. I was particularly interested in how other fields intersect with psychology—the classes I took on media studies, biology, and literature all enhanced my understanding of psychological concepts by providing different lenses through which to look at the issues involved.

2）直面挑战与困难

如果自身学习生涯并不轻松顺利，可以将其转化为一种优势，并将个人陈述转化为一个克服障碍的故事。比如自身的社会、文化或经济背景缺乏代表性，解释这或许会为未来研究提供独特的视角；缺乏个人经历或成绩低于理想水平，解释所面临的挑战以及如何应对挑战。

需注意：不能过分关注负面因素，而是要用挑战或困难来突出坚韧不拔、毅力十足等优良品质，从而使自己受到青睐，增加成功概率。

Growing up working class, urban decay becomes depressingly familiar. The sight of a row of abandoned houses does not surprise me, but it continues to bother me. Since high school, I have been determined to pursue a career in urban planning. While people of my background experience the consequences of urban planning decisions first-hand, we are underrepresented in the field itself. Ironically, given my motivation, my economic background has made my studies challenging. I was fortunate enough to be awarded a scholarship for my undergraduate studies, but after graduation I took jobs in unrelated fields to help support my parents. In the three years since, I have not lost my ambition. Now I am keen to resume my studies, and I believe I can bring an invaluable perspective to the table: that of the people most impacted by the decisions of urban planners.

3) 展示专业知识

如果正在申请博士学位或其他以科研为重点的项目，展示自身对学科相关专业知识或研究热点不失为一个不错的选择。可以陈述未来将专攻的领域或将探索的问题，并阐释其重要性；可以描述在学习中关注的话题或主题；可以讨论自身的学术成就或者相关学术观点。

需注意：个人陈述并非研究计划，所以不要过分强调细节，但这是展示自身对该领域的热情和自身原创思维能力的机会。

In applying for this research program, my intention is to build on the multidisciplinary approach I have taken in my studies so far, combining knowledge from disparate fields of study to better understand psychological concepts and issues. The Media Psychology program stands out to me as the perfect environment for this kind of research, given its researchers' openness to collaboration across diverse fields. I am impressed by the department's innovative interdisciplinary projects that focus on the shifting landscape of media and technology, and I hope that my own work can follow a similarly trailblazing approach. More specifically, I want to develop my understanding of the intersection of psychology and media studies, and explore how media psychology theories and methods might be applied to neurodivergent minds. I am interested not only in media psychology but also in psychological disorders, and how the two interact. This is something I touched on during my undergraduate studies and that I'm excited to delve into further.

4) 谈论职业理想

如果正在申请一个专业项目，关注具体目标以及该项目将如何帮助自身实现这些目标是不错的选择。如果职业生涯刚刚起步，展示自身性格如何适合该领域，并解释所申请的项目将如何帮助自身发展才能。如果已经从事该行业，展示到目前为止所取得的成就，并解释该项目将如何让自身迈出下一步。如果计划转行，解释做此决定的原因，以及现有经验将如何帮助自身取得成功。

需注意：不要仅陈述职业目标，应该阐释自身已对职业规划进行了大量思考，并证明自身适合该职业。

One thing that fascinated me about the field during my undergraduate studies was the sheer number of different elements whose interactions constitute a person's experience of an urban environment. Any number of factors could transform the scene I described at the beginning: What if there were no bus route? Better community outreach in the neighborhood? Worse law enforcement? More or fewer jobs available in the area? Some of these factors are out of the hands of an urban planner, but without taking them all into consideration, the planner has an incomplete picture of their task. Through further study I hope to develop my understanding of how these disparate elements combine and interact to create the urban environment. I am interested in the social, psychological and political effects our surroundings have on our lives. My studies will allow me to work on projects directly affecting the kinds of working-class urban communities I know well. I believe I can bring my own experiences, as well as my education, to bear upon the problem of improving infrastructure and quality of life in these communities.

就正文部分而言,不要总结自身的一切经历来重复个人简历,需明白个人陈述并非要列出自身的学术或专业经历,而是要反映、评估并将其与更广泛的主题联系起来。与其说自身有上进心,不如写下主动开始新项目的实习经历;与其说喜欢阅读,不如讲述改变了自身观点的小说或诗歌。建议将个人陈述写成故事,更有吸引力、说服力。

3. 结语部分

1) 期望收获

如果正在申请一所学校或一个科研项目,结语部分可以阐述:希望学到什么?为什么选择该学校/项目?也可以表达自身对某位老师的崇敬、喜爱、钦佩等。如:

In the course of this research program and beyond, I hope to pursue research into the relationship between media consumption and conditions like ADHD and autism. The work of Bernard Luskin on media psychology has been a major influence on my own research interests and was what first drew my attention to the faculty; the prospect of working among researchers committed to interdisciplinarity is highly attractive to me. I believe that the novel methods being developed in this department are crucial in illuminating how our minds adapt to a world of mass media, and my ambition is to contribute to advancing knowledge in this field.

2) 未来计划

如果正在申请一个专业培训项目,结语部分可以描述职业理想:未来将在社会中扮演什么角色?为什么这个项目是帮助自身实现该目标的最佳选择?如:

My ambition as an urban planner is to work with impoverished urban communities. I want to draw on my own and others' experience of these spaces rather than impose a prefabricated plan from above. I believe that by taking cues from the people affected, urban planning can more conscientiously shape the future of our cities. This master's degree is my path toward that goal.

就结语部分而言,不要重复前文已述内容。个人陈述篇幅有限,充分有效利用。尝试打开思维,表达个人愿望与学术研究甚至整个社会的关系。

（三）个人陈述样本

Personal Statement：Master of Business Administration（MBA）

I am currently a marketing manager for ××, a large cancer charity. I have held this position for three years. I am interested in studying an MBA to learn from industry leaders, and explore and share innovative ways of doing business through team projects. I am also keen to develop my management style and add consultancy and strategic thinking to my skills portfolio, in preparation for a business venture that I have in mind. This is to provide marketing consultancy to not-for-profit organizations.

During my business and marketing degree at ××× University, I took part in an enterprise challenge：to provide a social media marketing campaign for a local company. One of the judges was from ×××× and offered me a marketing assistant position, which I took up and worked in part-time for the duration of my degree. I was promoted within a year to marketing executive and completed my degree on a part-time basis to allow me to undertake this role.

My current role has involved devising a social media marketing strategy from scratch and, as a result, I contributed to a 10% increase in charitable donations over a two year period. This has required pro activity, negotiation skills and a great deal of diplomacy to persuade departments within the company to embrace a radical change in how the charity brands itself to an increasingly digital target audience. I lead a team of marketing executives and this has expanded as the company has boosted its online presence on tablets and smart phones. As I also see new marketing materials from inception to launch, I have to liaise with many departments in the company including technical specialists.

My strengths include innovation, excellent communication skills and an inclusive approach to team building. I devised an innovative way for members of the public to purchase e-greetings cards which incorporate a donation to the charity with information on how that money would be used locally. I also built up links with large companies who wished to be associated with ×× as part of their corporate social responsibility policy.

I have recently studied for the Chartered Institute of Marketing's（CIM）Professional Diploma in Marketing on a part-time basis while working. I have good time-management skills and a capacity for a heavy workload, and feel fully ready to take on study at an advanced level.

第三节　科技交流信函

科技交流信函由投稿信、邀请函、回复信件、电子邮件四部分组成。

（一）投稿信写作

投稿信（cover letter）由作者随科技论文原稿一起发送给期刊编辑，或上传到期刊投稿网站上的相应框中，是"推销"论文的重要机会。信中应表明作者对编辑的感谢，以及作者为本次投稿能够满足期刊要求所做的各种努力。

1.投稿信内容

（1）表示该论文在期刊主题范围内；

（2）注明稿件的标题和作者姓名；

（3）声明研究和论文的原创性；

（4）突出研究的创新点和价值；

（5）标记稿件中编辑可能会发问的所有要点，例如为什么论文的篇幅较长，为什么使用照片；

（6）表达你希望投稿论文论证充分，条理清晰；

（7）表示你期待审阅专家的建议。

2.投稿信中英样市（表7-5）

表7-5　投稿信中英样本

中文	英文
日期 管理编辑 《澳大利亚植物学杂志》 地址 亲爱的布朗先生， 附件为《辛普森沙漠南部丛枝菌根群落》原稿。这篇论文研究了生长在辛普森沙漠沙丘洼地系统不同土壤上的植物的菌根状态。很少有人对这片沙漠中的植物生态学进行研究，而且对于菌根群落是如何在澳大利亚沙漠植物中分布的也知之甚少。我们首次报道了47种植物的丛枝菌根状况。论文是根据期刊的作者须知准备的。我们相信这篇研究在您的期刊主题范围内，并希望您考虑将这篇论文收录在《澳大利亚植物学杂志》上。期待您的回复和审稿专家的意见。 此致， ××（署名）	Date … The Managing Editor *Australian Journal of Botany* Address … Dear Dr Brown, ***Please find attached the manuscript*** Arbuscular mycorrhizal associations of the southern Simpson Desert. ***This manuscript examines*** the mycorrhizal status of plants growing on the different soils of the dune-swale systems of the Simpson Desert. ***There have been few studies*** of the ecology of the plants in this desert and ***little is known about*** how mycorrhizal associations are distributed amongst the desert plants of Australia. We report the arbuscular mycorrhizal status of 47 plant species for the first time. ***The manuscript has been prepared according to the journal's Instructions for Authors***. We believe that this new work is within the scope of your journal and hope that you will consider this manuscript for publication in the *Australian Journal of Botany*. We await your response and the comments of reviewers. Yours sincerely, ×××

(二)邀请函写作

国际会议前,会议主持人或组织者应向该领域的著名学者和专家发出邀请函(letter of invitation),邀请他们作为会议的主讲人,参与会议相关内容。同时还需邀请其他作者在会议上展示他们的新想法、有价值的作品和正在进行的研究。这些信件是用于正式场合的正式信件,因此应包含有关场合的所有必要信息,并表达主人对与会者的最大诚意和欢迎。

1.邀请函内容

1)信头

信头是指作者(会议主持人)的完整地址,排列顺序由小到大:××号××路(Road),××区(District),××市(City),××省(Province),××国。邮政编码、电话号码、传真号码和电子邮件地址也可以包括在内。完整的信头信息通常在信件顶部,可以在左上角、右上角,或者顶部中心。

2)写信日期

在地址的正下方,写下完整的日期:日、月、年。通常的做法是将日期靠左顶格。信的日期应该一目了然。"年"填写完整;"月"使用英文书写,以避免引起误解;"日"用基数词或序数词书写,可以放在月份之前(英式)或之后(美式)。

3)封内地址

封内地址给出收信人的姓名和完整地址,左对齐。

4)称呼

这是对收信人的问候,例如尊敬的 Ann Mellon 女士(Dear Ms. Ann Mellon,当女性收信人的婚姻状况未知或她更喜欢 Ms. 时,使用 Ms.);John Wood 先生(Mr. John Wood);亲爱的 Williams 教授(Dear Professor Williams)。称呼语的位置也总是左对齐。

称呼语有以下三种:

(1)尊称。例如:夫人(Mrs.)、女士(Ms.)、小姐(Miss)、先生(Mr.)。

(2)职称。例如:博士(Dr.)、教授(Professor)。

(3)职务头衔。例如:经理(Manager)、董事(Director)等。

在英语国家中,称呼语一般出现在姓氏之前,一般做法是"称呼语+姓氏",而在中国,情况恰恰相反,一般做法是"姓氏+称呼语"。

5)正文

正文写清楚场合、时间、地点、邀请目的、会议主题/安排、期待赴会及与对方见面的心情。

6)结束语

结束语可以放在页面的左侧或右侧,第一个字母大写,后跟逗号。与称呼语一样，敬语应反映你与收件人的关系。以下为一些最常用的结尾敬语：

（1）正式：Sincerely yours，Respectfully yours，Very truly yours，Yours sincerely，Yours respectfully，Yours truly 等。

（2）非正式：Best regards，Best wishes，With best wishes，All the best，With respect 等。

7）署名

信件需要手写签名，应置于结束语和写信人印刷体签名之间，包括写信人的职位和单位。

8）附件（如果有）

可用于提醒收信人邀请函中附有其他材料，如会议议程。有些人更喜欢用缩写Encl. 或 Enc. 来注明。

2. 邀请函写作技巧

（1）邀请函的语气要亲切，否则可能会遭到拒绝。

（2）发出邀请函之前通知受邀者，让受邀者有足够的时间进行准备或预定。

（3）在邀请函的开头，先表示欢迎再描述会议细节，这有助于引起受邀者的兴趣。或者先简单介绍相关细节，让受邀者更好地了解该场合。

（4）请勿在正式邀请函中使用缩写，除非是 Mr.，Mrs.，Ms.，Dr. 等称谓。

（5）附上所有可能提供的食、住、行的交通路线和地图（可选）。

（6）提供联系人的姓名、电话号码和联系地址（包括电子邮件）。

（7）如果你邀请某人在会议/研讨会上发言，你还应该提及演讲的类型、主题或范围以及演讲时长。

（8）如需对方回复，请在邀请函末尾加上 R.S.V.P.（敬候赐覆），通常位于左下角。

（9）检查你的信件是否有拼写错误或其他语言错误，例如语法、结构等。

3. 邀请函写作句型

1）表达邀请（表 7-6）

表 7-6　表达邀请的中英例句

中文	英文
我很高兴邀请您参加我们将于 2005 年 11 月 1 日至 4 日在亚特兰大举行的化学教育年度会议。	I am pleased to invite you to attend our Annual Conference on Chemical Education to be held on November 1 – 4, 2005 in Atlanta.
很高兴邀请您参加第二届计算机年会。今年的会议将于 2007 年 3 月 23 日至 26 日在武汉举行。	It is with great pleasure that I invite you to the 2nd Annual Computer Conference. This year's conference will be held in Wuhan from March 23 to 26, 2007.

续表

中文	英文
我谨代表云南大学信息学院和昆明市科协，很高兴邀请您出席并主持将于 2006 年 8 月 24 日至 26 日在云南昆明举行的第十届国际计算机联合会议。	On behalf of the School of Information, Yunnan University and Kunming Association for Science and Technology, I am pleased to invite you to attend and chair a session of the forthcoming 10th Joint International Computer Conference to be held in Kunming, Yunnan, from August 24 to 26, 2006.
计算语言学协会第 36 届年会将于 2000 年 10 月 10 日至 25 日在香港举行，作为本次年会的联合主席，我写信是想询问您是否愿意作为受邀嘉宾在会议上用英文发表讲话。	As co-chair of the 36th Annual Meeting of the Association for Computational Linguistics, to be held in Hong Kong October 10-25, 2000, I am writing to ask whether you would be willing to present a talk in English at the conference as an invited speaker.
我很高兴邀请您参加即将于 2004 年 9 月 12 日至 13 日在北京举行的中国语境下的高等教育英语教学会议的小组讨论。	It is my pleasure to invite you to appear on a panel at the upcoming conference on English Teaching at Tertiary Level in the Chinese Context to be held in Beijing, September 12-13, 2004.

2）表明会议主题（表 7-7）

表 7-7　表明会议主题的中英例句

中文	英文
会议旨在汇集对化学工程领域感兴趣的工程师和研究人员，并促进他们之间就各自领域的最新发展交流思想和经验。	The conference aims at bringing together engineers and researchers with interests in the areas of chemical engineering and at promoting the exchange of ideas and experiences among them in the recent developments in their areas.
执行主席寻求/试图鼓励生活在美国中西部的亚洲人之间的学术交流，并在大学和中学层面促进亚洲研究。	The CE seeks/attempts to encourage scholarly interchange between Asians located in the Midwest and promote Asian studies both at the university and secondary levels.
2007 年第一届跨层设计国际研讨会为学术界、工业界和政府的研究人员提供了一个论坛，以展示关于跨层设计的新想法和有价值的研究。	The First International Workshop on Cross Layer Design 2007 provides a forum for researchers from academia, industry and government to present new ideas, valuable research on cross layer design.

3）传达期待（表 7-8）

表 7-8　传达期待的中英例句

中文	英文
我们真诚地希望您能接受这一邀请。	We sincerely hope that you can accept this invitation.

续表

中文	英文
我确实希望您能在百忙之中抽出时间参加会议，并在小组内分享您对这个主题的想法。	I do hope you can make time in your busy schedule to attend the conference and share your ideas on this topic on the panel.
我十分期待秋天与您相见于此地。	I very much look forward to meeting you here in the autumn.
我想借此机会呼吁贵组织参加这次非常重要的筹备会议。	I would like to take this opportunity to strongly encourage your organization to attend this very important preparatory meeting.
我们希望您能参加我们的会议，让我们从您的经验中获益。	We hope that you will be able to join us at this conference, and give us the benefit of your experience.

4）表明食宿安排（表7-9）

表7-9　表明食宿安排的中英例句

中文	英文
执行主席将提供从北京到会议地点的经济舱机票、会议期间的酒店住宿以及会议注册费。	The CE would provide the cost of an economy class airfare from Beijing to the conference, hotel accommodations during the conference, and free registration to the conference.
如果您参加研讨会，您的差旅费用，包括酒店住宿、餐饮和会议注册费将由组织者承担。	If you come to the symposium, your local expenses, including hotel accommodations, meals, and the conference fee will be covered by the organizers.
我们的部门会收取一定费用，当然，我们会报销您的旅行和酒店费用。	Our department offers a fee and will, of course, reimburse your traveling and hotel expenses.
您将获得往返机票和餐费补贴。	Your round-trip air ticket and meal expenses will be subsidized.
会议期间将向你提供生活津贴和住宿。	You will be provided with a subsistence allowance and accommodations for the duration of the conference.

5）表明附件或联系方式（表7-10）

表7-10　表明附件或联系方式的中英例句

中文	英文
随函附上会议通知副本一份。	We enclose a copy of the notice of the conference.
随函附上住宿、交通和登记信息，请查收。	Please find enclosed information on accommodations, transportation and registration.
随函附上两份……	Enclosed are two ...
有关会议的更多详情，请访问会议网站：……	For more details of the conference, please refer to / go to the conference website: ...

续表

中文	英文
如果您有任何疑问，请不要犹豫/随时联系我们的研究所协调员……或者访问我们的网站：……	If you have any enquiries, please do not hesitate / feel free to contact our institute coordinator at … or visit our website：…

4. 邀请函中英样本（表 7-11）

表 7-11　邀请函中英样本

中文	英文
第十九届国际化学教育会议邀请函	Invitation Letter for the 19th International Conference on Chemical Education
寄件人及地址	From …
日期	Date
收件人及地址	To …
亲爱的刘作明教授	Dear Professor Zuoming Liu,
我很高兴代表组委会邀请您参加将于 2006 年 8 月 12 日至 17 日在韩国首尔举行的第 19 届国际化学教育会议（第 19 届 ICCE）。我写信是想询问您是否愿意在会上用英语做报告。受邀演讲将持续一小时，然后是 20 分钟的问答环节。	It is my pleasure, on behalf of the Organizing Committee, to invite you to attend the 19th International Conference on Chemical Education (19th ICCE), to be held in upcoming August 12-17, 2006, in Seoul, the Republic of Korea. I am writing to ask whether you are willing to present a talk in English at the conference. Invited talks will be one hour long, followed by a 20-minute question and answer session.
第 19 届国际化学教育会议的主题是"为人类提供化学和化学教育"，旨在适应世界日新月异的变化，并不断拓展化学和化学领域的范围。化学是一种必不可少的工具和语言，是日常生活里大部分科学技术的基础知识，而且还是保障子孙后代生活质量的基本科学。	The theme of the 19th ICCE is "Chemistry and Chemical Education for Humanity", in keeping up with our fast-changing world and continually expanding scope of the chemistry and chemical field. Chemistry is not only an essential tool and language as well as basic knowledge for the most of science and technology of our everyday life, but also an essential science for future generations to ensure their quality of life.
为感谢您发表讲话，第 19 届 ICCE 将为您报销差旅费用，包括会议期间的酒店住宿、餐饮以及会议注册费。	In appreciation of your agreement to give a talk, the 19th ICCE will provide your local expenses, including hotel accommodations, and meals during the conference, and free registration to the conference.
期待与您在首尔相见。	I am looking forward to seeing you in Seoul.
此致，	Sincerely yours,
（署名）	(signature)
Choon. H. Do	Choon. H. Do
第十九届 ICCE 组委会主席	Chairman of the Organizing Committee of the 19th ICCE

(三)回复信件写作

受到邀请应及时回复,这是一种礼貌的表现。当你收到邀请并决定出席时,应尽早回复,通知会议主持人你接受邀请并出席会议。如果你因某种原因不能接受邀请,你也应该及时写信通知会议主持人。你的及时拒绝可以让他们有时间寻找补救方案及替补嘉宾。回复信件分为接受邀请的回信(letter of acceptance)和谢绝邀请的回信(letter of refusal)。

1.回信内容(表7-12)

表7-12　回信的基本格式

接受邀请的回信	谢绝邀请的回信
①信头	
②写信日期	
③封内地址	
④称呼	
⑤正文: A.表达感谢 B.表示接受 C.重述主要邀请内容、日期、时间和地点,致谢以及表达对会议的祝愿	⑤正文: A.说明不能参加的原因 B.表示遗憾 C.表达对会议的祝愿
⑥敬语	
⑦签名	

2.回信写作技巧

1)接受邀请的回信

(1)感谢词通常出现在信的开头,但有时也可以放在第一段的末尾。

(2)简要表明你接受邀请,重述邀请内容时也应该简略。

(3)如有必要,询问以下事项:会议期间的住宿,在会议上发表讲话或进行展示时的设备等。

(4)一旦你接受邀请,尽量避免高姿态,例如"我很忙,但我能应付"或是"如果情况允许,我会来的"。

2)谢绝邀请的回信

(1)态度礼貌且真诚,并给出令人信服的拒绝邀请的理由。

(2)给出其他补救方案。

(3)表达对未来合作的期待和祝愿。

3. 回信写作句型

1) 接受邀请的回信

(1) 表示感谢(表 7-13)。

表 7-13 表示感谢的中英例句

中文	英文
感谢您 5 月 23 日的来信。我十分高兴地告知您,我将参加今年 6 月的会议。	Thank you for your letter of May 23. I am pleased to confirm my participation in this year's conference in June.
感谢您邀请我参加 2005 年 8 月 23 日至 26 日在香港举行的"文化与翻译国际会议"。	Thank you for your invitation to attend the International Conference on Cultures and Translation to be held on August 23-26, 2005 in Hong Kong.
感谢您邀请我们参加 2003 年 7 月 7 日至 11 日在日本大阪 Senri 生命科学中心举行的国际会议。	Thank you for your invitation to attend the international conference to be held at Senri Life Science Center in Toyonaka, Osaka, Japan, July 7-11, 2003.
感谢您邀请我在研讨会上发言。	I would like to express my appreciation for the invitation to speak at your seminar.

(2) 表示接受(表 7-14)。

表 7-14 表示接受的中英例句

中文	英文
我很高兴接受您的邀请,并将在规定日期前将我的论文《认知语言学与话语分析》发送给论文委员会。	I am pleased to accept your invitation and will send my paper entitled *Cognitive Linguistics and Discourse Analysis* to the Paper Committee before the required date.
我已收到您 6 月 22 日的来信,邀请我 11 月 4 日至 6 日在北京举行的中国翻译协会第五届全国理事会开幕式上发言。我的主题是"全球化和多样性对译者意味着什么?"。感谢您的盛情邀请。	I have received your letter dated June 22, inviting me to speak at the Opening Ceremony of the Fifth National Council Meeting of Translators Association of China to be held on November 4-6, in Beijing. I will speak on *Globalization and Diversity: What Do They Mean for Translators*? Thank you for your kind invitation.

(3) 再次表示感谢以及美好祝愿(表 7-15)。

表 7-15 再次表示感谢以及美好祝愿的中英例句

中文	英文
再次感谢您的盛情邀请,感谢您为使本次会议取得成功所做的努力。	Thank you once again for your kind invitation and for your effort in making the conference a successful one.

中文	英文
我很高兴参加这次会议,并热切期待它的召开。	I am pleased to take part in the conference and look forward to it with pleasure.
我期待着访问伦敦,并在今年9月的会议上与您再次相见。	I look forward to visiting London and to seeing you again at the conference this coming September.

2)谢绝邀请的回信

(1)表示感谢(参照接受邀请的回信)。

(2)表明无法参加的原因(表7-16)。

表7-16　表明无法参加的原因的中英例句

中文	英文
很遗憾,我无法接受邀请,因为自今年夏天起我身体一直不好。	Much to my regret, I shall not be able to honor the invitation because I have been suffering from ill health this summer.
不幸的是,我事先已另有承诺,因此这次不能相助。如果您能在其他时间再次邀约,我很乐意发言。	Unfortunately, I have a previous commitment and thus can not help this time. I would be happy to speak if you would give me another opportunity at some other time.
非常遗憾,我无法出席会议,因为那时我必须主持在法国举行的一次会议。	Much to my regret, I shall not attend the conference because I have to chair a meeting to be held in France at that time.
我很抱歉地通知你,我将不能去加拿大。我刚刚得知,我原计划乘坐的特别航班已经取消,而普通机票的费用过于昂贵。	I am very sorry to inform you that I will be unable to go to Canada. I just have learned that the special flight that I had planned to take has been cancelled and the cost of a regular airline fare is prohibitive.

(3)再次表达歉意及美好祝愿(表7-17)。

表7-17　再次表达歉意及美好祝愿的中英例句

中文	英文
请接受我诚挚的道歉,如果WCA未来需要一位客座嘉宾,我希望您能考虑我。	Please accept my sincere apologies, and I hope you will think of me again if the WCA needs a guest speaker at some future date.
很遗憾,我错过了与您及其他许多知识经济领域的同事见面的机会。预祝会议圆满成功。	I feel very sorry to miss the opportunity of meeting you and many other colleagues in the field of the knowledge economy. I wish the conference a complete success.
但是,我期待着参加明年的会议。	However, I look forward to attending the conference next year.

4. 回信中英样本

1）接受邀请的回信（表7-18）

表7-18　接受邀请的回信的中英样本

中文	英文
寄件人的地址	（Your address）
2006年5月11日	May 11, 2006
亲爱的John Smith教授，	Dear Professor John Smith,
感谢您2006年4月23日的来信，邀请我参加将于2005年9月12日至14日在韩国首尔举行的第六届亚太风力工程会议。	Thank you for your letter of April 23, 2006, inviting me to attend the Sixth Asian-Pacific Conference on Wind Engineering to be held in Seoul, the Republic of Korea, September 12–14, 2005.
我很高兴接受邀请，并将在规定日期之前向文件委员会发送我的题为"气候和城市环境问题"的论文。再次感谢您的盛情邀请，我期待着在首尔与您会面。	I am pleased to accept the invitation and will send my paper entitled " Climate and Urban Environment Problems" to the Paper Committee before the required date. Thank you again for your kind invitation and I look forward to meeting you in Seoul.
此致，	Sincerely yours,
（署名）	（signature）
刘文	Liu Wen

2）谢绝邀请的回信（表7-19）

表7-19　谢绝邀请的回信的中英样本

中文	英文
寄件人的地址	（Your address）
2005年7月5日	July 5, 2005
亲爱的Chuck Taylor教授，	Dear Professor Chuck Taylor,
感谢您在2005年6月19日来信，邀请我于2005年12月6日至9日参加在新加坡国立大学举行的教育国际会议，会议是NUS百年庆典会议的一部分。	Thank you for your letter of 19 June, 2005, inviting me to attend the International Conference on Education to be held at the National University of Singapore, 6–9 December, 2005, as a part of the NUS Centennial Celebration Conferences.
我很抱歉地告知您，我无法赴约，因为最近一段时间我身体抱恙。我被告知，近期不要乘坐飞机长途旅行。	I am very sorry to inform you that I shall not be able to honor the invitation because I have been suffering from ill health for some time. I am firmly advised that it would be unwise to undertake any distance travel by air in the near future.
预祝会议圆满成功。	I wish the conference a successful one.

续表

中文	英文
此致，	Respectfully yours,
（署名）	（signature）
王飞龙	Feilong Wang

（四）电子邮件

随着信息技术的飞速发展，电子邮件的重要性与日俱增。现如今，许多机构/组织通过电子邮件发布会议通知、邀请、论文征集或论文接收/拒绝通知。当收到邀请信并决定参与学术会议或国外项目时，一般需要与组委会/机构进行沟通。而电子邮件快捷、实惠，已成为最常用的信息交流工具。

1. 电子邮件内容

（1）发件人。发件人的姓名或/和电子邮箱地址。

（2）收件人。收件人的姓名或/和电子邮箱地址。

（3）主题。邮件的重点或主题。

（4）正文。邮件的来意。

（5）结尾。告知下一步行动或者解释需要跟进什么。

（6）敬语。

（7）印刷体姓名。

2. 电子邮件写作技巧

电子邮件的正式程度因写作目的而异，或正式或口语化。在正式的电子邮件写作中应注意以下事项：

（1）开场白。表示感谢或表明来意。

（2）邮件主题。强化电子邮件中的重点，方便收件人了解收件原由。例如避免使用"工作坊（Workshop）"之类的范化表达，而代之以"7 月 2 日体育工作坊（Workshop on Physical Education on July 2）"这类具体表达。

（3）邮件目的。应明确邮件诉求，清楚表述发件人意愿。

（4）内容布局。重要信息放在第一段，将反复打磨的细节内容揉进第一句或第二句话中，以便收件人在海量信息中做出判断，节约阅读时间，提升阅读效率。

（5）措辞简洁。恪守单页面形式原则。

（6）附件。附件下载时间比纯文本电子邮件要长，并且可能携带病毒。出于安全考虑，许多电子邮件系统会拦截附件。确有必要添加附件，应在电子邮件正文中告知收件人，并明确指出附件文件名。

（7）突出显示。谨慎使用高亮等突出显示技术。多数电子邮件系统不支持粗体、斜体或下划线等操作,因为这些操作所需指令可能与收件人的计算机不兼容。在此情况下,消息可能会乱码。可以缩进电子邮件的讨论段落(使用 tab 键),然后在讨论中使用星号(*)或数字来设置逐项列表,并使用副标题作为新段落的导语。添加的空白会使信息清晰明了、重点突出。

(8)网络缩写。慎用网络缩写。缩写能使信息更简短,但对内容的呈现意义并不凸显,也不易于语用功能的实现。除少量已获公众认可的邮件缩略语之外,不建议过多使用。常见的电子邮件缩略语包括:

- BTW:by the way(顺便提一下)。
- FYI:for your information(供你参考)。
- U:you or university(你或大学)。
- WRT:with respect to(关于)。
- IMHO:in my humble opinion(依我浅见,在下认为)。
- TTYL:talk to you later(一会说)。

(9)排版拼写。可以在每段之间空出一行,同时确保语法、拼写和标点符号使用正确。

3. 电子邮件写作句型

1)表达邮件来意(表 7-20)

表 7-20 表达邮件来意的中英例句

中文	英文
我们衷心感谢史密斯教授提供了题为"大功率局部放电在线监测系统"的论文。	We wish to express our sincere thanks/gratitude to Prof. Smith for supplying the thesis entitled " System of PD On-line Monitoring for Large Power".
我代表会议秘书处很高兴地通知您,您的论文已收录在会议的张贴发言里。	On behalf of the conference secretariat, it is my pleasure to inform you that your paper has been accepted for presentation at the conference poster session.
感谢你们和全体教职员工在我们在贵校期间为我和我的家人提供了如此完美的安排和指导。	Thank you and your faculty members who provided such wonderful arrangements and guidance for me and my family during our stay at your university.
非常感谢您邀请我参加会议。这趟旅行非常美好,我现已回到中国。在我看来,您展现出出色的活动组织能力,大家对这次会议印象深刻,也很满意。	Thank you very much for inviting me to the conference. I am back in China and I have had a very good trip. From what I can tell, you did a great job in the organization and everybody was very much impressed by and satisfied with the conference.

2）告知收件人信息（表7-21）

表7-21　告知收件人信息的中英例句

中文	英文
我们很高兴地通知您，经过匿名审查，审查小组决定接受您提交的题为"中美城市化快速进程对比"的报告，并在中国城市化国际会议上宣读。	We are pleased to inform you that after anonymous review, the Review Panel decided to accept your submission entitled "Comparison of Rapid Urbanization Between America and China" for presentation at the International Conference on Urbanization in China.
您待会将会收到一封通知邮件。会议登记、酒店预订、教程、旅游和其他信息也可马上获悉。最终意见书必须在2003年5月23日前以电子版PDF格式提交。	A notification email will be following as well. The conference registration, hotel reservation, tutorial courses, tours and other information will also be available soon. Final submissions must be received in electronic PDF by May 23, 2003.
您的提交状态也可以通过会议网站http：…输入证件号码和姓氏查询。	The status of your submission may also be tracked through the conference website at http：… by using your paper number and family name.
非常感谢您积极参与我们的会议，但不幸的是，您的论文不符合本次会议主题。	Many thanks for your active participation in our conference, but unfortunately your paper does not fall within this conference category.
如果您需要进一步的帮助，请联系会议秘书……	If you require further assistance, kindly contact the conference secretary at …

3）提供和询问信息/行动（表7-22）

表7-22　提供和询问信息/行动的中英例句

中文	英文
如果您在访问会议网站时遇到任何困难，请通过电子邮件与我们联系，地址为……我们很高兴通过电子邮件附件向您提供信息支持。	If you have any difficulty accessing the conference website, please contact us through email at … and we'll be very glad to send you information via email attachment.
我们还有一个问题：您能给我们推荐一家在山东大学附近的酒店吗？我们俩将在济南住两晚。	We have one other question：Could you please suggest us a hotel near Shandong University? The two of us will stay two nights in Jinan.
你能打电话给约翰·史密斯（John Smith）确认我们星期一的会议吗？	Will you call John Smith to confirm our meeting on Monday?

4.电子邮件中英样市

1)顶格式

每段段首无缩进,靠左顶格书写,段落之间空一行,落款左对齐(表7-23)。

表 7-23 顶格式电子邮件中英样本

中文	英文
询问具体事项	Enquiring About Details
发件人 Joseph Nacino<Jnacino@ yahoo. com>	From Joseph Nacino<Jnacino@ yahoo. com>
收件人 Wanggang68@ yahoo. com	To Wanggang68@ yahoo. com
主题 研讨会时间	Subject Time for the Seminar
日期 2021 年 2 月 6 日	Date February 6, 2021
亲爱的王刚教授,	Dear Prof. Wang Gang,
我很高兴得知,您已同意在 2007 年 3 月进行为期几天的研究访问,并为我们的研究人员就研讨会发表介绍性论文。您打算谈论什么话题?	I am pleased to know that you have agreed to come for a research visit of a couple of days in March 2007 and hold an introductory paper on the seminar for our researchers. What topic are you going to talk about?
我们将支付您的机票和酒店费用(达 10,000 瑞典克朗)。据我所知,您需要一份签证,您可以向瑞典驻英国大使馆申请。为申请签证,您将需要我们的邀请函。在我撰写邀请函前,我们必须商量一个日期,3 月 15 日至 17 日您方便吗?	The faculty will cover your flight tickets and your hotel costs (up to an amount of 10,000 SEK). As far as I understand, you will need a visa which you could apply for at the Swedish Embassy in United Kingdom. In order to apply for a visa, you will need a letter of invitation from us. Before I can write such a letter, we will have to settle a date, on March 15-17? Would that be suitable for you?
此致,	Best regards,
Joseph Nacino	Joseph Nacino
Professor of Criminal Law	Professor of Criminal Law

2)缩进式

每段段首缩进4个字母,段落之间无空行,落款右对齐(表7-24)。

表 7-24　缩进式电子邮件中英样本

中文	英文
询问议程和住宿	Enquiring About Agenda and Accomodation
发件人 JohnWilliams@ yahoo. com	From JohnWilliams@ yahoo. com
收件人 LiangHong@ hotmail. com	To LiangHong@ hotmail. com
主题 会议议程	Subject Agenda of the Meeting
日期 2021 年 3 月 20 日	Date 20 March, 2021
亲爱的梁教授，	Dear Prof. Liang,
相信您已知道我们将分别于 4 月 13 日和 14 日在山东大学举行两场会议。再次感谢您的安排。然而这样一来，我们将面临一个难题，那就是我们在济南的时间紧张，是否还有机会组织客座讲座。	As you know we will now have two separate meetings at Shandong University, respectively on the 13th and 14th of April. Many thanks again to you for arranging this. In this respect, however, the question is whether there is still an opportunity to organize a guest lecture, despite our unfortunately limited time in Jinan.
按理说，Kamperman Sanders 教授(环境规划和管理)和我(环境破坏后的生物修复)都可以在 4 月 14 日发表演讲，但我们不知道时间是否允许。如果您认为我们这一计划可行，请通知我们。	In principle, either Prof. Kamperman Sanders (environmental planning and management) or me (biological repairing of destroyed environment) could give a lecture on April 14, but we do not know whether time permits this. Please let us know if you think we can still plan something in this respect.
另外，请问您能给我们推荐一家山东大学附近的酒店吗？我们俩将在济南住两晚。	We have one other question: Could you please suggest us a hotel in the area of Shandong University? The two of us will stay two nights in Jinan.
盼早日回复，提前致谢。	Thank you very much in advance for replying soon.
此致，	With kind regards,
John Williams	John Williams
PS：就我们与院长即将到来的会面，更多细节将很快公布。	PS：Further details regarding our upcoming meeting with the dean will follow soon.

第四节　期刊论文摘要

　　摘要是科技论文中非常重要的部分，摘要字数有限，但必须包括论文所有主要内容。有人将摘要比作论文的灵魂或是眼睛，其重要性不言而喻。摘要的重要性，表现在以下几方面：作者需要"推销"自己的论文，确定论文在学术方面是否有吸引力，是否能给读者提供完整和清晰的信息；读者能否很快检索到需要的论文，获取需要的信息；能否让杂志的编辑部初步认定论文的价值，获得送审的机会；能否让审稿人初步认定稿件的质量，获得发表或者修改以后发表的机会。

（一）摘要写作技巧

1. 时间

何时开始写摘要并没有统一规定，作者可以按照个人的具体情况来确定，一般有两种写法。第一种是在写好论文的其他部分，如引言、方法、结果和结论以后，掌握了系统而全面的论文信息，心中有数，再写摘要。另一种写法就是先写摘要草稿，根据论文提纲和构思来写，等到整个论文完成以后，再来修改定稿。第二种摘要写作方法同样适用于参加国家学术会议。

2. 长度

通常没有固定的长度。但是内容需要满足读者的需求，做到纲举目张。描述性摘要和信息性摘要的字数一般在 100 到 250 个单词之间，或者是论文正文长度的 5% 到 10% 之间；结构式摘要一般不超过 350 个字，按照小标题把摘要分成几小段，但也有一段式的结构式摘要。由于小标题一般都用黑体标出，比较醒目。

3. 布局

相较于遵循论文本身的章节顺序，作者应突出论文的新贡献，用精辟语句突出研究新发现、新理论、新成果。所谓新贡献包括新技术、新理论、新方法、新观点、新规律、纠正前人错误、解决争议、补充和发展前人成果等。这样，时间紧迫的读者即使只看了第一句话，也能知道作者的重点。

4. 人称

一般认为，学术论文要少用或尽量不用第一人称，以此体现其科学性和客观性。然而，根据上海交通大学外国语学院语言文字工程研究所陆元雯报道，在科技论文英文摘要语料库的词频统计中，第一人称复数 we 不仅在人称代词的使用频次上排名第一，在语料库的全部词汇中也是高频词之一，高居第 12 位。这也许是因为相对于被动语态或是以 this paper 或 this article 等客体为主语的句子，使用第一人称复数 we 作主语拉近了作者和读者之间的距离，容易使他们之间产生共鸣，同时也使摘要内容的表达更直接明了。因此，只要拟投期刊认可，可以放心使用第一人称。不过，如果拟投期刊另有规定，则按照规定。

5. 时态

陈述事实或描述论文所做的事情时，使用现在时态（如在描述性摘要中）。解释在研究中实际做过什么或发现了什么时，使用过去式（如在信息摘要中）。

(二)摘要写作句型

1. 表明目的(表7-25)

表7-25　表明目的的常用句型

中文		英文	
作者 笔者　+ 文本	旨在 描述 认为 研究 解决	The author The writer　+ The paper	attemps/seeks/aims/intends describes/defines argues/believes/holds/maintains investigates/explores/probes into/analyzes deals with/addresses/solves
本文/研究旨在……		The purpose of this paper is to … This study set out to investigate the usefulness of … The aim of this study was to develop a better understanding of … This study systematically reviews the data for …, aiming to provide … An investigation was designed to …	

2. 提出结论和建议(表7-26)

表7-26　提出结论和建议的常用句型

中文	英文
作者/本文得出……	The author/paper concludes that … This study has identified/shown … These findings illustrate how … These findings highlight the potential usefulness of … … provides strong empirical confirmation that …
建议……	It is suggested/recommended that … The paper suggests that … The thesis does not engage with …

(三)摘要类型

科技论文摘要主要分成三种类型：描述性摘要(descriptive abstract)、信息性摘要(informative abstract)和结构式摘要(structured abstract)。

1. 描述性摘要

1）描述性摘要内容

（1）目的（purpose）。

（2）方法（methods）。

（3）研究主题（scope of the paper）。

（4）研究课题（subject）。

2）描述性摘要中英样本（表7-27）

表 7-27 描述性摘要中英样本

中文	英文	分析
近年来，轴流压缩系统的建模与控制受到了广泛关注。本文旨在抑制旋转失速和喘振，扩大压缩机系统的稳定运行范围，并使用反馈控制方法扩大稳定平衡的吸引域。该研究领域取得成功后，将显著提高压缩机性能，从而提高未来的航空发动机性能。通过阅读研究文献，本文总结了这一活跃研究领域的主要进展，重点关注轴流压缩机旋转失速和喘振的建模和控制观点。	Modeling and control for axial flow compression systems *have received great attention* in recent years. *The objectives are to* suppress rotating stall and surge, to extend the stable operating range of the compressor system, and to enlarge domains of attraction of stable equilibria using feedback control methods. *The success of* this research field *will significantly improve* compressor performance and thus future aeroengine performance. *This paper surveys* the research literature *and summarizes* the major developments in this active research field, focusing on the modeling and control perspectives to rotating stall and surge for axial flow compressors.	要点提炼 • 首先解释研究领域、研究目的和研究的可能结果 • 继而说明作者已完成的工作 语言亮点 • 时态。一般现在时和一般将来时 • 学术词汇和句型。如 have received great attention; The objectives are to …; The success of … will …; This paper surveys … and summarizes …

2. 信息性摘要

1）信息性摘要内容

（1）目的（purpose）。

（2）方法（methods）。

（3）研究领域（scope of the paper）。

（4）结果（results）。

（5）结论（conclusion）。

（6）建议（recommendations）。

2）信息性摘要中英样本（表7-28）

表7-28　信息性摘要中英样本

中文	英文	分析
人类疱疹病毒6型（HHV-6）是皮疹的病原体，在免疫功能低下的患者中引起机会性感染，并与多发性硬化症和艾滋病（AIDS）进展有关。在这里，我们展示了两个主要的HHV-6亚组（A和B）使用人类CD46作为细胞受体。在HHV-6感染过程中记录了表面CD46的下调。HHV-6介导的急性感染和细胞融合均被CD46单克隆抗体特异性抑制；融合也被可溶性CD46阻断。对HHV-6融合和进入具有抗性的非人细胞在表达重组人CD46后变得敏感。普遍存在的免疫调节受体的使用为理解HHV-6的嗜性和致病性开辟了新的视角。	Human herpesvirus 6 (HHV-6) is the etiologic agent of exanthema subitum, causes opportunistic infections in immunocompromised patients, and has been implicated in multiple sclerosis and in the progression of AIDS. Here, we show that the two major HHV-6 subgroups (A and B) use human CD46 as a cellular receptor. Downregulation of surface CD46 was documented during the course of HHV-6 infection. Both acute infection and cell fusion mediated by HHV-6 were specifically *inhibited* by a monoclonal antibody to CD46; fusion was also *blocked* by soluble CD46. Nonhuman cells that were resistant to HHV-6 fusion and entry became susceptible upon expression of recombinant human CD46. The use of a ubiquitous immunoregulatory receptor opens novel perspective for understanding the tropism and pathogenicity of HHV-6.	要点提炼 ● 它首先对HHV-6下定义并解释了它的重要性 ● 给出研究目的、方法和结果 ● 以前景展望结尾 语言亮点 ● 时态。一般现在时（陈述和解释研究内容）和一般过去时（描述研究过程和结果） ● 学术词汇。相较于描述性摘要，这篇摘要拥有更多技术、主题相关术语，以及用于准确描述研究中发生的事情的特定动词（inhibit、block）

3.结构式摘要（structured abstract）

目前，全球生物医学类杂志及许多理工类杂志都推荐、鼓励或者要求作者采用结构式摘要。结构式摘要包括四段式、五段式、六段式、七段式及八段式等。下面将主要介绍四段式结构式摘要和八段式结构式摘要。

1）四段式结构式摘要

（1）四段式结构式摘要内容：

● 目的（objective）。简要说明研究的目的，表明研究范围、内容和重要性，常常涵盖文章的标题内容。

● 方法（methods）。简要说明研究课题的设计思路，使用何种材料和方法、如何对照分组、如何处理数据等。

● 结果（results）。简要介绍研究的主要结果和数据、有何新发现，说明其价值及局限。此外，还要给出结果的置信值、统计学显著性和检验的确切值。

● 结论(conclusion)。简要对以上的研究结果进行分析或讨论,并进行总结,给出符合科学规律的结论。

(2)四段式结构式摘要的中英样本(表7-29)。

表7-29　四段式结构式摘要的中英样本

中文	英文
①背景 由耐甲氧西林金黄色葡萄球菌(MRSA)引起的感染在世界各地的医院中愈加普遍。金黄色葡萄球菌仍是医院内菌血症的一种致病源。	① Background Infections due to methicillin-resistant *Staphylococcus aureus* have become increasingly common in hospitals worldwide. *S aureus* continues to be a cause of nosocomial bacteremia.
②方法 我们在一个拥有 2900 个床位的三级转诊医疗中心进行了回顾性队列研究,分析了耐甲氧西林金黄色葡萄球菌和甲氧西林敏感金黄色葡萄球菌(MRSA)菌血症的临床意义(死亡率)。本文使用生存分析和逻辑回归分析来确定影响死亡率的风险因素和预后因素。	② Methods We analyzed the clinical significance (mortality) of MRSA and methicillin-susceptible *S aureus* bacteremia in a retrospective cohort study in a 2900-bed tertiary referral medical center. Survival and logistic regression analyses were used to determine the risk factors and prognostic factors of mortality.
③结果 15 年期间,共有 1148 名患者诊断出患有医院内金黄色葡萄球菌菌血症。在逻辑回归分析中控制 MRSA 菌血症的潜在危险因素后,服务、感染菌血症前的入院天数、年龄、机械呼吸机和中心静脉导管(CVC)是 MRSA 的独立危险因素。感染金黄色葡萄球菌菌血症的粗死亡率为 44.1%。MRSA(49.8%)和 MSSA 菌血症(27.6%)的死亡率差异为 22.2%($P<0.001$),经 logistic 回归分析,MRSA 菌血症的死亡率是 MSSA 的 1.78 倍($P<0.001$)。其他预测的预后因素包括年龄、肿瘤、菌血症后住院时间、机械呼吸机的存在和 CVC 的使用。	③ Results During the 15-year period, 1148 patients were diagnosed with nosocomial *S aureus* bacteremia. After controlling potential risk factors for MRSA bacteremia on logistic regression analysis, service, admission days prior to bacteremia, age, mechanical ventilator, and central venous catheter (CVC) were independent risk factors for MRSA. The crude mortality rate of *S aureus* bacteremia was 44.1%. The difference between the mortality rates of MRSA (49.8%) and MSSA bacteremia (27.6%) was 22.2% ($P<0.001$). Upon logistic regression analysis, the mortality with MRSA bacteremia was revealed to be 1.78 times higher than MSSA ($P<0.001$). The other predicted prognostic factors included age, neoplasms, duration of hospital stay after bacteremia, presence of mechanical ventilator, and use of CVC.
④结论 具有对甲氧西林的耐药性是金黄色葡萄球菌菌血症患者重要的独立预后因素。	④Conclusions Resistance to methicillin was an important independent prognostic factor for patients with *S aureus* bacteremia.

2)八段式结构式摘要

(1)八段式结构式摘要内容:

● 目的(objective)。

● 设计(design)。

- 单位（setting）。
- 研究对象（participants）。
- 干预（intervention）。
- 初步结果（primary outcome）。
- 结果（results）。
- 结论（conclusion）。

（2）八段式结构式摘要的中英样本（表7-30）。

表7-30　八段式结构式摘要的中英样本

中文	英文
①目的 研究是否应建议患有慢性膝关节疼痛的老年患者使用局部或口服非甾体抗炎药（NSAID）。	① **Objective** To determine whether older patients with chronic knee pain should be advised to use topical or oral non-steroidal anti-inflammatory drugs（NSAIDs）.
②设计 随机对照试验和患者偏好研究。	② **Design** Randomised controlled trial and patient preference study.
③单位 26所全科诊室的病历档案。	③ **Setting** 26 general practices.
④研究对象 年龄≥50岁并患有膝关节疼痛者。其中，随机试验282人，偏好试验303人。	④ **Participants** People aged ≥50 with knee pain：282 in randomised trial and 303 in preference study.
⑤介入 建议局部使用或口服布洛芬。	⑤ **Interventions** Advice to use topical or oral ibuprofen.
⑥初步结果 西安大略和麦克马斯特大学（WOMAC）骨性关节炎指数，重大和轻度不良反应。	⑥ **Primary outcome measures** WOMAC（Western Ontario and McMaster Universities）osteoarthritis index, major and minor adverse effects.
⑦结果 一年内，全球WOMAC分数变化情况相当。在随机试验中，差异（局部减去口服）为2分（95%置信区间-2至6）；在偏好研究中，它是1分（-4到6）。对照实验间的重大不良反应没有差异。次要结果的唯一显著差异出现在随机试验中。口服组有更多的呼吸系统不良反应（17%对7%，95%差异置信区间 -17%至-2%），血清肌酐的变化为3.7 mmol/L（0.9 μmol/L 至 6.5 μmol/L）；更多的参与者因为不良反应而改变了治疗方法（16%对1%，-16%到-5%）。在局部治疗组中，更多的参与者在三个月时出现慢性疼痛 Ⅲ 级或 Ⅳ 级，更多的参与者因无效而改变治疗方案。	⑦**Results** Changes in global WOMAC scores at 12 months were equivalent. In the randomised trial the difference（topical minus oral）was two points（95% confidence interval -2 to 6）；in the preference study, it was one point（-4 to 6）. There were no differences in major adverse effects in the trial or study. The only significant differences in secondary outcomes were in the randomised trial. The oral group had more respiratory adverse effects（17% v 7%, 95% confidence interval for difference -17% to -2%）, the change in serum creatinine was 3.7 mmol/L less favourable（0.9 μmol/L to 6.5 μmol/L）；and more participants changed treatments because of adverse effects（16% v 1%, -16% to -5%）. In the topical group more participants had chronic pain grade Ⅲ or Ⅳ at three months, and more participants changed treatment because of ineffectiveness.

续表

中文	英文
⑧结论 使用口服或外用制剂在一年内对膝关节疼痛治疗效果相同，且口服 NSAIDs 的副作用更小。局部使用 NSAIDs 可能是口服 NSAIDs 的有用替代品。	⑧ **Conclusions** Advice to use oral or topical preparations has an equivalent effect on knee pain over one year, and there are more minor side effects with oral NSAIDs. Topical NSAIDs may be a useful alternative to oral NSAIDs.

（四）选择合适的摘要类型

每种期刊都有自己的传统和写作规范，投寄论文时，可自行检索拟投期刊规定的摘要格式。同时，期刊编辑将在这一点上提供指导。通常在撰写研究报告时，信息性摘要会更好，因为可以向读者提供事实信息以及主要观点。在一些情况下，描述性摘要是首选，例如，研究领域争议较多并且希望结果在读者读完整篇论文之前保密。摘要也可以杂糅描述性和信息性元素。而生物医学和理工类杂志更推荐作者使用结构式摘要。

（五）其他内容

（1）关键词。尽管关键词不属于摘要正文，但大多数期刊现在都希望作者在摘要中提供关键词。通常需要 5 到 10 个关键词，它们应该是最能反映论文内容的词。

（2）作者简介。许多期刊和会议现在还需要一份简短的作者简介，长度为 50～60 字。

（六）摘要质量管理

按照以下四个步骤撰写摘要，就应当可以保证摘要的质量。

（1）遵守要求。下载拟投期刊的作者须知并打印出来，认真阅读、消化和不折不扣地照办。

（2）借鉴模仿。了解拟投期刊的摘要要求，并参考拟投期刊近期发表的期刊摘要部分，进而认真模仿。

（3）内容撰写。动笔前，问自己三个问题：研究问题是什么？为什么它重要/有趣？主要结果是什么？捋清思路后完成摘要初稿写作。

（4）校对修改。使用 Word 的语法和拼写校对工具校对两次以上，以及人工校对两次，保证绝无语法和拼写错误。

（七）摘要校核表（表7-31）

表7-31　摘要校核表

序号	校核项目	回答	
		√	×
1	摘要是否严格遵守作者须知的规定		
2	摘要长度是否超标		
3	摘要是否包括论文的主要信息（背景、目的、方法、结果、结论），所用句型是否与正文雷同		
4	摘要是否避用了图表、示意图、公式、结构式、非公用的符号和术语，以及引证的参考文献		
5	摘要是否避用了生僻缩略语、代号、非法定计量单位、错误标点符号		
6	摘要是否有表达含混不清、模棱两可、冗长啰唆之处		
7	摘要是否有正文未涉及的内容		
8	摘要是否有不必要的自我评价，如 interesting、innovative、new、novel、valuable、fundamental 等		
9	摘要的文体（人称、时态、语态等）是否符合拟投期刊的要求		
10	关键词是否出现在标题和摘要中，保证读者利用摘要中的关键词能在数据库检索到论文		
11	摘要是否经过合作作者的"同行"评阅，并取得一致的认可		
12	如有可能，是否约请英语外教或者有经验的英语教师校阅或者润色		

第五节　研究计划写作

　　研究人员撰写并提交研究计划以证明研究的价值，证明自己的研究项目值得花费时间、精力和经费来资助。根据研究计划的不同目的，研究计划可能有不同的格式，但所有类型的研究计划都有一些共同点。

（一）研究计划结构

1.研究计划的标题

标题要包括表明研究对象、问题或方法等的关键词。该标题仅为临时标题，一旦研究计划获得批准，作者开始进入研究的下一个阶段，可以对其进行修改。

2.摘要

用 100~150 字的篇幅强调计划中最重要的内容。

3.问题陈述

使用准确的语言陈述研究项目打算解决的研究问题。可以提出一些重要的研究问题，进一步解释问题，提供问题的背景及严重性。

4.研究目的

使用要点快速介绍研究项目的主要目的。

5.研究项目的意义

明确陈述研究项目的理论价值、实践价值、社会价值等。

6.研究问题的文献综述/背景信息

利用最具针对性文献通过有效行文以描述当前研究现状，阐明已有研究的局限性。

7.研究方法/理论框架

用短文或要点介绍研究方法/理论框架，并解释方法/理论是如何适用于本研究项目的。

8.研究时间线

使用大纲格式描述每个主要阶段计划的时间框架，以及每个阶段要完成的工作/任务。

9.对结果/结论的预测

使用大纲格式或简短段落概括描述研究可能产生的结果/结论。

10. 预测研究项目的困难/障碍/挑战

使用大纲格式或短文描述方法、理论、应用、数据收集等方面的潜在障碍。

11. 参考文献

列出至少 10 个对研究项目至关重要和起支撑作用的高质量文献来源。

(二) 常用句型

1. 阐明研究问题(表 7-32)

表 7-32　阐明研究问题的中英例句

中文	英文
X 越来越被认为是一个严重的全球公共卫生问题。	X is increasingly recognised as a serious, worldwide public health concern.
X 及其后果是一个重要但尚未研究的问题。	X and its consequences are an important, but understudied, cause for concern.
迫切需要解决由……引起的安全问题……	There is an urgent need to address the safety problems caused by …
X 是一个主要的环境问题,也是……	X is a major environmental problem, and the main cause of …

2. 表明研究目的(表 7-33)

表 7-33　表明研究目的的中英例句

中文	英文
这项研究的目的是验证……	This research aims at examining …
本研究旨在比较……	This research intends to compare the different ways in which …
本项目的目的是为理解……提供一个新的模型……	The purpose of this project is to offer a new model for understanding …
这项研究将调查……的影响因素。	Thisresearch will investigate the factors that determine …
这个项目是描述设计和实施……	This project is to describe the design and implementation of …
本文试图通过分析……来解决这些问题。	This research seeks to remedy these problems by analysing the literature of …

3. 表明研究意义（表7-34）

表7-34　表明研究意义的中英例句

中文	英文
这项研究将提供一个机会来增进我们对……的了解。	This study will provide an exciting opportunity to advance our knowledge of …
希望这项研究有助于加深对……的理解。	It is hoped that this research will contribute to a deeper understanding of …
这项研究有望通过探索……促进相关研究的发展。	This study is expected to contribute to this growing area of research by exploring …
这个项目将提供一个重要的机会，促进我们对……的认识。	This project will provide an important opportunity to advance the understanding of …
本研究将通过……填补研究空白。	The present study fills a gap in the literature by …
理解 X 和 Y 之间的联系将有助于……	Understanding the link between X and Y will help …
这项调查将增进我们对……的了解。	This investigation will enhance our understanding of …

4. 说明研究方法（表7-35）

表7-35　说明研究方法的中英例句

中文	英文
通过采用定性的调查方式，将试图阐明……	By employing qualitative modes of enquiry, I attempt to illuminate the …
采用定性和定量的研究设计，以提供……	Qualitative and quantitative research designs will be adopted to provide …
本研究将利用口述历史访谈和档案资料。	This study will make use of oral history interviews as well as archival sources.
本研究拟采用定性和定量相结合的方法。	Both qualitative and quantitative methods will be used in this investigation.
采用整体方法，整合 X、Y 和 Z 材料，建立……	A holistic approach will be utilised, integrating X, Y and Z material to establish …
这项研究会以调查的形式进行，通过……收集数据。	The study will be conducted in the form of a survey, with data being gathered via …
这个项目将使用访谈和参与者观察来描述……	This project will use interviews and participant-observation to produce an account of …

5. 预测研究结果(表7-36)

表7-36 预测研究结果的中英例句

中文	英文
据预测这两种情况之间存在显著差异。	It is predicted that there was a significant difference between the two conditions …
预测结果是,报告 X 水平较低的受访者也报告 Y 水平显著较低。	Results are predicted as respondents who reported low levels of X also reported significantly lower levels of Y.
预测 X 和 Y 之间存在正相关性。	A positive correlation is predicted to be found between X and Y.
X 组和 Y 组之间的差异预计是显著的。	The difference between the X and Y groups is predicted to be significant.

(三)英文研究计划样本

Research Proposal

1. Title

A Study on Application of Dynamic Assessment in College English Translation Teaching

2. Abstract

The cultivation of translation competence is the essential goal of College English translation teaching at present. The research on the composition of translation competence and how to develop translation competence has become the academic focus of translation research. This research attempts to embed dynamic assessment as a teaching strategy into college English translation teaching, which will be conducted in the form of peer feedback after class. This study will carry out a quantitative research to identify the impact of dynamic assessment on students' translation competence. And this research is expected to give some entitlement on translation teaching and application of dynamic assessment to new field.

3. Statement of problem

(1) Traditional translation teaching model is not suitable for students' creative consciousness in translation because of the only presentation of reference version of translated text.

（2）Student-centered teaching model cannot be achieved because of large number of students and limited time.

（3） The development of translation competence（TC）is a dynamic process of interaction. Students' cognitive development and personal potentials during the translation process are usually neglected, leading to the failure that multiple sub-competences of TC do not develop synchronously.

（4）There are still many limitations of teaching methods and strategies of TC when they are carried out in real translation class.

Through a teaching experiment, the study will explore the impact of dynamic assessment on the development of students' translation competence, and four research questions were put forward as the following: Does dynamic assessment significantly improve students' general translation competence? Does dynamic assessment significantly improve students' strategic sub-competence? Does dynamic assessment significantly improve students' instrumental sub-competence? Does dynamic assessment significantly improve students' knowledge about translation sub-competence?

4. Research aim

（1） To prove if dynamic assessment（DA）can significantly improve students' TC through a teaching experiment.

（2）To avoid the limitations of the traditional classroom teaching by carrying out DA after the class, leaving students' enough time for assessment and interaction.

（3）To focus on the translation process instead of the translation products.

5. Significance of research project

（1）Theoretically, it will deepen the application of DA in translation studies through empirical research.

（2）Practically, it will not only analyze the feasibility of the method of "translation-process-centered" but also find out the students' problems in the process of learning translation, as well as accumulate certain experience for future practical application of DA in the development of TC.

6. Literature review

1）Studies on translation teaching and testing

In the past ten years, although the scope of translation teaching studies in China has been expanding and the research methods have gradually become mature and diversified, theoretical research always dominated the majority, and there is still a lack of quantitative and empirical research.

（1） In Mu's early study, she considered that there were many studies on the composition of TC and various components of TC, but the studies on TC testing and teaching were still rare.

（2）Miao argued that "TC was presented as cognitive competence which happened in the complex operation process in the human brain". She agreed with the process-based teaching method and put forward "translating in class" with small groups, which paid more attention to the translation process. Nevertheless, the experimental data to prove whether the process-based teaching method improved TC or not is insufficient.

（3）Xiao focused on the testing methods of TC and the validity of these methods, holding that TC is very abstract, which can be neither seen nor touched. Yu argued that when TC was measured, it should be broken down into some behaviors that we can observe directly to infer translator's TC. She also argued that most of the research focused on language expressions and text transformation, but little research involved a real social scene in translation.

2）Studies on dynamic assessment

In general, most of the studies on DA at home and abroad focus on the application of DA in Second Language Acquisition (SLA) such as English writing, vocabulary learning, oral English. Nevertheless, there are few studies on the application of DA in college English translation teaching.

（1）In the earlier studies, Han introduced the concept and model of DA and discussed its application in foreign language education. He also compared the similarities and differences between DA and static assessment.

（2）Many scholars proposed new ideas about the application of DA. For instance, Zhang claimed that DA, which went through the process of writing, should design a step-by-step "scaffolding teaching" intervention form based on the needs and development of learners, which developed the idea of promoting teaching by evaluation advocated in DA.

（3）Davin's study of 2016 extended his study of 2013 and explored the implementation of DA in an elementary foreign language classroom. Kamrood believed that compared to traditional non-dynamic testing, DA presents a more comprehensive account of human beings' abilities through addressing both the fully internalized abilities and the abilities that are in the process of being internalized.

7. Research method

56 non-English-major undergraduates from two intact classes of a university of science and technology will be selected as the subjects. These two classes will be randomly taken as experimental class and control class. The experiment will be conducted from September to December, lasting for one semester, 14 teaching weeks. During the experiment, we will conduct the pre-test and post-test of the self-assessment scale on TC, four translation tasks, peer feedback (interventionist and interactionist dynamic assessment), self-reflection, and

retrospective interview.

8. Predictions of results

（1）Dynamic assessment has a ·positive effect on students' strategic sub-competence, instrumental sub-competence, and knowledge about translation sub-competence.

（2）After the implementation of dynamic assessment, students' overall translation competencewill be improved.

9. Predictions of difficulties of the research project

（1）The persuasiveness of the experiment may be influenced due to the following reasons. First, it cannot last for a long time. Second, students' bilingual competence and extra-linguistic competence cannot be controlled.

（2）It is difficult to design a comprehensive self-reflection report form and peer feedback report form, as well as the questions in the retrospective interview to fully reflect all the students' ideas in translation.

10. References

杨志红, 王克非. 翻译能力及其研究[J]. 外语教学, 2010, 31(6): 91-95.

方红, 王克非. 动态系统理论下翻译能力的构成及发展模式研究[J]. 解放军外国语学院学报, 2014, 37(5): 124-130+160.

刘和平. 翻译能力发展的阶段性及其教学法研究[J]. 中国翻译, 2011, 32(1): 37-45.

孔文, 李敦东, 余国兴. L2 写作动态评估中同伴中介干预和教师中介干预比较研究[J]. 外语界, 2013(3): 77-86.

PACTE. Results of the Validation of the PACTE Translation Competence Model: Acceptability and Decision Making[J]. Across Languages and Cultures, 2009, 10(2): 207-230.

KAMROOD A M, et al. Diagnosing L2 Learners' Development Through Online Computerized Dynamic Assessment[J]. Computer Assisted Language Learning, 2019(1): 1-30.

LANTOLF J P. Dynamic Assessment: The Dialectic Integration of Instruction and Assessment[J]. Language Teaching, 2008, 42(3): 355-368.

DAVIN K J, DONATO R. Student Collaboration and Teacher-directed Classroom Dynamic Assessment: A Complementary Pairing[J]. Foreign Language Annals, 2013(46): 5-22.

LANTOLF J P, POEHNER M E. Dynamic Assessment: Bringing the Past into the Future[J]. Journal of Applied Linguistics, 2004(1): 49-74.

第六节　研究报告写作

(一)研究报告结构

研究报告通常由三个主要部分组成：前页；正文；附加材料。每个部分由几节组成，每节的主要内容各不相同，具体内容如表 7-37 所示。

表 7-37　研究报告结构

主要部分	节	内容
前页	标题	简要概括报告主要内容
	目录(可省略)	列出主要章节的标题及对应页码
	摘要/总结	简要概括报告内容，特别是发现的结果
正文	引言	介绍研究对象及原因
	文献综述(通常包含在引言部分)	介绍相应领域内的相关研究
	方法	介绍研究方法、研究过程
	结果	研究结果
	讨论	结果的相关性
	结论	概括研究发现
	建议(通常包含在结论部分)	根据研究发现可得出的相应启示或对未来研究的建议
附加材料	参考文献	包括报告中所引用的所有文献
	附录	研究中所使用的相关材料

(二)写作技巧

撰写研究报告需完成以下步骤：

1.分析写作任务

一般要分析以下几个问题：

(1)报告的目的是什么？(说服？分析？或报告调查、实验？)

(2)报告的目标读者是谁？

(3)字数限制是多少？(通常字数限制只包括报告的正文)

（4）报告的主题是什么？

（5）报告的格式是什么？

2.制订写作计划

使用章节标题来制订计划，同时写一篇论文陈述，阐明报告的总体目的。在相关部分记下你已经知道的有关该主题的任何内容。

3.撰写报告正文初稿

引言：说明研究目的、研究背景、报告大纲。

文献综述：若文献综述独立成节，可按照主题、时间等进行文献综述，以呈现条理性。

方法：清楚地概述研究材料、研究方法以及研究程序，多使用被动语态以客观描述。

结果：说明研究中发现的内容，展示研究结果，不要解释。

讨论：讨论结果的相关性，并说明研究发现如何与该领域的其他研究相联系。

结论：呈现研究最重要的结果或发现。切勿包含新的论点。可以指出研究存在的不足以及对未来研究的建议。

4.撰写补充材料

参考文献：包括报告中使用的所有参考文献或作为背景信息的参考文献。

附录：若涉及附录，则相关信息在正文中必须有所体现。每个附录要进行命名和编号。

5.撰写前页

报告标题：多用短语，清楚并准确地表明报告主题。

目录：列出所有章节、副标题及对应页码。

摘要/总结：以精简的形式对报告进行简短概述。

6.完善报告

检查、修改研究报告，以确保你已遵循相关的字数、格式要求。

（三）中英实验报告样本

实验报告也属于研究报告。实验报告可分为"非正式"和"正式"实验报告两类。正式或非正式只是程度的问题，正式实验报告通常采用研究论文格式，包括上文讨论的几个部分，而非正式实验报告通常采用标准备忘录格式。一份正式实验报告可能比一份非正式实验报告长得多。

MEMO

To：×××, Lab Instructor

From：×××

Subject：Lab Report—Heat and Reaction Rates

Date：11 June, 20××

Date：

Purpose：How does heat affect the rate of a reaction?

Hypothesis：If there is an increase in the heat (independent variable) of a reaction then the speed (dependent variable) of the reaction increases.

Materials：5 grams of instant coffee, 2 liters of water, a freezer, and hot water baths

Procedure：I made three cups of instant coffee and placed them into the freezer overnight. The next morning, I placed each cup in a different hot water bath. The baths were 35, 80 and 240 degrees Fahrenheit. I measured the time (speed) at which each frozen cup melted entirely and recorded my data. I compared my results with other students.

Data：

Temperature (℉)	Rate of melting in minutes	Observations
35	120	Very slow melting
80	27	
240	2	Immediate melting

Calculations：℃ = (℉−32) ∗ 0.56

Conclusion：I investigated the effect of different temperatures on the rates of reactions. To study the problem, I tested the melting rates of a frozen coffee at 3 different temperatures. My data supports the hypothesis but I have a few errors in data collection that could corrected by obtaining a more accurate themometer. I feel that further research in testing different compounds could aid in improving antifreeze for cars.

备忘录

收阅人：实验老师×××

写信人：×××

主题：实验报告——热与反应速率

日期：20××年 6 月 11 日

目的：热如何影响反应速率？

假设：如果热量（自变量）增加，那么反应速度（因变量）就会增加。

材料：5 克速溶咖啡，2 升水，冰箱和热水浴锅。

操作过程：冲泡三杯速溶咖啡，于冰箱中放置一整夜；翌日早将其放置于不同温度的浴锅中，浴锅的温度分别为 35℉、80℉和 240℉；测量每个冷冻杯子完全融化的时间（速度），记录数据；并与其他同学比较实验结果。

数据：

温度（华氏度℉）	融化时间（分钟）	备注
35	120	融化速度非常慢
80	27	
240	2	立即融化

计算：摄氏度℃ =（华氏度℉−32）∗ 0.56

结论：此实验调查了不同温度对反应速率的影响。为了研究这个问题，实验人员测试了冷冻咖啡在 3 种不同温度下的融化速度。实验数据证明如果热量（自变量）增加，那么反应速度（因变量）就会增加这一假设是成立的，但在数据收集过程中存在一些不恰当操作，可以采用更准确的温度计来纠正。进一步研究测试不同的化合物可以帮助改进汽车防冻剂。

第八章　科技文献检索

文献检索是打开人类知识宝库的钥匙，是科学活动的重要组成部分。科技文献可使科研人员在设计和生产中继承和借鉴前人的宝贵经验，减少人力和投资方面的重复与浪费。因此，利用数据库进行科技文献检索是科技工作者和当代大学生科研和学习的必备技能。

第一节　中英文数据库及检索方法

(一) 文献检索概念与分类

文献检索的概念有狭义和广义之分。狭义的文献检索是指依据一定的方法，从已经组织好的大量有关文献集合中，查找并获取特定的相关文献的过程。这里的文献集合，不是通常所指的文献本身，而是关于文献的信息或文献的线索。如果要获取文献中所记录的信息，那么还要依据检索所获得的文献线索索取原文。广义的文献检索包括存储和检索两个过程。存储是指工作人员将大量无序的文献信息集中起来，根据文献源的外表特征和内容特征，经过整理、分类、浓缩、标引等处理，使其系统化、有序化，并按一定的技术要求建成一个具有检索功能的工具或检索系统，供人们检索和利用。这里的检索是指运用编制好的检索工具或检索系统，查找出满足用户要求的特定文献。

(二) 国内数据库

目前我国主要应用的有以下几种全文数据库：中国知识资源总库（CNKI 中国知网）、博硕士优秀论文全文数据库、重要报纸全文数据库、万方全文数据库、重庆维普中文科技期刊全文数据库、人大报刊全文数据库、超星及书生提供的全文数据库等。

一般而言，数据库的检索有三种检索方式，即传统检索（初级检索）、高级检索（复合检索）、专业检索。传统检索是老用户习惯的检索方式，使用简单，但查准率低；高级检索是多种检索条件任意组合的限制性检索，文献命中率高；专业检索是对文章中图分类号进行检索，灵活限制检索范围。使用最多的是传统检索和高级检索。

（三）国外数据库

1. EI

美国《工程索引》（*The Engineering Index*，缩写为 EI），创刊于 1884 年，由美国工程信息公司（The Engineering Information Inc.）编辑出版，是世界著名的工程技术综合性检索刊物。登录网址为 http://www.engineeringvillage.com。

EI 名为索引，实为文摘期刊。它报道的文献主要为美国工程学会图书馆（The Engineering Society Library）收藏的各种期刊、会议录、技术报告、论文集、政府出版物和图书。所报道的文献几乎涉及工程技术各个领域。EI 收录的文摘精心挑选，只报道价值较大的工程技术论文，纯基础理论或者专利文献则不作报道。

2. SDOL

Elsevier 公司是全球最大的科学文献出版发行商，产品包括 2700 多种高质量的学术期刊、42000 多种电子书籍，涵盖科学、技术和医学等各个领域。Elsevier 公司出版的期刊是各个学科领域中公认的高品质期刊，SCI 2004 年所收录的 7973 种期刊中，有 1379 种是由 Elsevier 公司出版的。

Science Direct Online（SDOL）是 Elsevier 公司发行的最全面的电子全文文献数据库，涵盖了 3800 多种期刊，几乎涉及所有学科领域。SDOL 登录网址为 http://www.sciencedirect.com。

3. ProQuest Science Journals

ProQuest Science Journals 是由美国著名的 H. W. Wilson 公司出版的全文图像数据库。它收集了自 1994 年以来该公司出版的 450 多种期刊，主题范围包括声学、宇航科学、人工智能、大气科学、化学化工、土木工程、计算机技术及其应用、电子工程、海洋地质、光学计算、石油和燃气、物理、机器人、火与防火、食品和食品工业、地理、工业工程、海洋技术、数学、机械工程、金属学、采矿工程、固体技术、空间技术、通信、纺织等。该数据库每周更新，登录网址为 http://search.proquest.com。

4. Wiley-Blackwell 电子期刊数据库

John Wiley & Sons 出版公司于 1807 年在美国创建，在化学、生命科学、医学、材料学以及工程技术等领域学术文献的出版方面具有一定权威性。Blackwell 出版公司是全球最大的学术出版商,它所出版的学术期刊在科学技术、医学、社会科学以及人文科学领域具有一定权威性。

2007 年 2 月 John Wiley & Sons 出版公司收购 Blackwell 出版公司,并将其与自己的科学、技术以及医学业务(STM)合并组建 Wiley-Blackwell。Wiley-Blackwell 出版 1455 种同行评审的学术期刊及涵盖面广泛的书籍,涵盖学科领域包括科学、技术、医学、社会科学及人文。登录网址为 http://www.interscience.wiley.com。

5.其他常用的全文英文数据库

ACS(American Chemical Society),美国化学学会电子期刊和电子图书全文数据库。

AGU(American Geophysical Union),美国地球物理学会电子期刊(含过刊库)。

AIP(American Institute of Physics-Scitation ©),美国物理联合会期刊及会议录数据库。

Annual Reviews Journals,综合性期刊全文数据库。

APS(The American Physical Society),美国物理学会 APS 电子期刊。

ASM International E-Book,美国材料信息学会电子图书数据库(1984—2009 年,约 120 种图书)。

ASME(American Society of Mechanical Engineers),美国机械工程师学会电子期刊、电子图书、会议录全文数据库。

ASTM International(American Society for Testing and Materials International),美国材料与测试协会标准、科技报告、期刊全文数据库。

PQDT(ProQuest Dissertations and Theses-Full-Text),全球博硕论文全文库。

Science Online,美国《科学》杂志。

Springer Link,Springer 出版社电子期刊及电子图书。

RSC(Royal Society of Chemistry),英国皇家化学学会数据库平台。

第二节　科技报告的检索

科学技术报告又称科技报告、研究报告、技术报告或报告文献(狭义),最早产生于 20 世纪 20 年代,国家标准《科技报告编写规则》(GB/T 7713.3—2014)中对科学技术报告的定义为:进行科研活动的组织和个人描述其从事的研究、设计、工程、试验和鉴定等活动的进展或结果,或描述一个科学或技术问题的现状和发展的文献。总的来说,科技报告是指科研活动所产生的、按有关规定和格式撰写的,以积累、传播和交流为目的,能够完整而真实地反映科研活动的技术内容和经验的特种文献。

(一)科技报告的作用与类型

科技报告的内容新颖广泛、专业性强、技术数据具体,因而具有很高的使用价值。它在交流各种科研思路、推动发明创造、评估技术差距、改进技术方案、增加决策依据、避免科研工作中的重复与浪费、促进科研成果转化为生产力等方面具有积极的作用。

按研究进度可将科技报告划分为初步报告、进展报告、中间报告和终极报告等;按密级可将其划分为绝密报告、秘密报告、非密级限制发行报告、解密报告、非密公开报告等;按技术角度则可将其划分为技术报告(科研成果的总结,公开出版)、技术札记(报告新的技术工艺等,公开出版)、技术备忘录(试验报告、数据资料、会议记录等,不出版)、技术论文(准备在会议上宣读的论文的前身材料)、技术译文(翻译国外有价值的新技术)、合同报告(完成合同过程中的进展报告、研制报告等)、特殊出版物(会议文集、总结报告、资料汇编等)。

(二)中文科技报告的检索

1.中国科技成果数据库

万方的中国科技成果数据库是科技部指定的新技术、新成果查新数据库。其数据主要来源于各省(区、市)、部委的奖励成果、计划成果、鉴定成果,数据收录涉及自然科学各个学科领域,已成为我国最具权威的技术成果库。但该库只提供相关科技报告的题名、文摘、完成单位等信息的查询。

2.国家科技成果网(NAST)

创刊于 1963 年的印刷版《科学技术研究成果公报》曾经是科技部发布重要科学技术研究成果信息的政府出版物,是检索我国科学技术研究成果的工具。2004 年起,印刷版《科学技术研究成果公报》停刊。目前可通过"国家科技成果网"检索已经发布的我国重要科学技术研究成果信息资源。

国家科技成果网(http://www.tech110.cn)是由科技部创建的国家级科技成果创新服务平台,其中"科技成果"栏目拥有的全国科技成果数据库内容丰富,权威性高,收录全国各地区、各行业经省(区、市)以及部委认定的科技成果,库容量以每年 3 万~5 万项的数量增加,充分保证了成果的时效性。

3.国务院发展研究中心调查研究报告

国务院发展研究中心调查研究报告,简称国研报告,是国务院发展研究中心专门从事综合性政策研究和决策咨询的专家不定期发布的有关中国经济和社会诸多领域的调查研究报告,内容丰富,有很高的权威性和预见性。国研报告可登录国研网搜索平台（http://sl. drcnet. com. cn）搜索，或登录国务院发展研究中心信息网（http://www. drcnet. com. cn）浏览、下载。

4. 国家科技报告服务系统

国家科技报告服务系统（http://www. nstrs. cn）于 2014 年 3 月 1 日正式上线。系统开通了针对社会公众、专业人员和管理人员三类用户的服务。向社会公众无偿提供科研报告摘要浏览服务，社会公众不需要注册即可通过检索科技报告摘要和基本信息，了解国家科技投入所产出科技报告的基本情况。向专业人员提供在线全文浏览服务，专业人员需要实名注册，通过身份认证即可检索并在线浏览科技报告全文，但不可以下载保存。科技报告作者实名注册后，将按提供报告页数的 15 倍享有获取原文推送服务的"阅点"（用于获取全文推送服务的支付单位）。向各级科研管理人员提供面向科研管理的统计分析服务，管理人员通过科研管理部门批准注册，免费享有批准范围内的检索、查询、浏览、全文推送以及相应统计分析等服务。

（三）外文科技报告的检索

1. NTIS

NTIS（National Technical Information Service）是美国国家技术情报社出版的美国政府报告文摘题录数据库，主要收录美国政府立项研究开发的项目报告，可以检索 1964 年以来美国政府 AD（Accession Document）、PB（Publication Board）、NASA（National Aeronautics and Space Administration）、DOE（Department of Energy）四大报告的文摘索引信息，少量收录西欧、日本等地的科学研究报告，反映最新政府重视的项目进展。由于该库提供参照号，据此可以向有关机构索取报告的全文。该库 75% 的文献是科技报告，其他文献有专利、会议论文、期刊论文、翻译文献；25% 是美国以外的文献；90% 的文献是英文文献；专业内容覆盖科学技术各个领域。

2. Science. gov

Science. gov 是美国最大的政府科学门户网站（http://www. science. gov），由美国能源部（Department of Energy，DOE）主办，链接了 2000 多个科学网站供用户查询。它由来自美国 14 个主要科技部门的 17 个科技信息机构组成的联合工作组开发维护。Science. gov 最突出的特点是汇集了来自美国政府各部门的大量科技报告的全文资源。该网站默认为简单检索，也提供高级检索（可选择网站检索、数据库检索、网站与数据库复合检索，进行时间限制等）、主题检索、特色资源检索等检索途径。

3. NSTL 的国外科技报告数据库

NSTL（国家科技图书文献中心）的国外科技报告数据库主要收录 1978 年以来

的美国政府研究报告，即 AD、PB、DOE/DE 和 NASA 研究报告，以及少量其他国家学术机构的研究报告、进展报告和年度报告等。学科范围涉及工程技术和自然科学各专业领域，每年增加报告 2 万余篇，每月更新。进入 NSTL 网站（http://www. nstl. gov. cn）后，点击"国外科技报告"按钮，或由"文献检索"子系统选择国外科技报告数据库，均可检索我国收藏的美国政府报告及其他国家的科技报告，但只提供文摘。

4. 其他外文科技成果信息资源

NASA 科技报告数据库 NTRS（NASA Technical Report Server），是主要的检索世界航空、航天资料综合性检索工具。

Information Bridge 数据库由美国能源部的 Office of Science and Technical Information（OSTI）公开免费提供，可获得科技报告的全文。

美国国防科技报告（AD 报告）通过美国国防技术情报中心（Defence Technical Information Center，DTIC）在线平台 DTIC Online（http://www. dtic. mil/dtic/search/tr/tr. html）提供免费检索服务。

国际环境联合会研究服务报告（The Congressional Research Service Reports，CRS 报告）是 National Council for Science and the Environment（NCSE，原名"Committee for the National Institute for the Environment"）的站点，提供了许多环境方面的报告全文。

（四）科技报告原文的获取

通过数据库与免费网站检索到的科技报告绝大多数只有文摘，如果需要原文，可以通过以下途径获得：

（1）利用相关数据库直接从网上获取电子版全文。

（2）通过原文传递服务在国内科技报告的收藏机构获得。中国科技信息研究所是我国引进科技报告的主要单位；上海图书馆/上海科技情报研究所也有美国四大报告的原文馆藏；中国国防科技信息中心收藏有大量的 AD 报告和 NASA 报告；中国科学院文献情报中心是收藏美国四大报告尤其是 PB 报告最全的单位；中国核科技信息与经济研究院（由原中国核科学技术情报研究所等机构合并组建）收藏有较多的 DOE 报告；中国国防科技信息中心收藏有较多的美国四大报告全文；北京航空航天大学图书馆收藏有较多的 NASA 报告全文。

（3）直接从美国邮购。美国有两个科技报告收集发行中心，一是美国商务部所属的国家技术情报服务处，它搜集公开的美国科技报告；二是国防技术情报中心，它搜集有关军事的科技报告。另外，国内没有的，可根据 NTIS 订购号（入藏号）向 NTIS 直接订购报告复印件或微缩片。

附　录

附录 I　公制单位的前缀和缩略词

数目	前缀	缩略词
10^{-18}	atto	a
10^{-15}	femto	f
10^{-12}	pico	p
10^{-9}	nano	n
10^{-6}	micro	μ
10^{-3}	milli	m
10^{-2}	centi	c
10^{-1}	deci	d
10	deka	da
10^{2}	hecto	h
10^{3}	kilo	k
10^{6}	mega	M
10^{9}	giga	G
10^{12}	tera	T
10^{15}	peta	P
10^{18}	exa	E

附录 II　常用希腊字母的科技文体应用

大写	小写	英文读音	国际音标	意义
A	α	alpha	/ˈælfə/	角度,系数,角加速度
B	β	beta	/ˈbeitə/	磁通系数,角度,系数
Γ	γ	gamma	/ˈgæmə/	电导系数,角度,比热容比
Δ	δ	delta	/ˈdeltə/	变化量,屈光度,一元二次方程中的判别式
E	ε	epsilon	/epˈsilɒn/	对数之基数,介电常数
Z	ζ	zeta	/ˈziːtə/	系数,方位角,阻抗,相对黏度
H	η	eta	/ˈiːtə/	迟滞系数,效率
Θ	θ	theta	/ˈθiːtə/	温度,角度
I	ι	iota	/aiˈəute/	微小,一点
K	κ	kappa	/ˈkæpə/	介质常数,绝热指数
Λ	λ	lambda	/ˈlæmdə/	波长,体积,导热系数
M	μ	mu	/mjuː/	磁导系数,微,动摩擦系(因)数,流体动力黏度
N	ν	nu	/njuː/	磁阻系数,流体运动粘度,光子频率
Ξ	ξ	xi	/ksi/	随机数,(小)区间内的一个未知特定值
O	o	omicron	/əumaikˈrɒn/	高阶无穷小函数
Π	π	pi	/pai/	圆周率,$\pi(n)$表示不大于 n 的质数个数
P	ρ	rho	/rəu/	电阻系数,柱坐标和极坐标中的极径,密度
Σ	σ	sigma	/ˈsigmə/	总和,表面密度,跨导,正应力
T	τ	tau	/tau/	时间常数,切应力
Υ	υ	upsilon	/ʌpˈsailən/	位移
Φ	φ	phi	/fai/	磁通,角,透镜焦度,热流量
X	χ	chi	/kai/	统计学中有卡方(χ^2)分布
Ψ	ψ	psi	/psai/	角速,介质电通量
Ω	ω	omega	/ˈəumigə/	欧姆,角速度,交流电的电角度

附录Ⅲ　市制、公制、英制间的换算

市制	公制	英制
1 尺（chi）	1/3 米（meter）	1.0936 英尺（feet）
1 里（li）	1/2 公里（kilometer）	0.3107 英里（mile）
1 亩（mu）	1/15 公顷（hectare）	0.1644 英亩（acre）
1 两（liang）	50 克（grams）	1.7637 盎司（ounces）
1 斤（jin）	1/2 千克（kilogram）	1.1023 磅（pounds）
1 担（dan）	50 公斤（kilograms）	0.9842 英担（hundred-weight）（cwt） 0.0492 英吨（long ton）
1 担（dan）	1/20 吨（metric ton）	0.0551 美吨（short ton）
1 升（sheng）	1 公升（liter）	0.22 加仑（British gallon）
1 斗（dou）	10 公升（liters）	0.2 加仑（British gallon）

附录Ⅳ　科技文献常用动词

accelerate 加速	accommodate 适用	accompany 伴随
account for 说明	achieve 获得，实现	acquire 取得
adapt 适应	address 处理，解决	add 增加
adjust 调节	adopt 采用	affect 影响
allow 许可	alter 更改	analyze 分析
apply 应用	argue 主张	arise 出现
arrange 安排	assemble 组装	assess 评定，评估
assist 帮助，促进	associate 联系	assume 假定
attach 附加	attempt 试图	avoid 避免
bring about 实现	broaden 拓宽	calculate 计算
carry out 进行	categorize 分类	cause 引起
challenge 挑战	change 变更	choose 选择
claim 要求，声索	classify 分类	collect 收集
combine 结合	compare 比较	compensate 补偿
compute 计算	concentrate 浓缩	conclude 作出结论
concur 同时发生	conduct 进行	confirm 确认
connect to 连接	consider 考虑	consolidate 巩固
construct 建造	contradict 矛盾	contribute 助于
control 控制	convert 转变	correlate 相关
correspond 符合	corroborate 证实	create 创造
deal with 探讨	debate 辩论	decline 拒绝
decrease 减少	define 定义，规定	delay 延迟
demonstrate 显示	denote 表示，指示	derive 导出
describe 描述	design 设计	detect 探测
determine 决定	develop 发展	devise 设计
discard 报废	discover 发现	discuss 讨论
display 发挥	disprove 不同意	distribute 分配
divide 划分	drop 下降	effect 实现

elicit 引出	eliminate 消除	employ 利用
enable 使能够	enhance 提高	ensure 保证
establish 建立	estimate 估计	evaluate 评价
examine 检查	exist 存在	expand 膨胀
expect 期望	explain 说明	explore 探索
expose 暴露	extend 卷伸	extract 抽取
facilitate 有助于	fall 下降	filter 过滤
find 发现	focus on 集中于	formulate 制定
generate 发生	give rise to 引起	guarantee 保证
help to 帮助	identify 识别	illustrate 说明
immerse 沉浸	implement 实现	imply 意味着
improve 改进	include 包括	incorporate 包含
increase 增加	indicate 表明	influence 影响
inhibit 抑制	initiate 开始	insert 插入
install 安装	interpret 说明	introduce 介绍
invert 倒置	investigate 调查	isolate 绝缘
limit 限制	link 连接	locate 位于
maintain 维持	manage to 设法	match 匹配
maximize 最大化	measure 测量	minimize 最小化
mirror 反映	miscalculate 算错	misjudge 误判
misunderstand 误解	model 建模	modify 修改
monitor 监控	neglect 忽视	note 注意
observe 观察	obtain 得到	occur 发生
offer 提供	operate 运行	optimize 优化
originate 源于	outline 列举	outperform 胜过
overcome 克服	overlook 忽视	peak 达到峰值
perform 进行	position 定位	precede 领先
predict 预测	prefer 宁愿	prepare 准备
present 提出	prevent 防止	produce 生产
propose 提出	prove 证明	provide 提供
publish 发表	purchase 购买	put forward 提出

quantify 量化	realize 实现	recognize 承认
recommend 推荐	record 记录	reduce 减少
refine 提纯	refute 驳斥	regulate 调整
reinforce 增强	relate 相关	remove 排除
repeat 重复	report 报告	represent 代表
resolve 溶解	restrict 限制	retain 保留
reveal 显示	review 评审	revise 修改
rise 升起	sample 取样	score 获得
select 挑选	separate 分离	show 表明
simulate 模拟	solve 溶解	stabilize 稳定
state 陈述	study 研究	substitute 替代
succeed 成功	suggest 建议	support 支持
test 测验	track 跟踪	transfer 转换
treat 处理	trigger 引发	undertake 从事
use 使用	utilize 使用	validate 验证
vary 使不同	verify 验证	yield 产生

附录 V　常用表达替换

词/词组	替换表达
a considerable amount of	much
a considerable number of	many
a great deal of	much
a majority of	most
a number of	many, some
a small number of	a few
absolutely essential	essential
accounted for by the fact	because
adjacent to	near, next to
along the lines of	like
an adequate number of	enough
an order of magnitude faster	10 times faster
as a consequence of	because
as a matter of that	in fact(or leave out)
as a result of	because
as in the case	as happens
as of this date	today
as to	about(or leave out)
at a rapid date	rapidly, fast
at an earlier date	previously
at an early date	soon
at no case	never
at present	now
at the present time	now
at the conclusion of	after
at this point in time	now
based on the fact that	because
be of the same opinion	agree

续表

词/词组	替换表达
because of the fact that	because
by means of	by, with
causal factor	cause
completely full	full
consensus of opinion	consensus
contingent upon	dependent on
count the number of	count
definitely proved	proved
despite the fact that	although
due to the fact that	because
during the course of	during, while
during the time that	while
effectuate	cause
elucidate	explain
employ	use
end result	result
endeavor	try
entirely eliminate	eliminate
fabricate	make
facilitate	help
fewer in number	fewer
finalize	end
first of all	first
following	after
for the purpose of	since, because
for the reason that	because
from the point of view of	for
future plans	plans
give an account of	describe
give rise to	cause
have been engaged a study of	have studied

续表

词/词组	替换表达
have the appearance of	look like, resemble
have the capability of	can
have the potential to	can, may
having regard to	about
impact(v.)	affect
implement(v.)	start, put into action
important essentials	essentials
in a number of cases	sometimes
in a position to	can, may, able to
in a satisfactory manner	satisfactorily
in a situation in which	when
in a very real sense	in a sense(or leave out)
in case	if
in close proximity to	close, near
in connection with	about, concerning
in many cases	often
in most cases	usually
in my opinion it is not an unjustifiable assumption that	I think
in only a small number of cases	rarely
in order to	to
in relation to	toward, to
in respect to	about
in some cases	sometimes
in terms of	about
in the absence of	without
in the event that	if
in the possession of	has, have
in the not-too-distant future	soon
in view of the fact that	because, since
in as much as	for, as

续表

词/词组	替换表达
initiate	begin, start
in desirous of	wants
is detrimental of	harms
is similar to	resembles
it is apparent that	apparent
it is reported by Smith	Smith reported
it is believed that	I think (or who thinks)
it is clear that	clearly
it is clear that much additional work will be required before a complete understanding	I don't understand it
it is doubtful that	possibly
it is evident that a produced b	a produced b
it is generally believed that	many think
it is my understanding that	I understand that
it is often the case that	often
it is suggested that	I think
it is worth pointing out in this case that	note that
it may be that	I think
it may, however, be noted that	but
it should be noted that	note that (or leave out)
it was observed in the course of the experiment that	we observed
lacked the ability to	couldn't
large in size	large
majority of	most
make reference to	refer to
meet with	meet
militate against	prohibit
more often than not	often
needless to say	(leave out, and consider leaving out whatever follows it)
new initiative	initiative

续表

词/词组	替换表达
no later than	by
of great theoretical and practical importance	useful
of an efficient nature	efficient
of long standing	old
of the opinion that	think that
on a daily basis	daily
on account of	because
on behalf of	for
on the basis of	by
on the grounds that	since, because
on the part of	by, among, for
on those occasions in which	when
our attention has been called to the fact that	we belatedly discovered
owing to the fact that	because
perform	do
place a major emphasis on	stress, emphasize
pool together	pool
previous to	before
prior to	before
protein determinations were performed	proteins were determined
quite a large quantity of	much
quite unique	unique
rather interesting	interesting
red in color	red
referr to as	call
regardless of the fact that	even though
relative to	about
resultant effect	result
small in size	small
smaller in size	smaller
so as to	to

续表

词/词组	替换表达
subject matter	subject
subsequent to	after
sufficient	enough
take into consideration	consider
terminate	end
the great majority of	most, almost all
the opinion is advanced that	I think
the question as to whether	whether
the reason is because	because
the vast majority of	most, almost all
there is reason to believe	I think
this result would seem to indicate	this result indicates
through the use of	by, with
ultimate	last
utilize	use
until such time	until
was of the opinion that	believe
ways and means	ways, means (not both)
we have sufficient knowledge	we don't know
we wish to thank	we thank
whether or not to	whether to
with a view to	to
with reference to	about (or leave out)
with regard to	concerning, about (or leave out)
with respect to	concerning, about (or leave out)
with the exception that	except
with the possible exception of	except
with the result that	so that

附录 VI　常用科技英语词缀

1. 前缀

前缀	意义	例词
a-	在……之上，向	aboard 在飞机(火车、船)上 abroad 在国外 aside 在旁边
ab-	非，异，不	abnormal 异常的
aero-	空气，大气；气体；飞机；航空	aerospace 宇宙空间；航空航天学 aerodynamic 空气动力学 aeronautics 航空学
astro-	星，天体；宇宙	astronaut 宇航员 astronomer 天文学家 astrology 占星术
anti-	反，抗，阻；治，止；防止，中和	antibiotic 抗生素 antioxidant 抗氧化剂
auto-	自动的，自动调整的；自己，本身	automation 自动化，自动操作 auto-ignition 自燃 autofermentation 自然发酵 autoanalyzer 自动分析器 automatic 自动的
bi-	双	bilingual 双语的 bimetal 双金属的 binary 二进制的
bio-	生命；生物；生物学的	biopsy 活体检视 biodiversity 生物多类状态，生物多样性 biometric 计量生物学
bio-	生物的	biochemical 生物化学的，生化的 bioengineering 生物工程 biomass 生物物质
by-	附近，邻近，边侧	bypass 旁路 bypath 侧道 by-product 副产品

续表

前缀	意义	例词
circum-; circu-	周围，环绕，回转	circumference 圆周，周长 circuit 回路 circumstance 环境
co-	共同	coexistence 共存 cooperation 合作 co-oxidation 共氧化
cyber-	计算机的；互联网的	cyberspace 网络空间 cyberpunk 网络黑客
de-	离开；去除，减少；在下，向下	decline 下降 degrade 降级，降解 desalter 脱盐设备 descend 下降 derail 脱轨 detach 拆开
di-	二，二倍，二重；双，联	dioxide 二氧化物 diproton 双质子
dis-	不	dismount 拆卸 disconnect 断开
e-	电子	e-book 电子书 e-mail 电子邮件
elasto-	弹性的	elastomer 高弹体 elastomeric 弹性体的，高弹体的 elastometer 弹性计
electro-	电的；导电的；电解；电子	electrode 电极；电焊条 electrolyte 电解液，电解质 electromagnetic 电磁的 electromagnetism 电磁 electropyrometer 电阻高温计 electrospray 电喷射
en-	在内，进入	encode 编码 enlarge 放大 enrich 富集
ex-	外部，外	expand 膨胀 extend 延伸 extraction 提取

续表

前缀	意义	例词
fore-	预先，前	forecast 预测 foreground 前景 foresight 预见
geo-	地球；土地	geology 地质学 geoscience 地球科学
hetero-	杂，不同	heteroatomic 杂原子的 heterochromatin 异染色质 heterosugar 异糖
hexa-	六	hexabrominated 六溴化的 hexacene 并六苯 hexagonal 六方形的
hydro-	水的；氢的	hydrocarbon 碳氢化合物 hydroelectric 水电的 hydrocarbyl 烃基 hydrolysis 水解 hydroxide 氢氧化物 hydrology 水文学
im-	向内，在内	imbedded 镶嵌的 imbibe 喝，饮（酒等） import 进口
in-	向内，在内	inland 内地 inlet 入口 inside 在……之内
in-	非；无	inactive 非活动性的 instability 不稳定的
inter-	在……间，相互	interaction 互动；相互关系 interrelation 相互关系 internet 互联网
infra-	在下部；亚，低外	infra-red 红外线的 infrasonic 次声的
intra-	向内，在内，内侧	intracellular 分子内的 intraester 内酯 intratomic 原子内的
iso-	同，等；异	isoacetylene 异乙炔 isoamylase 异淀粉酶 isoamylene 异戊烯

续表

前缀	意义	例词
macro-	宏观的，大的	macromolecular 大分子的 macropore 大孔 macrosome 粗粒体
micro-	小，微；扩大，放大；微观的	microbe 微生物，细菌 microbiology 微生物学 microcomputer 微电脑，微机 microprocessor 微处理器 microscope 显微镜
mid-	中，中间	midposition 中间位置，中点 midsection 中间截面 mid-way 中间位置
milli-	毫	millimeter 毫米 milliampere 毫安 millivolt 毫伏
mono-	单，一	monochrome 单色复制，单色的 monocolor 单色的 monomer 单体 monochromator 单色仪 monocrystal 单晶
multi-	多量的，多元的，多样的	multipurpose 多目标的 multicentric 多中心的 multicolor 多色的 multimedia 多媒体 multipropellant 多元推进剂
neo-	新	neoantimycin 新抗霉素 neocardin 新卡氏菌素 neocarotene 新胡萝卜素
out-	在外面，在外部，在外	outlet 出口 outside 在外面 outweigh 胜过
over-	过于，在上面，在外部，向上	overestimate 低估 overlook 忽视 overhead 高架的
penta-	五	pentatomic 五原子的 pentabromide 五溴化物 pentachloride 五氯化物

续表

前缀	意义	例词
poly-	多，聚	polymer 聚合物 polyvinyl chloride 聚氯乙烯
post-	后，在……之后的	posthydrolysis 后水解 postreaction 补充反应 posttreatment 后处理
pre-	预先，之前的	predict 预报 preheat 预热 pretreatment 预处理
pro-	在前，向前	progress 进步 proceed 进行 propagation 传播
photo-	光；光电；照相	photon 光子，光量子 photosynthesis 光合作用
radio-	放射，辐射；无线电；射线	radioactivity 放射性，辐射能 radiology 放射学，辐射学 radiotherapy 放射疗法
quadri-	四	quadrilateral 四边形 quadrimolecular 四分子的 quadripole 四端电路
re-	重新，再	reaction 反应 reactor 反应器，反应堆 redistribution 再分配
self-	自动的；自我的	self-absorption 自动吸收 self-combustion 自燃 self-cleaning 自动净化
semi-	半；部分的，不完全的	semiconductor 半导体 semi-sphere 半球形
sub-	在……底下；从属，次要；分支；下面的，次的	sub-circuit 分支电路 subsonic 亚音速的 submarine 潜水艇 subway 地铁 subset 子集
super-	超，超级；超过，在……之上，上层	super-altitude 超高空 supersonic 超音速的 superfluid 超流体 supermarket 超市 superstructure 超晶格结构

续表

前缀	意义	例词
tele-	远距离；电信	telegram 电报 telecommunication 电信 telemetry 遥感勘测
tetra-	四	tetracene 并四苯 tetracid 四酸
trans-	转移；超越；跨越，移	transmission 传动装置 trans-gene 转基因 transformer 变压器 translation 翻译 transplant 移植
thermo-	热的	thermometer 温度计，体温表 thermostat 恒温调节器 thermocouple 热电偶 thermodynamics 热力学 thermodifussion 热扩散
tri-	三	triangle 三角形 trineutron 三中子 trioxide 三氧化物
ultra-	超，过；极端	ultrasound 超声波 ultra-filtration 超滤作用
ultra-	外，极	ultrasonic 超声的 ultrared 红外的 ultraviolet 紫外线
under-	在……下面，下的，不够	underestimate 低估 underground 地下的 underwater 水下的
uni-	单	unimolecular 单分子的 unipolar 单极的 unitary 单一的
up-	向上，向上面，在上	upside 上部，上边 upstream 上游 upward 向上

2. 后缀

(1)构成名词的常用后缀。

后缀	例词	
-(a)tion	construction 建设 operation 操作，运行	location 定位 rotation 旋转
-al	approval 赞同 denial 否认	arrival 到达 refusal 拒绝
-age	leakage 泄漏 shrinkage 收缩	shortage 短缺 usage 用途
-ance	acceptance 接受 reliance 依靠	allowance 允许 tolerance 公差
-dom	boredom 厌倦	freedom 自由
-ee	absentee 缺席人 referee 介绍人	employee 雇员 trainee 受训者
-ence	confidence 信心 difference 差异	dependence 依赖 reference 参考
-er	harvester 收割机 pain-killer 止痛剂	designer 设计员 programmer 程序员
-ese	Chinese 中文,中国人 Portuguese 葡萄牙文,葡萄牙人	Japanese 日文，日本人 Shanghainese 上海话，上海人
-ess	actress 女演员 lioness 母狮	hostess 女主人 waitress 女服务员
-ful	cupful 一杯 mouthful 一口	handful 一把 plateful 一盘
-hood	childhood 童年 likelihood 可能	falsehood 虚伪 motherhood 为母之道
-cian	mathematician 数学家 physician 内科医师	musician 音乐家 technician 技术员
-ing	building 大楼 painting 画	feeling 感觉 saying 谚语
-ion	decision 决策 expansion 膨胀	discussion 讨论 revision 修改
-ism	criticism 批评 optimism 乐观	heroism 英雄主义 socialism 社会主义

续表

后缀	例词	
-ist	chemist 化学家 physicist 物理学家	dentist 牙医 scientist 科学家，科研人员
-ity	activity 活动 possibility 可能性	humidity 湿度 reality 现实
-ment	argument 论证 judgment 判断	movement 运动 treatment 处理
-ness	coldness 冷却 happiness 幸福	nonobviousness 非显而易见性 illness 病
-or	actuator 促动器 semi-conductor 半导体	sailor 海员 transistor 二极管
-ship	hardship 困难 leadership 领导	relationship 关系 scholarship 学问
-th	health 健康 width 宽度	length 长度 truth 真理
-ty	capacity 能力 reliability 可靠性	creativity 创造性 safety 安全
-ure	disclosure 披露 pressure 压力	failure 故障 structure 结构
-y	difficulty 困难 inquiry 询问	discovery 发现 casualty 意外事故

（2）构成形容词的后缀。

后缀	例词	
-able	acceptable 可接受的 available 可利用的，有借的	applicable 可应用的 movable 可移动的
-al	accidental 意外的 critical 临界的	continual 继续的 professional 专业的
-an	American 美国的 European 欧洲的	Canadian 加拿大的 Russian 俄罗斯的
-ant	constant 经常的，常数的 radiant 辐射的	incessant 不停的 significant 重要的
-ar	cellar 细胞的 popular 普遍的	particular 特别的 vascular 血管的

续表

后缀	例词	
-ary	imaginary 想象的 secondary 次要的	ordinary 通常的 stationary 固定的
-ed	armed 武装的 landed 着陆的	educated 受过教育的 talented 有才华的
-en	earthen 地球上的 wooden 木质的	golden 金色的 woolen 羊毛的
-ent	adherent 附着的 dependent 依赖的	consistent 符合的 different 不同的
-ful	careful 仔细的 fruitful 有成果的	faithful 忠诚的 useful 有用的
-ible	feasible 可行的 responsible 负责的	permissible 允许的 reversible 可逆的
-ic	energetic 精力充沛的 realistic 现实的	logic 逻辑的 static 静态的
-ish	blueish 带青色的 reddish 微红的	brownish 带褐色的 Swedish 瑞典的
-ive	active 活跃的 negative 负的	destructive 破坏的 positive 正的
-less	careless 粗心的 jobless 失业的	colorless 无色的 waterless 无水的
-like	businesslike 有效率的 dish-like 像盘子的	childlike 孩子似的 manlike 像人的
-ly	friendly 友好的 hardly 几乎不的	daily 每日的 lively 生动的
-ous	cautious 小心的 erroneous 错误的	continuous 继续的 tremendous 巨大的
-some	burdensome 繁重的 tiresome 厌倦的	lonesome 寂寞的 troublesome 麻烦的
-y	cloudy 多云的 handy 手边的	dirty 脏的 rainy 下雨的

（3）还有一些构成动词、副词和数词的后缀。

词类	后缀	例词	
动词	-en	broaden 加宽 strengthen 加强	hasten 加速 widen 加宽
	-ify	amplify 放大 intensify 加强	electrify 电气化 verify 证实
	-ire	actualize 实现 modernize 现代化	globalize 全球化 pressurize 加压
副词	-ly	carefully 仔细地 simply 简单地	potentially 潜在地 theoretically 理论上
	-ward	backward 向后 forward 向前	eastward 向东 homeward 在归途上
	-wise	clockwise 顺时针地 likewise 同样地	lengthwise 纵长地 otherwise 否则
数词	-en	eighteen 十八 fourteen 十四	fifteen 十五 sixteen 十六
	-th	fourth 第四 ninth 第九	fifth 第五 twelfth 第十二
	-ty	fifty 五十 sixty 六十	forty 四十 twenty 二十